WITCHCRAFT

AND THE

BOOK OF SHADOWS

WITCHCRAFT

AND THE BOOK OF SHADOWS:

THE DEFINITIVE RECORD OF THE PRACTISES OF WICCA

GERALD B. GARDNER

EDITED AND COMPILED BY A. R. NAYLOR
WITH AN INTRODUCTION BY KATE WEST

I-H-O BOOKS

ISBN 1-872189-52-0

I-H-O Books © 2004
Essex House, Thame, England. OX9 3LS.

. . . for the name of this man is

GERALD BROSSEAU GARDNER,

and he is modern Europe's foremost witch.

His books on witchcraft, as the survival of an ancient pagan religion common to many peoples of the world, have thrown more light upon this strange subject than almost any others published for centuries. He is the very first practising witch to appear in print, saying what he wants to say. He has been praised, insulted, reverenced, quoted, televised, persecuted and vilified. Yet, despite all the high powered grinding of the twentieth century publicity machines, Gardner has remained a mysterious and almost aloof figure, holding steadily to his beliefs: beliefs which he finally came across at an age when many men have long sunk into the sullen reiterations of prejudice.

Gerald Gardner: Witch, J.L. Bracelin. p. 10

I HAVE been told by witches in England: "Write and tell people we are not perverts. We are decent people, we only want to be left alone, but there are certain secrets that you mustn't give away." So after some argument as to exactly what I must not reveal, I am permitted to tell much that has never before been made public concerning their beliefs, their rituals and their reasons for what they do; also to emphasize that neither their present beliefs, rituals nor practices are harmful.

I write only of what takes place in the North, South, East, and West of England today in covens which I know. I have in addition shown the origin of some at least of the stories which have been told about the craft. I can only repeat the words of Lucius Apuleius in the *Metamorphoses,* XL, 23, who wrote a long account of his own initiation into the mysteries in cryptic language, saying: "I have told you things of which, although you have heard them, you cannot know the meaning."

Witchcraft Today, Foreword. p. 11.

CONTENTS

PART THREE

INTRODUCTION

Introduction

by Kate West

Gerald Gardner and his contribution to modern Witchcraft need no introduction for many of the millions of practising Witches in the world today, nor indeed for serious students of the occult. For we grew up in a Craft which acknowledged him as the single individual most influential in bringing the practise of Witchcraft as a spiritual belief system back into the consciousness of the world. Having said that, because of the passage of years, and the recent rapid growth of Witchcraft as a living belief system, there are many today who are not really aware of just how important he is in the history of modern Witchcraft.

Biographical Information

Gerald Brousseau Gardner was born in 1884, the middle of three sons whose father was a Justice of the Peace. Although of Scottish descent; he traced his family roots back to Grizell Gairdner who was burned as a Witch in 1610, he was born near Liverpool, England. As a young man he worked in Ceylon, Borneo and Malaysia, before taking a position in 1923 as a British Government Inspector in the Far East until retiring and returning to England in 1936. However his vocation was as an amateur archaeologist and anthropologist.

On his return to England, Gardner lived in the New Forest area where he became involved with an occult/Masonic group called the Fellowship of Crotona. The inner circle of this group claimed to be an Hereditary Coven into which he was initiated by High Priestess Dorothy Clutterbuck (often referred to as Old Dorothy) in 1939. This Coven was amongst several which gathered together in 1940 and worked Magic to prevent Hitler's invasion of Britain. Many have disputed the existence of Old Dorothy but in 1980 Doreen Valiente, respected High Priestess of the Craft, Gardner's initiate and at one time High Priestess, undertook a documentary search to uncover the truth. After a search of over two years Valiente unearthed proof that Dorothy had been born in Bengal in 1880, had been an affluent and influential resident of the New Forest and had died leaving a substantial estate in 1951. Of course it is well-nigh impossible to prove the existence of this, or any other, Hereditary Coven, as even today these, and other Witches, still guard their secrets and anonymity very carefully.

Gerald Gardner was also an author, with his first book *Keris and Other Malay Weapons* written under the name of Scire and published in 1936; this was (as the title suggests) a treatise on Malay weapons. His next, *A Goddess Arrives* was first published in 1939. This novel, set in Cypress about the worship of Aphrodite, was inspired by dreams he had shortly after his initiation, inspirational dreams not being uncommon after Craft initiations, even today. However, Gardner's first book about the practice of Witchcraft was *High Magic's Aid* published in 1949, once more under the name of Scire. This was published as a fictional work, although even casual reading shows that there is much in its content which is also in his Book of Shadows. It is not known when Gardner first worked on his Book of Shadows, but the earliest available entries also date from 1949. It is important to note that at this time the Witchcraft Act of 1736 was still in force, it's repeal only coming in 1951, so it would have been sensible for any author to have presented their work as fictional, or as is the case of authors like Dr Margaret Murray, as anthropological.

Whilst Gardner wanted to write openly about the Craft there were many around him who felt this unwise, even after 1951. It was felt that to openly admit to the Craft would bring the reinstatement of the Witchcraft Act, as was indeed attempted in the 1960s and 80s, as well as a return to the persecution time of the Witch hunts. This division of opinion led to him leaving the New Forest Coven in 1951 and forming his own. He moved to Castletown on the Isle of Man, where Cecil Williamson had established a Museum of Magic and Witchcraft. For a while Gardner became the resident Witch, eventually buying the Museum. In 1953 he initiated Doreen Valiente and, with her assistance, crafted many of the Rituals we still practise today and generally developed and refined his earlier Book of Shadows.

In 1954 Gardner published his first non-fiction book; *Witchcraft Today,* under his own name. The ensuing publicity and adverse sensationalism by the media led to a rift within Gardner's Coven. Indeed, in 1957 Doreen Valiente drafted a set of amendments to the Book of Shadows which sought to make all members of the Coven, High Priest and High Priestess included, answerable to the Elders and included a prohibition against speaking to the press. It was at this disagreement, or just after, that Gardner and Valiente parted ways. His last work *The Meaning of Witchcraft* was published in 1959. Gerald Gardner's books still sell today and are an important legacy to the modern Craft.

In 1963 Gerald Gardner left England to over-winter in the Lebanon, but on his return voyage in 1964 he died of a heart attack on board ship and was buried in Tunis. Gardner left his museum of Witchcraft, his Ritual equipment, notebooks and copyrights to his then High Priestess, Monique Wilson (Lady Olwen) who, sadly, allowed them to be dispersed.

We can see from the above that there is every reason to suppose that Gerald Gardner was the linchpin between the remnants of the old Hereditary system of Witchcraft and the modern forms that we have today and not without good cause that he is referred to as the "Father of Modern Witchcraft". After Gardner's death his Covens continued to operate and it is from here that Gardnerian Witchcraft grew. Today's Gardnerian Witches can all trace their origins from one of Gardner's initiates. From Gardnerian Witchcraft sprang the Alexandrian Witches and nearly all forms of today's Craft. Hence any record or writing of his which has survived becomes a key to understanding not only our roots but the development of the modern Craft, and its future too.

Books of Shadows

In order to understand the relevance of Gerald Gardner's Book of Shadows we need firstly to understand what a 'Book of Shadows' is. In Gardner's own words: *"Keep this book in your own hand of write. Let brothers and sisters copy what they will, but never let this book out of your hands, and never keep the writings of another, for if it be found in their hand of write, they may well be taken and tortured. Each should guard his own writings and destroy them whenever danger threatens. Learn as much as you may by heart, and when the danger is past, rewrite your book. For this reason, if any die, destroy their book if they have not been able to, for, if it be found 'tis clear proof against them."* (The Warning, 1953, p. 150 this volume.) From this we see that, according to Gardner, the correct form of a Book of Shadows is one the Witch has copied from another, presumably more experienced, Witch. It can also be inferred, from the first word "Keep" that such a book will also be an ongoing project. Indeed, the versions to be found in this volume clearly demonstrate that Gardner himself updated and enhanced his Book of Shadows from time to time, but more of this later. Hence, a Book of Shadows is the individual Witch's record of the Rites, Rituals and rules of the Craft.

However, it is at this point that different branches of Witchcraft have slightly differing opinions as to its content. Gardnerian Witches hold strictly to the system of copying in the above way, and endeavour not to change the content or Rituals. Hence to them Gardner's Book of Shadows should be a definitive document. Alexandrians and others feel that a Book of Shadows should contain all the Rites and Rituals that the individual has performed, as well as the spells or magics they have worked and should also include the results of these, together with other information which is of reference to the Craft. For these Witches their Book of Shadows provides an invaluable personal record and reference for the future, whereas a Gardnerian Book of Shadows will be less personal and also less liable to have changed from the original.

I say less changed because no record which is subject to a combination of copying by hand with occasional references to memorized material, can be reasonably expected to remain static. A misplaced comma, an omitted word, a 'corrected' spelling, can all change the sense and content of even the shortest document. (As an author I can attest to the impact of even the tiniest alteration in text to the sense of my words!) Moreover, as I have mentioned above, it would seem that Gardner himself expected to see changes and development. In addition, whilst Gardner almost certainly allowed the copying of his Book of Shadows there were in fact several versions, as this volume explores. Furthermore, if we assume that Gardner's instructions in his Book of Shadows were carried out, as he would assuredly have wanted if not expected, his Book of Shadows would have been destroyed on his death, therefore any documentation available today ought to be a copy, if not a copy of a copy. All of which should lead us to the inescapable conclusion that there can be no such thing as The Book of Shadows, only many Books of Shadows, even if these be of differing 'value' to future generations of Witches. None of this alters the fact that for Witches today, whether Gardnerian or any another kind of Witch, whatever information we can find on Gardner's own Book of Shadows provides us with a link to the man who launched modern Witchcraft.

By the way, the term 'Book of Shadows' comes about because what the contents of the book are but a shadow of the reality.

This Volume

This volume is not simply yet another version of Gerald Gardner's Book of Shadows, like the many already published. Whilst it does include the texts of previously published versions, it also explores and examines them in context with his other published works on the Craft. I have deliberately not asked the editor for his purpose(s) in publishing it. Not because I don't want to know, a Witch always wants to know, but because I didn't want my introduction to be influenced by anyone else. Nor do I want to produce a series of 'excuses', a summary of its content, or piece which provides an advertisement for its reading. When I agreed to do this I was both flattered, terrified (of the responsibility) and conscious of the problems it might cause me.

There will be some who say that any Book of Shadows, let alone Gerald Gardner's, should never be published — but then all of the material included here (aside, perhaps from my own thoughts), is already in the public domain, whether in a book, text, or on the internet. There will be others who say that we should not examine Gardner's material, we should just accept it — but I believe that the craft is a dynamic, thinking belief system and that dogma leads to stagnation. Personally I am sure that there is more information in private hands, and whilst I would love to be allowed to examine it, I am not sure whether it would be better to publish it or to retain the mystique of the Craft. I do know that there are many traditions which have been handed down from Gardner which were never committed to paper, and perhaps they are better continued in that way.

What this volume does is to present the information available to us all, in a way which allows you, the reader, to examine it and to draw your own conclusions, rather than many of those previously published works which, whilst claiming to be objective, lead the reader to the author's own predetermined conclusions. It also, on the face of it, gives ammunition to the various detractors of the Craft, who seek to denigrate both Gerald Gardner and the modern Craft he gave form to:

> Those who point out inconsistencies in the various Gardnerian Books of Shadows do not realise that a living belief system will need to change to suit changing times. As I trust I have shown, Gardner intended Books of Shadows to change. Just as modern Christianity has changed by the inclusion of women priests, the changes wrought in the bible which convert 'dominion' to

'stewardship' and so on, all of which may well be responses to the rise of Witchcraft and Paganism. If we cannot change, from where would come our spells and magics to protect us in cars, or on other forms of transport?

- Those who feel that the obvious external influences of Masonic Rite and Templar Ritual, including the Seal of Solomon, must indicate a form of plagiarism. Christian Ritual, amongst those of other beliefs, also has it's origins elsewhere; for Christianity it lies in Hebraic conventions and the Jewish faith.
- Those who seek to prove evidence of Christianity in the Craft. (Gardner as a product of a Christian family and country must have been subjected to these strong formative influences in his younger years.) Many people take the phrase "Thou cans't be a Witch alone" as an instruction, but careful examination of the text will show that this is Gardner quoting the tormentors of the Witch Hunts – not a belief nor instruction to the Craft.
- Those who claim that Gardner made it all up. However, the fact that Gardner was writing about, and practising Witchcraft, before the Witchcraft laws were repealed signifies his strong beliefs in Witchcraft as a religion, rather than it being an invented cult.

There is no doubt in my mind that Gardner drew some of his material from the Seal of Solomon (he says so), and some has come from the

Masons and/or the Knights Templar, or they share the same sources (I have had the privilege of helping to transcribe some of their works). I equally have no doubt that his acquaintance with Aleister Crowley, and his reading of works by a number of the other serious occultists of his day, must have influenced his Rites and Rituals, as published here. But, and it's a very large but, wherever Gerald Gardner obtained the sources for his Rituals there is no doubt in my mind and the minds of many other Witches that they work!

The editor of this volume is a committed Christian, which makes his unbiased and open approach all the more refreshing. He does not guide us readers to any conclusion, but rather asks some very pertinent questions: it is perhaps up to us who are of the Craft to seek to answer them. He makes a number of valid points, e.g. the Editor raises the question about how Gardner could say there is no heaven and no hell, but then goes on later to consign the errant Witch to "the Christian hell". I may be biased, but my reading of this is that it is more a question of "You can't/won't follow the rules here – then go to the hell you think you're going to". Taken in the context of a Christian upbringing, and in a world where Christianity had pretty much a monopoly, this, to me, would be a sensible way of reading what is, to all intents and purposes, the exasperated outburst of the (probably highly frustrated and irritated) High Priest of a Coven! (Anyone who has had the privilege and grief of being a High Priest or High Priestess will appreciate the difficulties which come with the job!) Perhaps if we seek to answer these and other questions, we can truly come to an understanding of what modern Witchcraft is. Perhaps we can leave a legacy for future generations. One of Gardner's last communications shows that he was seriously concerned that the Craft would die out, not because of outside influences, but because the 'elders' of each generation are, a little like the Christian priesthood, frightened of letting go and seeing what the next generation can do.

A Personal Exploration

Working on this introduction has been for me, a journey of exploration. Despite coming through the Gardnerian 'line', it has been interesting and surprisingly informative to view Gerald Gardner's Book of Shadows, as presented in this volume, from the point of view of one who has been running Covens for a number of years. Perhaps I should explain my own background a little to put this into perspective. My original Craft contacts were in my childhood and the 'W' word was never mentioned, but the lore of the wise woman and cunning man were both an integral part of my informal education. In my youth I found the cycles of the Seasons, the phases of the Moon and the practise of the Magic came naturally. It was after this that I found my first mentor in the Craft. At that time I walked a Solitary path, guided by a Traditional Witch. It was only after this beginning that I found a Coven and became initiated into the Gardnerian tradition, and later still that I found the practice of the Alexandrian Craft. These days I practise a blend of Gardnerian, Alexandrian and Traditional Craft, far more suited to my circumstances and temperament. As a result of this 'mixed' heritage I find myself in a somewhat interesting position, able to see both the positive and negative effects of a volume such as this.

But to return to this volume, and the controversy it will almost certainly generate within the Craft today. The revisions seen here, alone speak volumes: Firstly there is the lessening of 'High Magic' or ceremonial magic techniques and the perceptible return to the nature based feel of the true Craft. As any High Priestess or High

Priest will tell you, whilst formal Ritual has much to commend it there comes a time when the experienced Witch does not need the formality, they can work in far less constrained circumstances, especially when theirs becomes an experienced Coven. Secondly, a good many of the revisions to Gardner's Book of Shadows show the, almost inevitable, 'tightening of the reins' that many a High Priest or High Priestess finds necessary as their Coven grows in size, and it's members become more inclined to think and act for themselves. All of which find me feeling a far greater admiration for Gerald Gardener than I have felt for a while, for it shows him to be human and fallible, just like the rest of us. Another thing that researching this has taught me is that Gardener, whilst a product of his generation and upbringing, was in fact genuinely far sighted — for he was probably the first Witch to really understand that, by hiding away and keeping the Craft a 'secret' we would have been doing ourselves a disservice. He was the first Witch to open the doors to the 'public' via the medium of writing and publicity and because of that, he was The Witch who has enabled so many of us to discover our true beliefs and calling.

Like the above 'objections' to Gardner's Book of Shadows, there are those who would point out that Gerald Gardner had many personal traits which we today might consider strange, or even anti-social, but we have to remember that he was, like you and me, a product of his upbringing and his time. Gerald Gardner was no saint, nor did he pretend to be. He had many personality faults and adverse character traits, but whatever Gerald Gardner's personal idiosyncrasies or faults there is no doubt in my mind that he is the Father of Modern Witchcraft and for that he deserves the acknowledgement of every generation of Witch, past, present and future. Personally I feel that Gardner would be pleased by both the modern growth of the Craft and by the ongoing debate which this volume will undoubtedly generate.

Whatever your interest in Witchcraft, Gerald Gardener or his Book of Shadows, I trust that you, like me, will find this volume an interesting journey of exploration, as is the Craft itself.

Blessings

Kate West)O(

BOOK OF SHADOWS

PROLEGOMENA

NOTE:

- There is much debate regarding 'Gardner's sources' for *The Book of Shadows* but one thing always evolves another, always a little different, mutating through selection and experience. Today, 'Witchcraft' has gained considerable momentum and therefore such arguments are somewhat spurious. Accordingly, Gardner's texts are presented herein as IS, without a measure or any BECAUSE — whatever else may be said of Gardner none can deny that these texts ARE the very foundation stones of 'modern witchcraft' in all its divers forms.

- The text and footnotes throughout are the work of Gerald Gardner except, 1) where clearly identified as the work of another, 2) an 'Editor's Note' or, 3) references or text in square brackets [for example].

- All citations referring to Gardner's *Witchcraft Today, The Meaning of Witchcraft* and *High Magic's Aid* refer to the versions published by I-H-O Books.

- This volume is primarily intended for use as a reference book and as a consequence some short passages of Gardner's text are repeated within different sections (although every effort has been made to keep such repetition to a minimum).

A. R. Naylor

Thame, 2004

'The Old Gods are not dead. They think we are.'

The unseen Powers that have interested man most in his early history have been the powers of fertility and of contact with the spirit world; of Life and Death. These are the elementary powers that became the divinities of the witches, and their worship is as old as civilisation itself. The meaning of witchcraft is to be found . . . in the deepest levels of the human mind, the collective unconscious, and in the earliest developments of human society. It is the deepness of the roots that has preserved the tree.[1]

And this statement, I think, is more or less true of all peoples. But the two great realities with which all ancient people were faced were essentially the unchanging, unending ones of Life and Death; and these it was, together with that third elusive thing, magical power, which the Gods held in Their hands. Consequently, wherever men have formulated for themselves figures of Divinity, these have ever been the archetypes: the Lady of Life, the Lord of Death and What Lies beyond; and between them the web of magic has been spun.[2]

There are very few real witches left, and those keep themselves very much to themselves. They are generally the descendants of witch families, and have inherited a tradition which has been preserved for generations. This is, indeed, the traditional way in which witchcraft was spread and preserved; the children of witch families were taught by their parents, and initiated at an early age.[3]

They are the people who call themselves the Wica, the "wise people", who practise the age-old rites and who have, along with much superstition and herbal knowledge, preserved an occult teaching and working processes which they themselves think to be magic or witchcraft. . . . These Wica generally work for good purposes and help those in trouble to the best of their ability.[4]

They were the people, the priests and priestesses of the Old Goddess. [5]

Witchcraft is a religion[6] — It has suffered badly by reason of the modern disease of "meddle-o-mania" or "delirium interferens", which may be defined as a morbid desire to run other people's lives for them; so that people dare not initiate their children as they used to do in the good old days (and even dared to do in the bad old days, the "burning time"), for fear of finding some paid snooper from "the authorities" or a representative of the "Sunday Hysterical" on their doorstep. Yet, in spite of all, it survives; because there exists, even in the Welfare State, a spirit of romance, a love of the spice of life, and a dislike of smug respectability.[7]

Witchcraft is a system involving both magic and religion. This in itself is an indication of great age, because in primitive times magic and religion were closely inter-related.[8]

The foundation of magical beliefs, of which witchcraft is a form, is that unseen Powers exist, and that by performing the right sort of ritual these Powers can be contacted and either forced or persuaded to assist one in some way. People believed this in the Stone Age, and they believe it, consciously or not, today. It is now well-known that most superstition is in fact broken-down ritual. [9]

Witchcraft is not anti-Christian[10] — Witchcraft is certainly not black magic, because witches do not even believe in the devil, let alone invoke him. The Old Horned God of the witches is *not* the Satan of Christianity, and no amount of theological argument will make him so. He is, in fact, the oldest deity known to man, and is depicted in the oldest representation of a divinity which has yet been found, namely the Stone Age painting in the innermost recess of the Caverne des Trois Freres at Ariege. He is the old phallic god of fertility who has come forth from the morning of the world, and who was already of immeasurable antiquity before Egypt and Babylon, let alone before the Christian era. Nor did he perish at the cry that Great Pan was dead. Secretly through the centuries, hidden deeper and deeper as time went on, his worship and that of the naked Moon Goddess, his bride, the Lady of Mystery and Magic and the forbidden joys, continued sometimes among the great ones of the land, sometimes in humble cottages, or on lonely heaths and in the depths of darkling woods, on summer nights when the moon rode high. It does so still.[11]

Of course, the Craft of the Wica is not the only group which seeks to contact the Gods. There are other occult groups which use a similar technique, and their aims are the same, namely to bring through the Divine power to help, guide and uplift mankind at this dangerous and exciting turning-point in human history. But, so far as I know, these groups generally work with the Egyptian and Greek Gods and Goddesses, and I cannot think that these contacts are as powerful here as they would be upon their native soil; whereas the divinities of the Craft of the Wica are the Ancient Ones of Britain, part of the land itself. (For a country exists not merely upon the physical plane, and man does not live by bread alone.)

Nor is the veneration of the Wica for the old sacred places such as Stonehenge and Glastonbury mere sentiment. Those who are sensitive to atmosphere will know that these places possess a life of their own, and, from what we have been told by seers, these too exist not only upon the material plane. They are focusing points for influence and the power from the Inner Planes, places where the Veil is thinner than elsewhere; and the "superstition" that it is dangerous to remove or injure the Old Stones is founded on fact. [12]

Now I am an anthropologist, and it is agreed that an anthropologist's job is to investigate what people do and believe, and not what other people say they should do and believe. It is also part of his task to read as many writings as possible on the matter he is investigating, though not accepting such writings uncritically, especially when in conflict with the evidence as he finds it. Anthropologists may draw their own conclusions and advance any theories of their own, but they must make it clear that these are their own conclusions and their own theories and not proven facts; and this is the method I propose to adopt. In dealing with native races one records their folklore, the stories and religious rites on which they base their beliefs and actions. So why not do the same with English witches?

I must first explain why I claim to speak of things not generally known. I have been interested in magic and kindred subjects all my life, and have made a collection of magical instruments and charms. These studies led me to spiritualist and other societies, and I met some people who claimed to have known me in a past life.[13]

They were also interested in the fact that an ancestress of mine, Grizel Gairdner, had been burned as a witch. They kept saying that they had met me before. We went through everywhere we had been, and I could not ever have met them before in this life; but they claimed to have known me in previous lives. Although I believe in reincarnation, as many people do who have lived in the East, I do not remember my past lives clearly; I only wish I did. However, these people told me enough to make me think. Then some of these new (or old) friends said, "You belonged to us in the past. You are of the blood. Come back to where you belong."

I realised that I had stumbled on something interesting; but I was half-initiated before the word "Wica" which they used hit me like a thunderbolt, and I knew where I was, and that the Old Religion still existed. And so I found myself in the Circle, and there took the usual oath of secrecy, which bound me not to reveal certain things.

In this way I made the discovery that the witch cult, that people thought to have been persecuted out of existence, still lived. I found, too, what it was that made so many of our ancestors dare imprisonment, torture and death rather than give up the worship of the Old Gods and the love of the old ways. I discovered the inner meaning of that saying in one of Fiona MacLeod's books: '*The Old Gods are not dead. They think we are* .'[14]

1. *Meaning of Witchcraft*, Chapter I: The Witch Cult in Britain. p. 20.
2. *Meaning of Witchcraft*, Chapter XI: Who were the Gods of Britain? p. 165
3. *Meaning of Witchcraft*, Chapter I: The Witch Cult in Britain. p. 11.
4. *Witchcraft Today*, Chapter X: What are Witches. p. 88.
5. *Meaning of Witchcraft*, Chapter VI: Witchcraft in Roman and Saxon Times. p. 89.

6. *Witchcraft Today,* Chapter I: Living Witchcraft. p. 15.
7. *Meaning of Witchcraft,* Chapter XVII: The Future. p. 255.
8. *Meaning of Witchcraft,* Chapter I: The Witch Cult in Britain. p. 18.
9. *Meaning of Witchcraft,* Chapter I: The Witch Cult in Britain. p. 20.
10. *Witchcraft Today,* Chapter III: The Witch Beliefs. p. 34.
11. *Meaning of Witchcraft,* Chapter I: The Witch Cult in Britain. p. 19.
12. *Meaning of Witchcraft,* Chapter XVII: The Future. p. 258.
13. *Witchcraft Today,* Chapter I: Living Witchcraft. p. 16.
14. *Meaning of Witchcraft,* Chapter I: The Witch Cult in Britain. p. 8.

Death: Afterlife and Reincarnation

[see also *Skull and Cross Bones*]

In the Stone Ages man's chief wants were good crops, good hunting, good fishing, increase in flocks and herds and many children to make the tribe strong. It became the witches' duty to perform rites to obtain these things. This was probably a matriarchal age, when man was the hunter and woman stayed at home making medicine and magic. Historically, the matriarchal period has been tentatively dated from the middle of the ninth to the middle of the seventh millennium B.C., during which time caves, trees, the moon and stars all seem to have been reverenced as female emblems. So the myth of the Great Mother came into existence and woman was her priestess. Probably at the same time the men had a hunter's god, who presided over the animals. Later, perhaps, came the idea of a future life and thoughts of the next world as being an unhappy place unless you could attain to the abode of the gods, a sort of paradise. This was thought of as a place of rest and refreshment where one would grow young again ready for reincarnation on earth.

Primitive man feared to be born again outside his own tribe, so his ritual prayers to his god were that he might be born again in the same place and at the same time as his loved ones, and that he might remember and love them again. The god who rules this paradise must, I think, have been Death, but somehow he is identified with the hunting god and wears his horns. This god of death and hunting, or his representative, seems at one time to have taken the lead in the cult, and man became the master. But it is emphasized that because of her beauty, sweetness and goodness, man places woman, as the god placed the goddess, in the chief place, so that woman is dominant in the cult practice.

What probably happened was this: there was an organized tribal religion, with a male tribal god, and an order of priestesses and their husbands who looked after the magic. The chief priest of the tribal cult was dominant when he attended their meetings, but in his absence the priestess ruled. My witches speak of him as god of "Death and what lies beyond": by this they not only mean the life in the next world but resurrection (or reincarnation). He rules a sort of happy hunting ground, where ordinary folk go and forgather with like-minded people; it may be pleasant or unpleasant according to your nature. According to your merits you may be reincarnated in time, and take your chance where and among whom this takes place; but the god has a special paradise for his worshippers, who have conditioned their bodies and natures on earth, who enjoy special advantages and are prepared more swiftly for reincarnation which is done by the power of the goddess in such circumstances as to ensure that you will be reborn into your own tribe again. This is taken nowadays to mean into witch circles. It would seem to involve an unending series of reincarnations; but I am told that in time you may become one of the mighty ones, who are also called the mighty dead. I can learn nothing about them, but they seem to be like demigods — or one might call them saints.[1]

Nearly all primitive people had initiation ceremonies and some of these were initiation into priesthoods, into magic powers, secret societies and mysteries. They were usually regarded as necessary for the welfare of the tribe as well as for the individual. They usually included purification and some test of courage and fortitude — often severe and painful — terrorization, instruction in tribal lore, in sexual knowledge, in the making of charms, and in religious and magical matters generally, and often a ritual of death and resurrection.[2]

I do not think that primitive people were as afraid of death as many people are today. Living closer to nature, their psychic powers were more active, and they were used to the idea of communicating with their dead relatives and friends. They looked upon it as quite a natural thing. Hence the witches, among whom this ancient creed is still preserved in a fragmentary form, do not regard the Horned God in his form as lord of the Gates of Death as a terrifying being, nor have they any conception of a burning "Hell" such as some Christians envisage[†].[3]

Exactly what the present-day witch believes I find it hard to say. I know one who goes to church at times, though she is, at best, only an occasional conformist. She firmly believes in reincarnation, as many Christians do. How she or they reconcile it with the Church's teaching I do not know. But, to begin with, the belief in many different heavens, each with their different god, is not unusual. The cult god is thought of as the god of the next world, or of death and resurrection, or of reincarnation, the comforter, the consoler. After life you go gladly to his realms for rest and refreshment, becoming young and strong, waiting for the time to be reborn on earth again, and you pray to him to send back the spirits of your beloved dead to rejoice with you at your festivals.

That they believe something of this sort is clear from the myth of the goddess which forms the central part of one of their rituals. It is a sort of primitive Spiritualism.

---

† Editor's Note: This statement regarding 'Hell' is not true — in *The Book of Shadows* there are a number of references to the Goddess as 'Hell's dark mistress' and 'Queen of Hell'. Furthermore, with direct reference to the Christian Hell, *3.1 The Old Laws* warns "the Curse of the Goddess shall be upon them, so they never be reborn on earth, and may remain where they belong, in the Hell of the Christians." See *Appendix: Witchcraft, Devil Worship and Christianity* for further details.

Witches have no books on theology, so it is difficult for me to discover all they actually believe. With all the thousands of books there are on Christianity I find it difficult to define Christian beliefs. Transubstantiation, for instance. On the other hand, it is easy to give the central idea or myth, which I believe is defined as being a story which affects people's actions. Strictly speaking, in this sense the Myth of Christianity lies in the Crucifixion and Resurrection, and few Christians differ about this. The Myth of Witchcraft seems to be the story of the goddess . . . [see *4.2. The Descent of the Goddess*] . . . This myth upon which its members base their actions is the central idea of the cult. Perhaps it was coined to explain ideas and rituals already conceived, and to explain why the wiser, older and more powerful god should give his power over magic to the goddess. It is very easy to say this is only the story of Istar descending into hell, but the point of the story is different. Again you can say it is simply Siva, the god of Death and Resurrection; but here again the story is different. It is quite possible that the stories of Istar and Siva have influenced the myth, but I think that its origin is most likely Celtic. In Celtic legends the Lords of the Underworld did prepare you for rebirth, and many living people are said to have entered their regions, formed alliances with them and returned safely, but it needed great courage; only a hero or a demigod dared to risk it. Celtic mysteries assuredly contained rituals of death and resurrection, and possibly visits to the underworld with a safe return. I think St Patrick's Purgatory in Lough Derg was a Christianized version of this legend.[4]

The Goddess's gift is rebirth in a new body, reincarnation. "With sturdier limbs and brighter brain, the old soul takes the road again."

Incidentally, this may be the inner meaning of the old British tale of Avalon, the Place of Apples. Every old Celtic tale speaks of the after-world as a place of apple-trees, but nobody seems to know just why. If the reader cares to make the experiment of slicing an apple across, he will see the answer: the core forms the sign of the Pentagram, the symbol of the Goddess of Rebirth and Resurrection. "Avalon" was the place where souls went to rest between incarnations on earth. To this day, in the witch ritual, the Priestess first stands with her arms crossed on her breast and her feet together, to represent the God of Death, and then opens out her arms and stands with feet apart to represent the Goddess of Resurrection. In this position the human body resembles the figure of the Pentacle, or Pentagram. Because it was the place from which the old and weary soul was reborn in a young body, with its strength and courage renewed; Avalon was also called in the Celtic "Tir-nan-Og", the land of Youth.[5]

* * * * *

It is believed by witches that by acting a part you really take on the nature of the thing you imitate. This is really the basis of the cave-man's magic. By making the clay image of the animal you wish to kill, and by knowing its name, you establish a link between them, so that when he stuck spears into it it gave him power to kill it when he hunted it. That these beliefs may seem rather like children's games to some does not alter the fact that primitive men do behave like this, and so do the witches. By acting the part of the goddess the priestess is thought to be in communion with her; so the priest, acting as the god, becomes at one with him in his aspect of Death, the Consoler, the Comforter, the bringer of a happy after-life and regeneration. The initiate in undergoing the god's experiences becomes a witch.[6]

It must be understood clearly that witchcraft is a religion. Its patron god is the Horned God of hunting, death and magic, who, rather like Osiris of Egypt, rules over the After-World, his own Paradise, situated in a hollow hill, or at least in a place which is only approached through a cave, where he welcomes the dead and assigns them their places; where they are prepared, according to their merits and wisdom, for rebirth into a new body on this earth, for which they will be made ready by the love and power of the Goddess, the Great Mother, who is also the Eternal Virgin and the Primordial Enchantress, who gives rebirth and transmutation, and love on this earth, and in whose honour and by means of ritual the necessary power is raised to enable this to be done. They think that the God and the Goddess assist them in making their magic, as they assist the God and the Goddess in their turn by raising power for them by their dances and by other methods. In fact, they seem to consider the gods as being more like powerful friends than deities to be worshipped.[7]

The After-Life is rather that of a place of rest and refreshment, where people await their turn to be born again on this earth. This, of course, is the concept of reincarnation, which is widely held among primitive people of all kinds. To them, the most logical place for the souls of new-born babies to have come from is the Land of the Dead, where there are plenty of souls awaiting another body. Hence the Lord of the Gates of Death is also the phallic deity of fertility, the Opener of the Door of Life. This is why the witches' god was incorporated into the Roman pantheon as Janus, the two-faced god who was Guardian of the Gates. He and his consort Diana are two of the oldest deities of Western Europe, and Diana is named in the Canon Episcopi of the early tenth century as being the goddess of the witches.[8]

The modern witches believe that at death the "Mighty Ones", the Old Ones of the cult, come for faithful followers and take them to a favoured place among other initiates who have gone before.

By now, I think, this body of primitive belief and practice had become a real religion. Whether they had only two gods, the old hunting god and the new god of death and resurrection, one cannot say; but there is a natural tendency to amalgamate gods, to regard two different gods as being really different manifestations of the same deity, and it appears to me that at some time the Great Hunter and the god of Death and What Lies Beyond became one and the same. Also, the Great Mother became amalgamated with the witch-wife who brought her slain husband to life again, the personification of feminine allure and excitement, "The World's Desire".[9]

Now, we have seen that Janus or Dianus was a form of the God of the Witches; the two faces depict his dual nature. As the witch ritual says, "Thou art the Opener of the Doorway of the Womb; and yet, because that which is born must also die, that it may be renewed, therefore art Thou Lord of the Gates of Death." Being the consort of Diana, he was the King of the Wood, and as the Phallic God, he was the renewer of life. It is evident that the bust which Lady Raglan illustrates depicts him as the renewer of life in spring, the green leaves take life from his mouth. Closely akin to him are Faunus and Silvanus, and Pan, who was hailed in Hellas as "Pamphagë, Pangenetor", "All-Devourer, All-Begetter"; and as "Chairë Soter Kosmou", "Beloved Saviour of the World", yet from whose name was derived "panic" as a term of terror. Priapus, too, was the Phallic God and the God of Gardens. The concept of fertility, of eternal, ever-renewing, upspringing life, is the basis of them all.

May we venture to suggest that the foliate mask is not merely derived from the figure of "Jack in the Green", but that both are derived from the same source — the Old God of Fertility?[10]

Herne the Hunter, with his helmet crowned with stag's antlers, his wild band of followers, his association with "fairies", and the huge oak tree, now apparently destroyed, beneath which he used to appear, is the British example *par excellence* of a surviving tradition of the Old God of the Witches.

The dual nature of the Old God will be noticed. He is the giver of fertility, both of the ground and of humans and animals; but he is also Lord of the Gates of Death. This dual nature has caused some students of comparative religion to equate him with Janus, who was in very ancient times the consort of Diana, and who was depicted with two faces. There is also an obvious resemblance to the Indian Shiva, who is the Phallic God as well as the Destroyer, and who is the consort of the Great Mother Goddess, Shakti.

The witches explain this duality by a ritual in which they invoke the Old God: "Thou art the Opener of the Doorway of the Womb; and yet, because all things that are born must also die, that they may be renewed, therefore art thou Lord of the Gates of Death."

In the Magical Legend of the Witches, which I gave in *Witchcraft* . . . the Old God explains to the Goddess that Age and Fate (i.e. Karma) against which he is powerless (because they are Cosmic Law) cause all things to wither and die: "But when men die at the end of time, I give them rest and peace, and strength so that they may return", i.e. be reborn upon the earth, or reincarnated.[11]

1. *Witchcraft Today,* Chapter II: There have been Witches in all ages. p. 26.
2. *Witchcraft Today,* Chapter I: Living Witchcraft. p. I7.
3. *Meaning of Witchcraft,* Chapter III: The Stone Age Origins of Witchcraft. p. 43.
4. *Witchcraft Today,* Chapter III: The Witch Beliefs. p. 36.
5. *Meaning of Witchcraft,* Chapter VIII: Magic Thinking (cont.). p. 115.
6. *Witchcraft Today,* Chapter XIII: Recapitulation. p. 122.
7. *Meaning of Witchcraft,* Chapter II: Witches' Memories and Beliefs. p. 25.
8. *Meaning of Witchcraft,* Chapter III: The Stone Age Origins of Witchcraft. p. 43.
9. *Meaning of Witchcraft,* Chapter III: The Stone Age Origins of Witchcraft. p. 47.
10. *Meaning of Witchcraft,* Chapter XII: Signs and Symbols. p. 173.
11. *Meaning of Witchcraft,* Chapter XI: Who were the Gods of Britain. p. 162.

Coven

[see also 3.1 *The Old Laws*]

First I must make it clear — I am a humble member of a coven. I am not its head or leader in any way, and I have to do what I am told. People often speak as if I owned a coven and could call it up to perform for them in public. I can and have occasionally introduced people to a witch, when the witch was willing and agreeable. More than this I cannot do.[1]

Each coven is independent[2] — the coven traditionally consists of twelve witches and a leader, probably because it is a lucky number and because there are thirteen moons in a year.

I think I must make this clear: that the word *coven* is used in two senses. First, it is a band which may be of any number of initiated people who have a common leader, who hold meetings and celebrate the rites. The leader may be a man or a woman, but a high priestess (whom they may borrow from another coven, if they have not got one of their own available) must be present to celebrate the rites. In the old days there were numbers of people who would come to the meetings who were of the faith but were uninitiated (not received into the circle, or taught the secrets). I think that in the old days there was no real secrecy about what the initiation consisted of; anyone could see and hear it much as one may see a baptism or marriage. But unless you undergo the marriage or baptismal rites you are not married or baptized; neither does knowing how a marriage is performed give you power to marry someone else.

Secondly, a coven can also mean the people who celebrate the rites in the circle. Traditionally, this consists of six perfect couples and a leader; preferably the couples are husbands and wives, or at least betrothed. That is, they should be lovers, in sympathy with each other, as this gives the best results. They can give me no reason for this number of thirteen, except custom and that "more would make the rite too long, as each has to do certain things in turn". Also six couples and a leader is the most that can work in a nine-foot circle — and you do not become giddy so easily in a larger one.[3]

A popular belief about witchcraft, which is nevertheless erroneous, is the idea that a witches' coven must consist of thirteen people. Actually, it may consist of more or less than thirteen people; but thirteen is considered to be the ideal number.[4]

In these degenerate days six perfect couples are not always available, so others are taken in to make up the numbers. These are all "purified" as soon as they enter the circle; other initiates present, and children, would sit outside and watch the proceedings. Later these would probably be purified and taken into the circle to receive the sacred meal. When the rites in the circle were finished, all would join in the feast and dance. If there were, say, twenty initiates present with two qualified priestesses and there was enough room, they tell me they might form two covens and have two circles, with one common leader to keep them in time, and that in the old days at large meetings in the open air they might have many such circles; but I have never seen more than one. Nowadays numbers are so few that practically everyone comes into the circle, though I have seen a man sit outside, refusing to come in because his girl was not there that night.

They tell me that in the old days they often used to choose the prettiest young girl suitable to represent the goddess at large meetings. She was known as the Maiden. She was made a sort of acting high priestess and treated with the greatest honour and would often act as sort of hostess to distinguished visitors (i.e. the Devil if he turned up), but the real power remained in the hands of the true priestess, who usually worked all the magic. Often the Maiden was the high priestess's daughter and would take the place of her mother in time and there was sometimes some mystification over this; seeing the resemblance at a distance ignorant visitors believed that the high priestess became young again at the meetings.

They say that in the old days there were rules that there must not be more than one large coven in a certain area, so as to prevent arguments as to who should belong to whom; but they are uncertain about these rules now. It is certain that long ago there was some sort of central authority, exercised by a common leader, whom the Church called the Devil, but they know nothing of this nowadays and would not know how to recognize him if he turned up.[5]

I think that I must make it clear that, as far as my experience goes, while the coven should traditionally have six couples and a leader in the circle, nowadays it may often have less. At a meeting, if there were more than thirteen initiated people present they would sit outside with any uninitiated and watch the religious rite. If for certain reasons they were required in the circle, others would step outside to make room, and those without would then be purified and taken inside. When the rites were finished and the circle closed, all took part in the dance and feast. If there were, say, twenty initiated and enough room, they would probably form two covens, each in their own circle, with one leader or timekeeper. If there were still more, they would form three circles. Nowadays, no uninitiated persons are ever present and the ceremonies are usually indoors, where there is seldom room for more than one circle. Also, though the witch ideal is to form perfect couples of people ideally suited to each other and so in perfect sympathy, and to cause people to be suited to each other, nowadays this is not always possible; the right couples go together, the others go singly and make do as they can. Witchcraft today is largely a case of "make do".[6]

1. *Witchcraft Today,* Chapter XIII: Recapitulation. p. 116.
2. *Witchcraft Today,* Chapter X: What are Witches. p. 97.

3. *Witchcraft Today*, Chapter X: What are Witches. p. 98.
4. *Meaning of Witchcraft*, Chapter I: The Witch Cult in Britain. p. 16.
5. *Witchcraft Today*, Chapter X: What are Witches. p. 98.
6. *Witchcraft Today*, Chapter XI: Some Other Matters. p. 106.

Passwords

In Italy witches are said to say "six and seven" as a password, because it would be dangerous to say thirteen; these numbers of course add up to thirteen. In England I could understand their saying five and eight for the same reason, but actually they mostly know each other in the coven and so do not need passwords; they very often do not know of the existence of other covens.

They say that in the old days there were rules that there must not be more than one large coven in a certain area, so as to prevent arguments as to who should belong to whom; but they are uncertain about these rules now. . . . They have no regular system of passwords, that I could discover, to recognize each other by. But at initiations there are certain words required to pass you into the circle and there are certain catch-phrases that could be used as such; of course a knowledge of the mysteries would prove you were initiated.[1]

Postulant: "I have two Passwords: Perfect Love and Perfect Trust."

Magus drops the sword point, saying,

"All who approach with perfect love and perfect trust are doubly welcome."

Going around behind her, he blindfolds her, then putting his left arm around her waist and his right arm around her neck, he pulls her head back, says,

"I give you the 3rd password, a Kiss to pass through this dread Door,"

and pushes her forward with his body, through the doorway and into the circle. Once inside, he releases her saying,

"This is the way all are first brought into the circle."[2]

1. *Witchcraft Today,* Chapter X: What are Witches. p. 99.

2. 1.4.1a First Degree

Meetings

> Listen to the words of the Great Mother, who of old was also called among men Artemis, Astarte, Dione, Melusine, Aphrodite and many other names. At mine altars the youth of Lacedaemon made due sacrifice.
>
> Once in the month, and better it be when the moon is full, meet in some secret place and adore me, who am queen of all the magics. . . .[1]

What interests me is the fact that numbers of people meet every year and perform witch rites because they believe in them. A critic has suggested to me: "These people are not witches; they only do witch rites because it gives them pleasure and because they are superstitious." If that is to be the touchstone, is not a superstition a belief?[2]

Actually, witch meetings today may take place anywhere that is convenient, and only people who have been initiated into the cult are allowed to be present.[3]

[In the old days there were numbers of people who would come to the meetings who were of the faith but were uninitiated (not received into the circle, or taught the secrets).][4]

What happens at our meetings? There is the little religious ceremony, the greeting of the Old Gods; then any business which has to be talked over, or perhaps someone wants to do a rite for some purpose; next there is a little feast and a dance; then you have to hurry for the last bus home![5]

The spiral or meeting dance is sometimes performed if there is room. This is a sort of "follow my leader" dance, the priestess usually leading, dancing round in a right-hand spiral to the centre, when she suddenly turns and unwinds the spiral. As she does this, she kisses each man she meets and all the other girls do the same. They say it is called the meeting dance because in the old days people came from distant parts and did not know each other, and this was designed to get them acquainted. But one man told me he had danced it at a church hall when he was a boy; so it may simply be an old children's game which the witches have taken over, or vice versa. Nowadays the only music they can have is a gramophone, or sometimes a sistrum, a rattle, or a small drum, played softly.[6]

I have attended many of these cult rites . . . there may be a fertility dance, but the other rites are simple, and with a purpose, and in no way resemble those of the Roman Catholic or any other Church that I know. True, sometimes there is a short ceremony when cakes and wine are blessed and eaten. (They tell me that in the old days mead or ale was often used.) This may be in imitation of the early Christian Agape, the Love Feast, but there is no suggestion that the cakes turn into flesh and blood. The ceremony is simply intended as a short repast, though it is definitely religious. The priestess usually presides. Candles are used, one to read the book by and others set round the circle. This does not in any way resemble the practice of any other religious sect I know. I do not think that can be called "imitation of the Church's pageantry". There are no crucifixes, inverted or otherwise, no sermons, mock or otherwise, and no absolution or hosts save for the cake and wine mentioned. Incense is used, but this has a practical purpose. There is no praise or homage to the Devil, no liturgy, evil or otherwise, nothing is said backwards, and there are no gestures with the left hand; in fact with the exception that it is a religious service and all religious services resemble one another, the rites are not in any way an imitation of anything I have ever seen. I do not say there have never been diabolists. I only say that, as far as I know, witches do not do the things of which they have been accused, and knowing what I do of their religion and practices I do not think they ever did.[7]

Of course, witch rites today are somewhat different from what they used to be many centuries ago. Then the great meetings, called Sabbats, used to be attended by large numbers of the population, who arrived provided with the wherewithal to cook a meal for themselves (hence the "hellish Sabbat fires" we have heard so much about), and prepared to spend a night on the heath in merrymaking, once the more serious rites were over. In fact, most traditional country merrymakings have some connection with the Old Religion; the Puritan Stubbes, in his *Anatomie of Abuses*, fiercely denounces the people who stayed out all night in the woods "Maying" on the old Sabbat date of May Eve; and Christina Hole, in her *English Folklore*, notes how the Northamptonshire "guisers" — folk-dancers dressed in fantastic costumes — are called "witch-men" to this day. Such instances might be greatly multiplied.

The English climate, of course, did not always permit these gatherings to be held on the heath; and I think that in this event they probably took place in someone's barn, or in the hall of a great house whose owner was friendly to the cult. In the Basque country of Pays de Labourd in 1609 the official investigator from the Parlement of Bordeaux, Pierre de Lancre, was horrified to find that the Sabbat was sometimes held in the local church, apparently with the priest's consent. He was particularly scandalised to find how many Basque priests sympathised with the Old Religion.[8]

We are often told horrid tales of witch meeting in churchyards, and of witches who, in the words of Robert Burns, "in kirkyards renew their leagues owre howkit dead." But in the old times the churchyard was the regular place for village merrymakings. In those days a churchyard was not, as it is today, a place of gravestones, but simply a green sward. From M.C. Anderson's *Looking for History in British Churches*[9] we may see that dancing in the churchyard was quite feasible in the old days as the author says that it was not the practice to erect gravestones to those who were buried there. "The great folks were buried beneath sculptured tombs within the church. . . . The little people remained anonymous in death before the 17th century."

Eileen Power, in her book, *Mediaeval People*[10] says, speaking of the peasants:

> They used to spend their holidays in dancing and singing and buffoonery, as country folk have always done until our own more gloomier, more self-conscious age. They were very merry and not at all refined, and the place they always chose for their dances was the churchyard; and unluckily the songs they sang as they danced in a ring were old pagan songs of their forefathers, left over from old Mayday festivities, which they could not forget, or ribald love-songs which the Church disliked. Over and over again we find the Church councils complaining that the peasants (and sometimes the priests, too) were singing 'wicked songs with a chorus of dancing women', or holding 'ballads and dancings and evil and wanton songs and such-like lures of the devil'; over and over again the bishops forbade these songs and dances; but in vain. In every country in Europe, right through the Middle Ages to the time of the Reformation, and after it, country folk continued to sing and dance in the churchyard.

She continues:

> Another later story still is told about a priest in Worcestershire, who was kept awake all night by the people dancing in his churchyard, and singing a song with the refrain 'Sweetheart have pity', so that he could not get it out of his head, and the next morning at Mass, instead of saying 'Dominus vobiscum', he said, 'Sweetheart have pity', and there was a dreadful scandal which got into a chronicle.[11]

However, I have never heard of a present-day witch meeting being held in a churchyard; I think those sensation-mongers who have described present-day witches as forgathering in graveyards are guessing, and their guess is a few centuries out.[12]

"You may wish to talk of nothing but the last meeting, and long for nothing save the next." It is what the "Wica" suffered torture and death for rather than give up. It is the foretaste of the "Promised City" which we may now enter today — the "Witches' Circle."[13]

1. 1.3.a *Lift Up the Veil*
2. *Witchcraft Today,* Chapter IV: Witch Practices. p. 46.
3. *Meaning of Witchcraft,* Chapter I: The Witch Cult in Britain. p. 14.
4. *Witchcraft Today,* Chapter X: What are Witches. p. 98.
5. *Meaning of Witchcraft,* Chapter I: The Witch Cult in Britain. p. 10.
6. *Witchcraft Today,* Chapter XIII: Recapitulation. p. 119.
7. *Witchcraft Today,* Chapter I: Living Witchcraft. p. 19.
8. De Lancre, *Tableau de LIInconstance des Mauvais,* Paris, 1612.
9 John Murray, 1951.
10. Penguin Books, 1951.
11. The chronicle in question was that of Giraldus Cambrensis, *Gemma Ecclesiastica,* pt. 1, c. XLII.
12. *Meaning of Witchcraft,* Chapter I: The Witch Cult in Britain. p. 13.
13. *Meaning of Witchcraft,* Chapter XII: Signs and Symbols. p. 180.

High Priestess

The High Priestess shall rule her Coven

as representative of the Goddess and

the High Priest shall support her

as the representative of the God.

Acting the part of the goddess the priestess is thought to be in communion with her.[1]

She has the position of authority, and may choose any man of sufficient rank in the cult to be her High Priest.[2]

Someone asked me the other night, "why do women take the chief place in witchcraft?" I had to say, "I don't know." No one knows. To say that it has always been so is not an answer. The easiest thing is to say it is a survival of matriarchy. It may well be, but I doubt if it is the true answer; because we do not know exactly what was the origin of matriarchy. I think the best explanation is because women represent the Goddess; and this probably originated when the cult of the Goddess was superimposed on the original cult of the Old God of Hunting and Death.

It must be clearly realised that not all women are regarded as representatives of the Goddess. It is only those who are recognised as being young and lovely, loving and generous, motherly and kind. In fact, those who possess all those qualities which can be summed up in the one word "sweetness". They should be Man's Ideal; in that way they may be worthy to have the spirit of the Goddess invoked to descend upon them.

The poet sings:

> O Woman! In our hours of ease
> Uncertain, coy, and hard to please,
> And variable as the shade
> By the light quivering aspen made,
> When pain and anguish wring the brow,
> A ministering angel thou!

Now, that is not quite the witch ideal. She should be steadfast, trusty and easy, otherwise she is not fit to have the Goddess descend upon her. If she is cross and selfish and ungenerous, it is certain she will never receive that divine blessing. Our Lady of Witchcraft has a high ideal set before her; she must be fresh and kindly and always the same to you. In any case, she will always receive the honour and respect which witches give to every woman, but to receive the high honours she must be worthy of them.

Among the virtues she must have is the realisation that youth is among the requisites necessary for the representative of the Goddess, and that she must be ready to retire gracefully in favour of a younger woman in time. She will then become one of the Elders, whose decisions are powerful in council.

But as the Old God told the Goddess, "Age and Fate wither all things, and against them I am helpless. But when men die and come to me I give them rest and peace so that they may return."

So a true Priestess realises that gracefully surrendering pride of place now is one of the greatest virtues, and she will return to that pride of place the next time, in another incarnation, with greater power and beauty. In a sense, the witch religion recognises all women as an incarnation of the Goddess, and all men as an incarnation of the God; and for this reason every woman is potentially a priestess, and every man potentially a priest; because to the witch the God and the Goddess are the Male and Female, the Right and the Left, the Two Pillars which support the Universe and every manifestation of male and female is a manifestation of Them.[3]

There is a tradition in the witch cult that a priestess may impersonate either the God or the Goddess, but that a male priest may only impersonate the God.[4]

1. *Witchcraft Today,* Chapter XIII: Recapitulation. p. 122.
2. *Meaning of Witchcraft,* Chapter I: The Witch Cult in Britain. p. 16.
3. *Meaning of Witchcraft,* Chapter IX: Why? p. 123.
4. *Meaning of Witchcraft,* Chapter VIII: Magic Thinking (cont.). p. 117.

High Priest

"He is whoever the high priestess appoints to take this position."

In practice, she always appoints her husband if he has sufficient rank; but she may appoint anyone who is eligible, including herself; she belts on a sword and acts as a man. In the old days it was often a distinguished visitor who was appointed.[1]

The priest, acting as the god, becomes at one with him in his aspect of Death, the Consoler, the Comforter, the bringer of a happy after-life and regeneration.[2]

The High Priest of a witch coven is, as we have seen, chosen by the Priestess. He is the person whom the Inquisitors and witch-hunters of old times used to call "the Devil", as being either an actual supernatural devil or else his human representative. Witches are constantly being accused of "worshipping the Devil". Now, when we use that word "Devil", what picture automatically forms itself in most people's minds? Is it not that of a strange-looking being who seems to be partly human and partly animal, having great horns on his head, and a body covered with hair, although his face is human? Have you ever stopped to wonder why this picture should automatically come into your mind in this way? *There is not one single text in the Bible which describes 'the Devil' or 'Satan' in this manner.* The only place in which you will find such a personage described is, curiously enough, among the gods of the ancient peoples, Here you will find quite a number of Horned Gods, and sometimes Horned Goddesses too, who were not, however, beings of evil, but deities beneficent to man. The reason why people picture "the Devil" in this way is because from the very earliest times the Church has taught that the Old God who possessed these attributes was the enemy of the Christian God, and hence must be Satan; and people have got so used to this concept that they have never stopped to question it.

It is evident from early pictures and descriptions (the earliest being the famous cave paintings found at Ariege in the Caverne des Trois Freres, done by men of the Stone Age), that the High Priest who was the god's representative sometimes wore a ritual disguise, consisting of a head-dress bearing the horns of a stag or a bull, and a kind of robe of animal skins; sometimes, too, a mask which concealed his features.

This custom seems to have been more particularly followed at the big Sabbats, when many people gathered outside the circle who were not actual initiates of the witches' mysteries, but came "for luck" (i.e. for the blessing of the Old Gods) or simply to enjoy themselves. It made the proceedings more impressive, and at the same time safer, if the god's representative was masked and disguised, so that he could not be recognised. The horned figure, seen dimly by moonlight or by the light of torches, would have seemed to the outsiders to be a supernatural being, and the initiates would not have undeceived them. When only initiates were present, there was less need for the ritual disguise, so the custom of wearing it has tended to fade out.[3]

1. *Witchcraft Today,* Chapter XII: Who is the Devil. p. 110.
2. *Witchcraft Today,* Chapter XIII: Recapitulation. p. 122.
3. *Meaning of Witchcraft,* Chapter I: The Witch Cult in Britain. p. 17.

Oaths

The charge I think came from the time when Romans or strangers came in; it explains a little which would not be known to all in the old days, and identifies the goddess with goddesses of other lands. I think a similar charge was a feature of the ancient mysteries.

I am forbidden to give any more; but if you accept her rule you are promised various benefits and admitted into the circle, introduced to the Mighty Dead and to the cult members.

There is also a small "frightening", an "ordeal" and an "oath"; you are shown certain things and receive some instruction. It is all very simple and direct.[1]

[First Degree]

Magus: "Art armed?"

Witch: "With a knife in my hair."

Magus: "Then on that knife wilt thou swear absolute secrecy?"

Witch: "I will."

Magus: "Then say after me. 'I, (name), in the presence of the Mighty Ones, do of my own will and accord, most solemnly swear that I will ever keep secret and never reveal the secrets of the Art, except it be to a proper person, properly prepared, within a circle such as I am now in. All this I swear by my hopes of a future life, mindful that my measure has been taken, and may my weapons turn against me if I break this my solemn oath.'"

Magus now unbinds her feet, unties the Cable Tow from the altar, removes the blindfold, and helps her up to her feet.[2]

"When may we advance, Morven, and how many degrees are there?"

"There is but one degree more," she said. "Where you take an oath and are made to use the working tools, but after that, there is what is called a degree. There is no oath, and all who have taken the second degree are qualified to work it, but 'tis the quintessence of Magic, and 'tis not to be used lightly, and then only with one whom you love and are loved by, may it be done, all else were sin. To misuse it were the greater death, in this world, as in the next."[3]

[Second Degree]

Magus: "To attain this sublime degree, it is necessary to suffer and be purified. Art ready to suffer to Learn?"

Witch: "I am."

Magus: "I prepare thee to take the great oath."

He strikes three knells on the bell, and again gives the series of three, seven, nine, and 21 strokes with the scourge as before.

Magus: "I now give thee a new name: _______. [kiss]

Magus: "Repeat thy new name after me, <saying> 'I, (name), swear upon my mother's womb and by mine Honour among men and among my brothers and sisters of the Art, that I will never reveal to any at all any of the secrets of the Art, except it be to a worthy person, properly prepared, in the centre of a Magic Circle, such as I am now in. This I swear by my hopes of Salvation, my past lives, and my hopes of future ones to come, and I devote myself to utter destruction if I break this my solemn oath."[4]

In the event of any member resigning from the Craft, he or she will honourably observe the Oath of Secrecy taken at initiation, and will also return to the Elders any written matter relating to the Craft which may be in his or her possession.[5]

1. Witchcraft Today, Chapter III: Witch Beliefs. p. 36
2. 1.4.1a *First Degree Initiation*
3. *High Magic's Aid*, Chapter XVII: The Witch Cult. p. 186.
4. 1.4.2a Second-Degree
5. 3.1 Supplement: The "Proposed Rules for the Craft"

BOOK OF SHADOWS

PART ONE

1.1.a Casting the Circle (1949)

- Having chosen a place proper, take the sickle or scimitar of Art or a Witch's Athame, if thou mayest obtain it, and stick it into the centre, then take a cord, and 'twere well to use the Cable Tow for this, and loop it over the Instrument, four and one half feet, and so trace out the circumference of the circle, which must be traced either with the Sword, or the knife with the black hilt, or it be of little avail, but ever leave open a door towards the North. Make in all 3 circles, one within the other, and write names of power between these.
- First draw circle with Magic Sword or Athame.
- Consecrate Salt and Water: Touch Water with Athame, saying, "I exorcise thee, O creature of Water, that thou cast out from Thee all the impurities and uncleannesses of the Spirits of the World of Phantasm, so they may harm me not, in the names of Aradia and Cernunnos."
- Touching Salt with Athame, say, "The Blessings of Aradia and Cernunnos be upon this creature of Salt, and let all malignity and hindrance be cast forth hencefrom, and let all good enter herein, for without Thee man cannot live, wherefore I bless thee and invoke thee, that thou mayest aid me."
- Then put the Salt into the Water.
- Sprinkle with exorcised Water.

- Light candles; say, "I exorcise thee, O Creature of Fire, that every kind of Phantasm may retire from thee, and be unable to harm or deceive in any way, in the names of Aradia and Cernunnos."
- Caution initiate (if any); warn companions; enter circle and close doors with 3 pentagrams.
- Proclaim object of working
- Circumambulate 3 times or more before commencing work.
- Summon: "I summon, stir, and Call thee up, thou Mighty Ones of the East, South, West, and North." Salute and draw pentacle with Magic Sword or Athame, the first stroke being from the top down to the left.

NOTES

[A *fictional* description of 'Casting the Circle' from *High Magic's Aid.*]

. . . for the stars were well aspected, and that night they were to attempt the great experiment, making the Great Circle.

". . . All who enter the Circle with me come as my helpers, and must help me by thinking correctly, to give me strength and so increase my power, for if there are any in the Circle who lets his thoughts stray from the matter in hand, he not only weakens me and so defeats his own ends, but brings danger upon us all."

. . . With some soberness of spirit, because of the great things before them, they mounted the stairs to the chamber above where stood the tub of water, each man carrying a bucket of hot water which they mixed with the cold already in the tub. Thur stripped and exorcised the water thus:

"I exorcise thee, O creature of water, that thou cast out from thee all the impurities and uncleanlinesses of the spirits of the world of phantasms, so they may harm me not. Through the Virtue of God the Almighty, Who reigneth through the Ages of Ages. By the names of Mertallia, Musalia, Dophalia, Nnemalia, Zitanseia, Goldaphaira, Dedulsaira, Gheninairea,

Geogropheira, Cedahi, Gilthar, Godieb, Ezoiil, Musil, Grassil, Tamen, Puri, Godu, Hoznoth, Astroth, Tzabaoth, Adonai, Asla, On, El, Tetragramaton, Shema, Ariston, Anaphaxeton, Segilaton, Primeuraton. Amen." Then he washed himself thoroughly, saying as he did so:

"Purge me, O Lord, with hyssop and I shall be clean. Wash me and I shall be whiter than snow."

Then he took salt and blessed it, saying:

"The blessings of the Father Almighty be upon this creature of salt, let all malignity and hinderance be cast forth therefrom, and let all good enter therein, wherefore do I bless Thee, that Thou mayest aid me. Amen."

Casting this exorcised salt into the water, he washed himself again, saying as he did so:

"Imanel, Arnamon, Imato, Memeon, Vaphoron, Gardon, Existon, Zagverinm, Momerton, Zarmesiton, Tilecon, Tixmion. Amen."

As the invocation ended he stepped out, dried himself and donned a clean white linen robe.

While all this was in progress, Jan was obediently fixing his mind upon Fitz-Urse and his castle, but Olaf's attention was fixed on Morven, who had now entered the bath and splashed about.

Then Thur poured water over her, saying solemnly:

"I conjure thee, O creature, being a young girl. By the Most High God, the father of all creatures, by Father Elohim and by Father Elohim Gebur and by Father Elion, that thou shalt neither have the will or the power to hide anything from me, and that thou shall be faithful and obedient to me. Amen."

Then he poured water over again, saying:

"Be thee regenerate, cleansed and purified, so that the spirits may neither harm thee nor abide in thee. Amen."

Then he had the two Bonders strip and get into the tub together: silently they obeyed, watching him covertly as they scoured their bodies with an earnestness that made them glow. Thur smothered a smile at this cleansing, accomplished as never before. Taking water from the tub and pouring it over their heads so it flowed in a cascade to their feet, saying as he did so over each: "Be ye pure and regenerate, cleansed and purified in the name of the Ineffable, Great and Eternal God from all your iniquities, may the Virtue of the Most High descend upon you and abide with you always, so that you may have power and strength to win the desires of your heart. Amen."

When they stepped out and dried themselves, much subdued by the solemn strangeness of this unusual stress upon purification, Thur pointed to two clean white robes and motioned to them to don them. Then he said: "It is needful that you wear these Talismans upon your breasts," and hung about Jan's neck a Pentacle of Iron for Mars, and upon Olaf a thin disc of beaten gold, for Leo. Morven already had her own, the Pentacle of Jupiter of silver. Each of these Pentacles was engraved with the Kabalistic signs appropriate to its ruling spirit.

Upon his own breast Thur then suspended three of the Pentacles of Iron he had made for Bartzebal, together with his own individual Talisman of Mercury, formed of brass. The Pentacles of Bartzebal he covered with a kerchief. He then censed the three disciples and himself, then censed again the Talismans upon their breasts and upon his own, saying: "These are the Talismans and Pentacles, perfumed with the proper fumigations, by which being assured and encouraged ye may enter into this matter without fear or terror, and shall be exempt from all perils and dangers provided thou obey my commands and do all I shall ordain. All things shall go according to my desires."

After a moment of silence he spoke again. "Jan and Olaf, you will need your swords; Morven hath her Athame. Each weapon hold in your right hands when in the Circle."

As he spoke he picked up the lighted lantern and turned to ascend the ladder leading to the loft above. They all followed. The rays of the lantern faintly illuminated the great loft. Thur lighted a great candle upon the Altar, placed in the midst of the Great Circle, saying: "I exorcise Thee, O Creature of Fire, in the Name of the Sovereign and Eternal Lord, by his Ineffable Name which is JHVH, by the name Jah and by the name of Power which is El, that thou mayest enlighten the hearts of all Spirits which we may call into this Circle, so that they may appear before us without fraud and deceit, through HIM, who hast created all things."

Then, going sunwise, he lighted other candles round the Circle. When he had finished there was a soft and steady illumination; meanwhile Morven had been following him around lighting the charcoal in braziers set at the four cardinal points, and putting incense thereon.

As the candles were lighted, details of the place of experiment leapt into being, the vast oak beams, springing from the floor, and sloping upwards to the peak of the roof, wisps of reeds from the thatch increased in shadow to fingers of clutching hands; Kabalistic signs chalked on beams, which as they sprang to their attention, struck the mind with all the force of a physical blow by reason of their mystery and the awfulness of their import. As the little points of light grew, the creamy satin-smoothness of Morven's body, like a fine pearl, concentrated them and drew them to itself to send them forth again in iridescent lustre at which Jan resolutely refused to look. The markings of the Great Circle could now be seen in all its complicated detail.

In all there were four circles, the outer, a double one, was fifteen feet in diameter, a second was drawn a foot inside this, and a third a foot within this again. Thus the inner circle was eleven feet in diameter.

Outside the Great Circle but just touching it, were four small double circles, two feet in diameter, around the braziers at the cardinal points. A triangle was drawn outside the Circle at the south. A doorway was marked into the Great Circle by drawing two parallel lines two feet apart, from the outer to the inner circle. The three disciples stood waiting his pleasure. To Morven, Thur gave a censer and a basket of incense. In her right hand she held her Athame, and she slung the handle of the basket on her arm. Jan was given a mighty parchment and a flask of perfume; to Olaf a pen, parchment and a small horn of ink, which, together with his sword, he clutched with a desperate firmness of determination not to drop them.

Meanwhile Thur, standing in the centre of the circle, facing eastwards, crossed himself, saying; "Atoh, Malkus, ve Gevruah, vr Gedulah, le Olam."

Then, going to the eastern side of the Circle, said;

"I summon stir and call thee up, thou Mighty Ones of the East, to guard this Circle." He then made the same proclamations to the Mighty Ones of the South, West and North in turn. Then, with the point of his consecrated sword, he retraced every line of the Great Circle, but carefully raised the point of his sword in the form of an arch each time he passed the doorway, so the Circle was left incomplete at these points. Then he wrote names of power between the Circles. In the south-east, he wrote JHVH (Jehovah); In the south-west AHIA, at the north-west, ALVIN; and in the north-east, ALH. Within the second and inner circle he wrote at the east, AL; at the south, AGLA; at the west, JA, and at the north, ADNI. All in Hebrew characters, Pentacles were traced between these names around the circumference of the Circle. All this accomplished, Thur went to each brazier in turn, from the east passing southwards, the way of the sun, fanning up the coals, followed by Morven casting upon them fresh incense of aloes, nutmeg, gum-bengerman and musk. Before the Altar was a large brazier, this was now lighted and incense set on it.[1]

* * * * *

Casting the Circle.

I am also permitted to tell for the first time in print the true reason why the important thing in all their ceremonies is "Casting the Circle". They are taught that the circle is "between the worlds", that is, between this world and the next, the dominions of the gods.

The circle such as it is shown in pictures may or may not be used. It is most convenient to mark it with chalk, paint or otherwise, to show where it is;

but marks on the carpet may be utilized. Furniture may be placed to indicate the bounds. The only circle that matters is the one drawn before every ceremony with either a duly consecrated Magic Sword or a Knife, the latter being the Witches' Athame or Black-Hilted Knife, with magic signs on the hilt, and this is most generally used. The circle is usually nine feet in diameter, unless made for some very special purpose. There are two outer circles, each six inches apart, so the third circle has a diameter of eleven feet. When drawn, this circle is carefully purified, as also are all who celebrate the rites. Witches attach great importance to this, for within the circle is the gods' domain.

It is necessary to distinguish this clearly from the work of the magician or sorcerer, who draws a circle on the ground and fortifies it with mighty words of power and summons (or attempts to summon) spirits and demons to do his bidding, the circle being to prevent them from doing him harm, and he dare not leave it.

The Witches' Circle, on the other hand, is to *keep in* the power which they believe they can raise from their own bodies and to prevent it from being dissipated before they can mould it to their own will. They can and do step in and out if they wish to, but this involves some loss of power, so they avoid doing so as much as possible.

People try to make me say that in the rites skulls and other repulsive things are used. I have never seen such things; but they tell me that in the old days sometimes, when the High priest was not present, a skull and crossbones was used to represent the god, death and resurrection (or reincarnation). Nowadays the High Priestess stands in a position representing the skull and crossbones, or death, and moves to another position, a pentacle, representing resurrection, during the rites. [2]

1. *High Magic's Aid,* Chapter xvi, Making The Great Circle. p. 164.
2. *Witchcraft Today,* Chapter1: Living Witchcraft. p. 22.

1.1.b A Revision of the Casting Procedure (1957)

- All Are Purified
- Magus consecrates salt and water.
- High Priestess kneels at Altar, takes up Sword, says, "I conjure thee, O Sword of Steel, to serve me as a defence in all Magical Operations. Guard me at all times against mine enemies, both visible and invisible. Grant that I may obtain what I desire in all things wherein I may use Thee, Wherefore do I bless Thee and invoke Thee in the names of Aradia and Cernunnos." Gives Sword to Magus.
- Magus kneeling hands her vessel of consecrated Water and Aspergillum. He Casts the Circle, three circles, on the lines marked out, starting at the East and returning to the East. High Priestess follows, Asperging Circle (sprinkling it to purify it) and all present and finally herself. Then she goes round again censing it. (Everyone in the circle must be sprinkled and censed.) She returns vessel, etc., to Magus, who places them on altar, or convenient place, and hands her Sword [handwritten].
- She walks slowly round Circle, saying, "I conjure Thee, O Circle of Space, that thou be a Boundary and a Protection and a meeting place between the world of Men and that of the Dread Lords of the OUTER SPACES, that Thou be cleansed, Purified, and strengthened to be a Guardian and a Protection that shall preserve and contain THAT POWER which we so

earnestly desire to raise within thy bounds this night, wherefore do I bless thee and entreat thee to aid me in the endeavour, in the names of Aradia and Cernunnos." Hands sword to Magus.

Magus then summons the Mighty Ones as usual.

High Priestess stands in front of Altar (which may be pushed back for this). High Priestess assumes Goddess position (arms crossed). Magus kneeling in front of her, draws pentacle on her body with Phallus-headed Wand, Invokes (Drawing down the Moon), "I Invoke and beseech Thee, O mighty MOTHER of all life and fertility. 'By seed and root, by stem and bud, by leaf and flower and fruit, by Life and Love, do I invoke Thee' to descend into the body of thy servant and High Priestess (name)." (The Moon having been drawn down, i.e., link established, Magus and all male officers give fivefold kiss; all others bow.)

High Priestess in Goddess position says, (arms crossed),

"Mother, Darksome and Divine,
    Mine the Scourge and Mine the Kiss,
    The Five-point Star of Love and Bliss;
Here I charge ye in this Sign.
(Opens out Arms to pentacle position)

Bow before my Spirit bright (All bow)
    Aphrodite, Arianrhod,
    Lover of the Horned God,
Queen of Witchery and Night.

Diana, Brigid, Melusine,
Am I named of old by men,
Artemis and Cerridwen,
Hell's dark mistress, Heaven's Queen.

Ye who ask of me a boon,
Meet ye in some hidden shade,
Lead my dance in greenwood glade
By the light of the full moon.

Dance about mine altar stone,
Work my holy magistry,
Ye who are fain of sorcery,
I bring ye secrets yet unknown.

No more shall ye know slavery
Who tread my round the Sabbat night.
Come ye all naked to the rite
In sign that ye are truly free.

Keep ye my mysteries in mirth,
Heart joined to heart and lip to lip.
Five are the points of fellowship
That bring ye ecstasy on Earth.

No other law but love I know;
By naught but love may I be known,
And all that liveth is my own:
From me they come, to me they go.

1.2. Drawing Down the Moon (1949)

High Priestess stands in front of Altar, assumes Goddess position (arms crossed).

Magus, kneeling in front of her, draws pentacle on her body with Phallus-headed Wand, invokes,

> "I Invoke and beseech Thee, O mighty Mother of all life and fertility. By seed and root, by stem and bud, by leaf and flower and fruit, by Life and Love, do I invoke Thee to descend into the body of thy servant and High Priestess [name]."

The Moon having been drawn down, i.e., link established, Magus and other men give Fivefold Kiss:

(kissing feet)

> "Blessed be thy feet, that have brought thee in these ways";

(kissing knees)

> "Blessed be thy knees, that shall kneel at the sacred altar";

(kissing womb)

> "Blessed be thy womb, without which we would not be";

(kissing breasts)

> "Blessed be thy breasts, formed in beauty and in strength";

(kissing lips)

"Blessed be thy lips, that shall speak the sacred names."

Women all bow.

If there be an initiation, then at this time the Magus and the High Priestess in Goddess position (Arms Crossed) says the Charge while the Initiate stands outside the circle.

NOTES

It is believed by witches that by acting a part you really take on the nature of the thing you imitate. This is really the basis of the cave-man's magic. By making the clay image of the animal you wish to kill, and by knowing its name, you establish a link between them, so that when he stuck spears into it it gave him power to kill it when he hunted it. That these beliefs may seem rather like children's games to some does not alter the fact that primitive men do behave like this, and so do the witches. By acting the part of the Goddess the priestess is thought to be in communion with her; so the priest, acting as the god, becomes at one with him in his aspect of Death, the Consoler, the Comforter, the bringer of a happy after-life and regeneration. The initiate in undergoing the God's experiences becomes a witch.

Witches quite realize that this communion does not occur every time one assumes the goddess position, but they very soon realize that by doing so they begin to receive thrills which are apt to grow more and more intense when the trance comes on. They KNOW! It is no use saying: "This is only suggestion, or the subconscious mind." They reply: "We quite agree; suggestion or the subconscious mind are simply some of the tools which we use to help to open the Door."

It is the old case of: 'Unless you experience it yourself you will never believe. When you have experienced it, you don't believe, you KNOW.'

And, when you have once known the goddess, does anything else really matter? To attain this state there are many roads, and dancing is perhaps the easiest; the calls and chants help, the attitude of the other members is of the greatest assistance — but the true secret is within oneself, and also to some extent in one's partner or assistant in the art, and it is not a thing that can be forced. A quiet knowledge that you will do it, and a steady and regular performance of the rites, are all that is really necessary, although other things help. Short cuts are useful, but you must use them carefully as they are apt to lead you astray and to involve more work in the end. You must first believe it is possible; then, use the method, or preferably a combination of the various methods that may be used together. When you have once attained the ecstasy you know that it exists and may be attained again. You must banish all feelings of *can't*, fix in your mind: "*I can and will.*"

There are a number of spiritual powers which many people do not recognize as such, e.g. the various forms of inspiration, music and poetry, clairvoyance and magical awareness; but the greatest of all these is love. All these aids should be employed under instruction, as there are difficulties and dangers in their undiscriminating use.[1]

1. *Witchcraft Today,* Chapter XIII: Recapitulation. p. 122.

1.3.a "Lift Up the Veil" (1949)

THE CHARGE (1949)

Doreen Valiente, High Priestess of Gardner's coven (1953–1957), rewrote this as *The Charge of the Goddess*.

Magus:	"Listen to the words of the Great mother, who of old was also called among men Artemis, Astarte, Dione, Melusine, Aphrodite, Cerridwen, Diana, Arianrhod, Bride, and by many other names."
High Priestess:	"At mine Altars the youth of Lacedaemon in Sparta made due sacrifice. Whenever ye have need of anything, once in the month, and better it be when the moon is full, ye shall assemble in some secret place and adore the spirit of Me who am Queen of all Witcheries and magics. There ye shall assemble, ye who are fain to learn all sorcery, yet have not won its deepest secrets. To these will I teach things that are yet unknown. And ye shall be free from slavery, and as a sign that ye be really free, ye shall be naked in your rites, both men and women, and ye shall dance, sing, feast, make music, and love, all in my praise. There is a Secret Door that I have made to establish the way to taste even on earth the elixir of immortality. Say, 'Let ecstasy be mine, and joy on earth even to me, To Me,' For I am a gracious Goddess. I give unimaginable joys

on earth, certainty, not faith, while in life! And upon death, peace unutterable, rest, and ecstasy, nor do I demand aught in sacrifice."

Magus: "Hear ye the words of the Star Goddess."

High Priestess: "I love you: I yearn for you: pale or purple, veiled or voluptuous. I who am all pleasure, and purple and drunkenness of the innermost senses, desire you. Put on the wings, arouse the coiled splendour within you. Come unto me. For I am the flame that burns in the heart of every man, and the core of every Star. Let it be your inmost divine self who art lost in the constant rapture of infinite joy. Let the rituals be rightly performed with joy and beauty. Remember that all acts of love and pleasure are my rituals. So let there be beauty and strength, leaping laughter, force and fire by within you. And if thou sayest, 'I have journeyed unto thee, and it availed me not,' rather shalt thou say, 'I called upon thee, and I waited patiently, and Lo, thou wast with me from the beginning,' for they that ever desired me shall ever attain me, even to the end of all desire.

This much of the rites must ever be performed to prepare for any initiation, whether of one degree or of all three.

NOTES

Before an initiation a charge is read beginning: *Listen to the words of the* Great Mother, who of old was also called among men Artemis, Astarte,

Dione, Melusine, Aphrodite and many other names. At mine altars the youth of Lacedaemon made due sacrifice. Once in the month, and better it be when the moon is full, meet in some secret place and adore me, who am queen of all the magics. . . .

For I am a gracious goddess, I give joy on earth, certainty, not faith, while in life; and upon death, peace unutterable, rest and the ecstasy of the goddess. Nor do I demand aught in sacrifice. . . .

The charge I think came from the time when Romans or strangers came in; it explains a little which would not be known to all in the old days, and identifies the goddess with goddesses of other lands. I think a similar charge was a feature of the ancient mysteries.

I am forbidden to give any more; but if you accept her rule you are promised various benefits and admitted into the circle, introduced to the Mighty Dead and to the cult members.

There is also a small "frightening", an "ordeal" and an "oath"; you are shown certain things and receive some instruction. It is all very simple and direct.[1]

1. *Witchcraft Today,* Chapter III: Witch Beliefs. p. 36

1.3.b The Prose Charge (1957)

THE CHARGE, to be read while the initiate stands, properly prepared before the Circle.

Magus: "Listen to the words of the Great mother, who was of old also called among men, Artemis, Astarte, Dione, Melusine, Aphrodite, Cerridwen, Diana, Arianrhod, Bride, and by many other names."

High Priestess: "At mine Altars the youth of Lacedaemon in Sparta made due sacrifice. Whenever ye have need of anything, once in the month, and better it be when the moon is full. Then ye shall assemble in some secret place and adore the spirit of Me who am Queen of all Witcheries. There ye shall assemble, ye who are fain to learn all sorcery, yet who have not won its deepest secrets. To these will I teach things that are yet unknown. And ye shall be free from slavery, and as a sign that ye be really free, ye shall be naked in your rites, and ye shall dance, sing, feast, make music, and love, all in my praise.' "For mine is the ecstasy of the Spirit, and mine is also joy on earth. For my Law is Love unto all beings. "Keep pure your highest ideals. Strive ever towards it. Let naught stop you or turn you aside. "For mine is the secret which opens upon the door of youth; and mine is the cup of the Wine of

Life: and the Cauldron of Cerridwen, which is the Holy Grail of Immortality. "I am the Gracious Goddess who gives the gift of Joy unto the heart of Man. "Upon Earth I give the knowledge of the Spirit Eternal, and beyond death I give peace and freedom, and reunion with those who have gone before. Nor do I demand aught in sacrifice, for behold, I am the Mother of all things, and my love is poured out upon earth."

Magus: "Hear ye the words of the Star Goddess, She in the dust of whose feet are the hosts of Heaven, whose body encircleth the universe."

High Priestess: "I who am the beauty of the green earth; and the White Moon amongst the Stars; and the mystery of the Waters; and the desire of the heart of man. I call unto thy soul: arise and come unto me. "For I am the Soul of nature who giveth life to the Universe; 'From me all things proceed; and unto me, all things must return.' Beloved of the Gods and men, thine inmost divine self shall be enfolded in the raptures of the infinite. "Let my worship be within the heart that rejoiceth, for behold: all acts of love and pleasure are my rituals; and therefore let there be Beauty and Strength, Power and Compassion, Honour and Humility, Mirth and reverence within you. "And thou who thinkest to seek me, know that thy seeking and yearning shall avail thee not unless thou know the mystery, that if that which thou seekest thou findest not within thee, thou wilt never find it without thee, for behold; I have been with thee from the beginning, and I am that which is attained at the end of desire."

1.4. Initiation

Introductory Notes

From an early date recruits were admitted only from people who were of the blood; that is, from a witch family. The various rituals of worship, secrets of herbal lore, and the Great Secret of what they call magic, have been handed down to what has become more or less a family secret society.[1]

It is a family group, if you like; but not all of the family belongs to it, only those who are initiated, and people of non-witch families are at times introduced and initiated. While it is unusual for members of the cult today to think of themselves as a "caste", they certainly regard themselves as a kind of "family" apart.[2]

Gomme, in *Folklore as a Historical Science* (p. 201 *et seq*), stresses the importance of the act of initiation as applied to the witch cult. "It emphasises the existence of a caste apart from the general populace. The existence of this caste long before, where they did practise their powers, carrying back this act of initiation age after age. It is clear that the people who were from time to time introduced into the witch caste carried on the practices and assumed the functions of the caste even though they came into it as novices and strangers. We thus arrive at what might be termed an artificial means of descent into a peculiar group of superstitions. This was influenced in the Middle Ages by beliefs of the carrying on of traditional practices by certain families and groups of people who could only acquire such practices by initiation and family teaching." This is, of course, exactly what happened.

At a witch meeting, where I was present, a visit to a nudist club was discussed, and a woman said, "I wouldn't like that". I said, "Why not?" And the reply was, "I don't care *here*, of course; but I wouldn't go before other people". The exact "caste" feeling![3]

Being initiated into the witch cult does not give a witch supernatural powers but instructions are given, in rather veiled terms, in processes which develop various clairvoyant and other powers, in those who naturally possess them slightly. If they have none they can create none. Some of these powers are akin to magnetism, mesmerism and suggestion, and depend on the possibility of forming a sort of human battery, as it were, of combined human wills working together to influence persons or events at a distance. They have instructions in how to learn to do this by practice. It would take many people a long time, if I understand the directions aright. If these arts were more generally practised nowadays, we should call most of them spiritualism, mesmerism, suggestion, E.S.P., Yoga or perhaps Christian Science; to a witch it is all MAGIC, and magic is the art of getting results. To do this certain processes are necessary and the rites are such that these processes may be used. In other words, they condition you. This is the secret of the cult.[4]

The witches tell me: "The law always has been that power must be passed from man to woman or from woman to man, the only exception being when a mother initiates her daughter or a father his son, because they are part of themselves." (The reason is that great love is apt to occur between people who go through the rites together.)[5]

Plato says, "Of what the disease of the spirit consists, from what cause it is dulled, how it can be clarified, may be learned by philosophy. For by lustrations of the Mysteries the soul becomes liberated and passes into divine condition of being, hence discipline willingly endured becomes of far greater utility for purification. . . . On entering the interior part of the Temple, unmoved, and guarded by the sacred rites, they genuinely receive into their bosoms divine illumination, and divested of their garments they participate in the divine nature." The same ideas are found in the Speculations of Thales. Proclus, in his *On the Theology of Plato,* says, "the mind is affected and agitated in death, just as in initiation into the Mysteries, and word answers word, as well as thing to thing; for to die, and to be initiated, is the same. With hymns, dances, and sublime and sacred knowledge crowned and triumphant, they walk the regions of the blessed."[6]

1 *Witchcraft Today,* Chapter II: There have been Witches in all Ages p. 28

2. *Meaning of Witchcraft,* Chapter VIII: Magic Thinking (cont.) p. 119

3. *Meaning of Witchcraft,* Chapter VIII: Magic Thinking (cont.) p. 119

4. *Witchcraft Today,* Chapter I: Living Witchcraft p. 24

5. *Witchcraft Today,* Chapter VI: How the Little People became Witches . . . p. 57

6. *Meaning of Witchcraft,* Chapter VIII: Magic Thinking (cont.) p. 120

1.4.1a First Degree (1949)

Magus leaves circle by the doorway, goes to Postulant, and says,

"Since there is no other brother here, I must be thy sponsor, as well as priest. I am about to give you a warning. If you are still of the same mind, answer it with these words: 'Perfect Love and Perfect Trust.' " Placing the point of the sword to the Postulant's breast, he says, "O thou who standeth on the threshold between the pleasant world of men and the domains of the Dread Lords of the Outer Spaces, hast thou the courage to make the Assay? For I tell thee verily, it were better to rush on my weapon and perish miserably than to make the attempt with fear in thy heart."

Postulant: "I have two Passwords: Perfect Love and Perfect Trust."

Magus drops the sword point, saying,

"All who approach with perfect love and perfect trust are doubly welcome."

Going around behind her, he blindfolds her, then putting his left arm around her waist and his right arm around her neck, he pulls her head back, says,

"I give you the 3rd password, a Kiss to pass through this dread Door," and pushes her forward with his body, through the doorway and into the circle. Once inside, he releases her saying,

> "This is the way all are first brought into the circle."

Magus closes the doorway by drawing the point of the sword across it three times, joining all three circles, saying,

> "Agla, Azoth, Adonai,"

then drawing three pentacles to seal it. Magus guides Postulant to south of altar, and whispers,

> "Now there is the Ordeal."

Taking a short piece of cord from the altar, he ties it around her right ankle, saying,

> "Feet neither bound nor free."

Taking a longer cord, he ties her hands together behind her back, then pulls them up, so that the arms form a triangle, and ties the cord around her neck, leaving the end dangling down in front as a Cable Tow. With the Cable Tow in his left hand and the sword in his right hand, the Magus leads her sunwise around the circle to the east, where he salutes with the sword and proclaims,

> "Take heed, O Lords of the Watchtowers of the East, (name), properly prepared, will be made a Priestess and a Witch."

Magus leads her similarly to the south, west, and north, making the proclamation at each quarter. Next, clasping

Postulant around the waist with his left arm, and holding the sword erect in his right hand, he makes her circumambulate three times around the circle with a half-running, half-dancing step. He halts her at the south of the altar, and strikes eleven knells on the bell. He then kneels at her feet, saying,

> "In other religions the postulant kneels, as the Priests claim supreme power, but in the Art Magical, we are taught to be humble, so we kneel to welcome them and say:
>
> "Blessed be thy feet that have brought thee in these ways." (He kisses her feet.)
>
> "Blessed be thy knees that shall kneel at the sacred altar." (He kisses her knees.)
>
> "Blessed be thy womb, without which we would not be." (He kisses her Organ of Generation.)
>
> "Blessed by thy breasts, formed in beauty and in strength." (He kisses her breasts.)
>
> "Blessed be thy lips, which shall utter the sacred names." (He kisses her lips.)

Take measure [height, around forehead, across the heart, and across the genitals]. Magus says,

> "Be pleased to kneel,"

and helps her kneel before the altar. He ties the end of the Cable Tow to a ring in the altar, so that the postulant is bent sharply forward, with her head almost touching the floor. He also ties her feet together with the short cord. Magus strikes three knells on the bell and says,

	"Art ready to swear that thou wilt always be true to the Art?"
Witch:	"I am."
Magus:	strikes seven knells on the bell and says,
	"Before ye are sworn, art willing to pass the ordeal and be purified?"
Witch:	"I am."
Magus:	strikes eleven knells on the bell, takes the scourge from the altar, and gives a series of three, seven, nine, and 21 strokes with the scourge across the postulant's buttocks and says, "Ye have bravely passed the test. Art always ready to help, protect, and defend thy Brothers and Sisters of the Art?"
Witch:	"I am."
Magus:	"Art armed?"
Witch:	"With a knife in my hair."
Magus:	"Then on that knife wilt thou swear absolute secrecy?"
Witch:	"I will."

Magus: "Then say after me. 'I, (name), in the presence of the Mighty Ones, do of my own will and accord, most solemnly swear that I will ever keep secret and never reveal the secrets of the Art, except it be to a proper person, properly prepared, within a circle such as I am now in. All this I swear by my hopes of a future life, mindful that my measure has been taken, and may my weapons turn against me if I break this my solemn oath.' "

Magus now unbinds her feet, unties the Cable Tow from the altar, removes the blindfold, and helps her up to her feet.

Magus says, "I hereby sign thee with the triple sign.

"I consecrate thee with oil." (He anoints her with oil on the womb, the right breast, the left breast, and the womb again.)

"I consecrate thee with wine." (He anoints her with wine in the same pattern.)

"I consecrate thee with my lips" (he kisses her in the same pattern), "Priestess and Witch."

Magus now unbinds her hands and removes the last cord, saying,

"Now I Present to thee the Working Tools of a Witch.

"First the Magic Sword. With this, as with the Athame, thou canst form all Magic Circles, dominate, subdue, and punish all rebellious Spirits and Demons, and even persuade the Angels and Geniuses. With this in your hand you are the ruler of the Circle.

[Here "kiss" means that the initiate kisses the tool, and the Magus then kisses the Witch being initiated.]

"Next I present the Athame. This is the true Witch's weapon and has all the powers of the Magic Sword. [kiss]

"Next I present the White-Handled Knife. Its use is to form all instruments used in the Art. It can only be properly used within a Magic Circle. [Kiss]

"Next I present the Wand. Its use is to call up and control certain Angels and Geniuses, to whom it would not be mete to use the Magic Sword. [Kiss]

"Next I present the pentacles. These are for the purpose of calling up appropriate Spirits. [Kiss]

"Next I present the Censer of Incense. This is used to encourage and welcome Good Spirits and to banish Evil Spirits.[kiss]

"Next I present the scourge. This is a sign of power and domination. It is also to cause suffering and purification, for it is written, to learn you must suffer and be purified. Art willing to suffer to learn?"

Witch: "I am." [Kiss]

Magus: "Next, and lastly I present the Cords. They are of use to bind the sigils in the Art, the material basis, and to enforce thy will. Also they are necessary in the oath. I Salute thee in the name of Aradia and Cernunnos, Newly made Priestess and Witch."

Magus strikes seven knells on the bell and kisses Witch again, then circumambulates with her, proclaiming to the four quarters,

"Hear, ye Mighty Ones, (name) hath been consecrated Priestess and Witch of the Gods."

Note: if ceremony ends here, close circle with

"I thank ye for attending, and I dismiss ye to your pleasant abodes. Hail and farewell."

If not, go to next degree.

NOTES

[A *fictional* initiation from *High Magic's Aid.*]

. . . she re-drew the Circle with her Athame, leaving a doorway, then circumambulated three times sunwise, with a dancing step, as she did so calling on the Mighty Ones of the east, south, west and north to attend, then after dancing around several times in silence, she chanted;

"Eko; Eko; Azarak. Eko; Eko; Zomelak."

"Bagabi Lacha bachabe

Lamac cahi achababe

Karrellyos

Lamac lamac Bachalyas

Cabahagy sabalyos

Baryolos

Lagoz atha Cabyolas

Samahac atha famolas

Hurrahya"

She then left the circle by the doorway, and going to Jan said:

"As there is no other brother here I must be thy sponsor as well as priest. I am about to give you a warning, if you are still of the same mind, answer it with these words 'Perfect Love and perfect Trust.'"

Then, placing the point of her Athame to his heart said:

"O Thou who standest on the threshold, between the pleasant land of men and the domains of the dread lords of the Outer Spaces, hast Thou the courage to make the assay? For I tell thee verily, it were better to rush on my weapon and perish miserably than make the attempt with fear in thy heart."

Jan answered: " I have two passwords. Perfect Love and perfect Trust."

Morven dropped the knife's point saying:

"All who bring such words are doubly welcome," then going behind him she blindfolded him, then clasping him from behind with her left arm around his waist, and pulling his right arm around her neck, and his lips down to hers, said: "I give you the third password; 'A kiss.' "

So saying she pushed him forward with her body, through the doorway, into the Circle.

Once inside she released him whispering. "This is the way all are first brought into the Circle."

She then carefully closed the doorway by drawing the point of her Athame across it three times, joining all the circles.

Then leading him to the south of the Altar, whispered: "Now there is the Ordeal."

Taking a short piece of cord from the Altar she bound it round his right ankle, leaving the ends free, whispering; "Feet neither Bond nor Free."

Then with a longer cord she bound his hands firmly behind his back, then pulling them up into the small of his back, tied the cord round his neck, so his arms made a triangle at his back, leaving an end of cord hanging in a cable tow in front.

With this cable tow in her left hand and the Athame in her right, she led him Sunways round the Circle to the east, where saluting with the Athame she proclaimed;

"Take heed, O Lords of the Watchtowers of the East. Jan, properly prepared, will be made a priest and witch."

She then led him in turn to the south, west and north, where similar proclamations were made.

Then, clasping him round the body with her left arm, Athame erect in right, she made him circumambulate three times round the Circle with a half run, half dance step. Bound, blindfold, running round and round in so small a space, Jan's brain reeled giddily, tightly bound as he was he could do nothing but strive to keep his feet.

Suddenly he was pulled to a stop, at the south side of the Altar, where he stood swaying, his head reeling.

Morven struck eleven strokes on a little bell, then knelt at his feet, saying: "In other religions, the postulant kneels as the Priests claim supreme power. But in the Art Magical, we are taught to be humble, so we say:

Kissing his feet.	"Blessed be thy feet that have brought thee in these ways."
Kissing knees.	"Blessed be thy knees that shall kneel at the Sacred Altar."
Kissing phallus.	"Blessed be the Organ of Generation, without which we would not be."
Kissing breasts.	"Blessed be thy breasts, formed in beauty and in strength."
Kissing lips.	"Blessed be thy lips, which shall utter the sacred names."

She then made him kneel at the Altar, tying the cable tow to a ring so he was bending forward, and could scarcely move. She then tied his feet together with the cord on his right ankle.

Then, ringing three knells on the little bell, said:

"Art ready to swear thou wilt always be true to the Art?"

Jan replied; "I will."

Morven struck seven knells on the bell saying;

"Thou first must be purified."

Taking the scourge from the Altar, she struck his buttocks, first three then seven, then nine, then twenty one strokes with the scourge (forty in all).

They were not hard, but blindfold and bound as he was, their effect was startling, they helped to rouse him from the dazed condition he was in from running around the Circle.

As he came more to his senses he realised how utterly helpless he was. In Morven's power, he belonged to her, he was part of her, the blows that were raining on his buttocks gave her power over him, but he did not resent it, she had power over his mind, but that was as it should be, all he wanted was her, if he was hers he would be part of her, and that was all he wanted.

Then the blows ceased, and Morven's voice came.

"Art always ready to protect, help and defend thy brothers and sisters of the Art?"

Jan: "I am."

"Then say after me:

"I, Jan, in the presence of the Mighty Ones of the Outer Spaces, do of my own free will most solemnly swear that I will ever keep secret and never reveal the secrets of the Art, except it be to a proper person, properly prepared, within such a Circle as I am in now, and that I will never deny the secrets to such a person, if they be properly vouched for, by a brother or sister of the Art. All this I swear by my hopes of a future life and may my weapons turn against me if I break this my solemn oath.'"

He felt the cords loosed from his feet, then the cord from the Altar, the blindfold was whisked off, and hands still bound, he was assisted to his feet, where he stood, blinking, dazed and yet somehow, he felt so happy.

Morven knelt before him; he heard her voice as in a dream.

"I hereby consecrate thee with oil,"

"I hereby consecrate thee with wine,"

"I hereby consecrate thee with my lips, Priest and Witch," and he felt the touches, first the phallus and then right breast, then phallus again, forming a triangle. Then she rose and loosed his hands, saying:

"Now I present thee with the working tools of a witch."

Handing him a sword from the Altar, and motioning him to touch it.

"First, the Magic Sword. With this as with the Athame, thou canst form all Magic Circles, dominate, subdue and punish all rebellious Spirits and demons, and even persuade the angels and geniuses. With this in thy hand thou art the ruler of the Magic Circle," and she kissed him.

"Next I present the Athame. This is the true Witches' Weapon, it has all the powers of the Magic Sword." (Again a kiss.)

"Next I present the White Handled Knife. Its use is to form all instruments used in the Art. It can only be properly used within a Magic Circle." (Again a kiss.)

"Next I present the Censer of Incense, this is to encourage and welcome good spirits and to banish evil spirits." (A kiss.)

"Next I present the Scourge, this is a sign of Power and Domination, it is also to cause suffering and purification, for it is written: To learn thou must suffer and purified. Art willing to suffer to learn?"

Jan; " I am." (Again a Kiss.)

"Next and lastly I present the Cords. They are of use to bind the Sigils, the material basis, and to enforce thy will, also, they are necessary in the Oath."

Morven again kissed him, saying; "I salute thee in the name of the Gods. Newly made Priest and Witch."

They then both circumambulated the Circle, Morven proclaiming at the four quarters;

"Hear Ye, Mighty Ones, Jan hath been consecrated Priest and Witch." [1]

"When may we advance, Morven, and how many degrees are there?"

"There is but one degree more," she said. "Where you take an oath and are made to use the working tools, but after that, there is what is called a degree. There is no oath, and all who have taken the second degree are qualified to work it, but 'tis the quintessence of Magic, and 'tis not to be used lightly, and then only with one whom you love and are loved by, may it be done, all else were sin. To misuse it were the greater death, in this world, as in the next."[2]

1. 1949 : *High Magic's Aid,* Chapter xvII, The Witch Cult. p. 180.
2. 1949 : *High Magic's Aid,* Chapter xvII: The Witch Cult. p. 186.

* * * * *

A NOTE REGARDING THE AUTHENTICITY OF *HIGH MAGIC'S AID:*

"It has been said that only the words spoken by Morven, this book's heroine, are to be understood as truly authentic. This is interesting in view of what Gerald said when he presented me with a copy of *High Magic's Aid* in 1960, "Darling, take notice of Morven's words, they will teach you much."

Then, too, Gerald, himself, says at the end of his Introduction to this book, under Note. The Magical Rituals are authentic, partly from the Key of Solomon (MacGregor Mather's Translation) and partly from Magical MSS in my possession. (my emphasis)

And now, in 1992, forty-three years after this novel was written — 4 + 3 = 7 the number of Saturn, the Lord of Time; a letter has come to light in America. It is a handwritten letter from Gerald Gardner, to a Mr. Gordon B . . . . and contains these relevant passages. " . . . Actually, I wanted to write about a witch and what she'd told me, and she wouldn't let me tell anything about witchcraft, but I said why not let me write from the Witch's point of view. You are always persecuted and abused . . . So she said I might if I didn't give any Witch's magic, and it must only be as fiction. So, as I had to give some magic, I simply copied it from Jewish Ritual Magic, chiefly *The Key of Solomon the King*. It was thought that King Solomon could command the spirits and make them work for him. And if you know these words and sigils you could do the same. This key is usually in Latin or Hebrew, but there is an English translation by MacGregor Mathers. But personally I don't believe that it works. It's all very difficult and complicated . . . ."

So, in the end, (or the beginning), Gerald has confounded Time and substantiated his own words and actions from across the gulf of the years.

Patricia Crowther, Foreword to *High Magic's Aid*

1.4.1b First-Degree (1957)

Draw Circle with Magic Sword or Athame.

Sprinkle with Exorcised Water.

Go round Circle with Magic Sword or Athame, saying,

> "I conjure thee, O Circle of Power, that thou beest as a Boundary and a Protection to contain the magic power which I will raise within thy bounds. So do I bless thee, in the names of Aradia and Cernunnos."

Go round, saying at East, South, West, and North,

> "I summon, stir, and call thee up, ye Mighty Ones of the East (South, West, North), to witness the rites and to guard the circle."

[Editor's note: Later revisions by Gardner include, at this point, the rite of 'Drawing Down the Moon' followed by the 'Cabalistic Cross' (the Christian doxology spoken in Hebrew "Ateh Malkuth ve-Geburah ve-Gedulah le-Olahm, Amen. — For thine is the kingdom, and the power, and the glory forever, Amen. Mt 6.13b.)]

Read Charge, then say,

> "O thou who standest on the threshold between the pleasant world of men and the dread domains of the lords of the outer spaces, hast thou the courage to make the assay?" (Place point of the Magic Sword or Athame to Postulant's heart.) "For I say verily it were better to rush on my blade and perish

than to make the attempt with fear in thy heart."

Postulant: "I have two perfect words: perfect love, and perfect trust."

Say, "All who have are doubly welcome."

Entering position: "I give you a third to pass you through this dread door." Gives it [kiss].

Leading postulant, proclaim at four quarters,

"Take heed, ye Lords of the Watchtowers of the East (South, West, North), that (name) is properly prepared to be made a priestess and a witch."

Three times round the Circle with Dance step and chant.

Place Postulant in East; say,

In other religions the postulant kneels while the priest towers above him, but in the Art Magical we are taught to be humble, and so we kneel to welcome them, and we say:

"Blessed be the feet that have brought you in these ways; [kiss]

"Blessed be the knees that shall kneel at the sacred altar; [kiss]

"Blessed be thy womb (or organ of generation), without which we would not be; [kiss]

"Blessed be thy breasts, erected in beauty and in strength; [kiss]

"Blessed be thy lips, which shall utter the sacred names; [kiss]

"Before ye are sworn, art willing to pass the ordeal and be purified?"

Postulant "I am."

Take measure.

Secure.

Three strokes on bell.

Scourge 3, 7, 9, 21.

Say, "Ye have bravely passed the test. Art ready to swear that thou wilt always be true to the Art?"

Postulant "I am."

"Art always ready to help, protect, and defend thy brothers and sisters of the Art?"

Postulant "I am."

"Then say after me:

I, (name), in the presence of the mighty ones of the outer spaces, do of my own free will most solemnly swear that I will ever keep secret and never reveal the secrets of the Art, except it be to a proper person, properly prepared, within such a circle as I am in now, and that I will never deny the Secrets to such a person if they be vouched for by a brother or Sister of the Art. All this I swear by my hopes of a future life, and may my weapons turn against me if I break this my solemn oath."

Assist to rise.

"I hereby sign thee with the triple sign . . .

[the point-down triangle formed by touching the genitals, the right breast, the left breast, and the genitals again.]

. . . I consecrate thee with oil. I consecrate thee with wine. I consecrate thee with my lips, Priest (Priestess) and Witch."

Remove Cords. [kiss]

"I now present to you the working tools. First the magic sword. With this, as with the athame, thou canst form all magic circles, dominate, subdue, and punish all rebellious spirits and demons, and even persuade angels and good spirits. With this in your hand, you are ruler of the circle." [kiss]

"Next I present to you the athame. This is the true witches' weapon, and has all the powers of the magic sword." [kiss]

"Next I present the white-handled knife. Its use is to form all instruments used in the Art. It can only be used in a magic circle." [kiss]

"Next I present the wand. Its use is to call up and control certain angels and genie to whom it would not be meet to use the sword or athame." [kiss]

"Next I present the pentacle. This is for the purpose of calling up the appropriate spirits." [kiss]

"Next I present the censer of incense. This is used to encourage and welcome good spirits, and to banish evil spirits." [kiss]

"Next I present the scourge. This is a sign of power and domination. It is also used to cause purification and enlightenment, for it is written, 'To learn you must suffer and be purified.' [kiss]

"Art willing to suffer to learn?"

Postulant: "I am."

"Next and lastly I present the cords. They are of use to bind the sigils of the art, also the material basis. Also they are necessary in the oath." [kiss]

> "I now salute you in the names of Aradia and Cernunnos, Newly made Priestess and Witch."

Lead round and proclaim to four quarters,

> "Hear, ye Mighty Ones, (name) has been consecrated a priestess of the Goddess."

To close circle proclaim to four quarters,

> "Ye Mighty Ones of the East (South, West, North), I thank you for attending and, ere ye depart for your lovely realms, I say hail and farewell."

1.4.2a Second Degree (1949)

Magus binds Witch as before, but does not blindfold her, and circumambulates with her, proclaims to the four quarters,

> "Hear, ye Mighty Ones, (name), a duly consecrated Priestess and Witch, is now properly prepared to be made a High Priestess and Witch Queen."

Magus now leads her thrice around the circle with the half-running, half-dancing step, halts south of the altar, has the Witch kneel, and ties her down to the altar as before.

Magus: "To attain this sublime degree, it is necessary to suffer and be purified. Art ready to suffer to Learn?"

Priestess Witch: "I am."

Magus: "I prepare thee to take the great oath."

He strikes three knells on the bell, and again gives the series of three, seven, nine, and 21 strokes with the scourge as before.

Magus: "I now give thee a new name: ________. [kiss]

Magus: "Repeat thy new name after me, <saying> 'I, (name), swear upon my mother's womb and by mine Honour among men and among my brothers and sisters of the Art, that I will never reveal to any at all any of the secrets of the Art, except it be to a worthy person, properly prepared, in the centre of a Magic Circle, such as I am now in. This I swear by my hopes of Salvation, my past lives, and my hopes of future ones to come, and I devote myself to utter destruction if I break this my solemn oath."

Magus kneels, placing left hand under her knees and right hand on her head, thus forming magic link.

Magus: "I hereby will all my power into you." Wills.

Magus now unties her feet, unties the Cable Tow from the altar, and helps the Witch to her feet.

Magus: "I hereby sign and consecrate you with the great Magic Sign. Remember how it is formed and you will always recognize it."

"I consecrate thee with oil."

(He anoints her with oil on her womb, right breast, left hip, right hip, left breast, and womb again, thus tracing a point-down pentacle.)

"I consecrate thee with wine."

(He anoints her with wine in the same pattern.)

"I consecrate thee with my lips"

(He kisses her in the same pattern),

"High Priestess and Witch Queen."

Magus now unbinds Witch's hands and removes the cord, saying,

"Newly made High Priestess and Witch Queen" [kiss]

"you will now use the working tools in turn.

First, the Magic Sword; with it you will scribe the Magic Circle [kiss]

"Secondly, the Athame" (Form Circle) [kiss]

"Thirdly, the White Handled Knife" (use) [kiss]

"Fourthly, the Wand" (Wave to 4 Quarters) [kiss]

"Fifthly, the Pentacle" (Show to 4 Quarters) [kiss]

"Sixthly, the Censer of Incense" (Circle, cense) [kiss]

"Seventhly, the cords; bind me as I bound you."

Witch binds Magus and ties him to Altar.

Magus: "Learn, in Witchcraft, thou must ever return triple. As I scourged thee, so thou must scourge me, but triple. So where you received 3, return 9; where you received 7, return 21; where you received 9, return 27; where you received 21, return 63."

Witch scourges Magus as instructed, 120 strokes total.

Magus: "Thou hast obeyed the Law. But mark well, when thou receivest good, so equally art bound to return good threefold."

Witch now unbinds Magus and helps him to his feet.

Magus, taking the new Initiate by the hand and holding the Athame in the other, passes once round the Circle, proclaiming at the Four Quarters,

"Hear, Ye Mighty Ones, (name) hath been duly consecrated High Priestess and Witch Queen."

Note: if ceremony ends here, close circle with

"Hail and farewell."

If not go to next degree.

1.4.2b Second-Degree (1957)

Form Circle in usual manner, invoking the Mighty Ones at the Four Quarters. The Initiate should be properly prepared and bound with the Cords.

All are purified, including Initiate.

Circle once, proclaiming at the Four Quarters:

> "Hear Ye Mighty Ones, . . . (N), a duly consecrated Priestess and Witch is now properly prepared to be made a High Priest and Magus (High Priestess and Witch Queen)."

Circle three times, with dance step and chant.

Initiate then kneels before the Altar and is secured with the Cords.

Priestess or Magus:

> "To attain to this sublime Degree it is necessary to suffer and be purified. Art willing to suffer to learn?"

Initiate: "I am."

Priestess or Magus:

> "I purify thee to take this great oath rightly."

Strike three strokes upon the bell. Scourge 3, 7, 9, 21.

> "I now give thee a new name: . . ." [kiss]

"Repeat thy new name after me, saying, 'I, . . ., swear, upon my mother's womb and by mine honour among men and my brothers and sisters of the Art, that I will never reveal to any at all any of the secrets of the Art, except it be to a worthy person, properly prepared, in the centre of a Magic Circle such as I am now in. This I swear by my hopes of salvation, my past lives and my hopes of future ones to come and I devote myself and my measure to utter destruction if I break this my solemn Oath.' "

Kneel.

Place Left Hand under Initiate's Knee and Right Hand on Head, thus forming Magic Link, saying:

"I will all my power into thee."

WILL.

Loose, assist to rise.

Consecrate: "I consecrate thee with oil, I consecrate thee with wine, I consecrate thee with my lips, High Priest and Magus (High Priestess and Witch Queen)."

Loose remaining cords. [kiss]

"You will now use the working tools in turn, "First the Magic Sword. (Form Circle) [kiss]

"Second the Athame. (Form Circle) [kiss]

"Third the White-Handled Knife. (use) [kiss]

"Fourth the Wand. (Wave to 4 Quarters) [kiss]

"Fifth the Pentacle. (Show to 4 Quarters) [kiss]

"Sixth the Censer. (Circle, cense) [kiss]

"Seventh the Cords. (Use) [kiss]

"Eighth the scourge. In witchcraft you must ever give as you receive, but ever triple. So where I gave thee 3, return 9, where I gave 7, return 21, where I gave 9, return 27, where I gave 21, return 63." (Use, 9, 21, 27, 63; i.e., 120 in all. [kiss])

"Thou hast obeyed the law. But mark well, when thou receivest good, so equally art bound to return good threefold."

The Priestess or Magus is then loosed from the cords and says:

"Having learned thus far, you must know why the Wicca are called the Hidden Children of the Goddess."

Then the Legend of the Goddess is either read or acted out. If it is possible to act it out, the new Initiate may take one of the parts. One of the Coven should act as Narrator, and another as Guardian of the Portal. The Priestess, or another woman, may act the part of the Goddess, and the Magus, or another man, may act the part of the God. The Priestess — or whoever is taking the part of the Goddess — takes off her necklace and lays it on the Altar. Then she goes outside the circle and is dressed in a veil and jewellery. The Magus — or whoever is taking the part of the God — is invested with a horned crown and girds on a sword, which he draws and stands in the God position with sword and scourge, by the altar.

Narrator: "In ancient times our Lord, the Horned One, was, as he still is, the Consoler, the Comforter; but men knew him as the Dread Lord of Shadows — lonely, stern, and hard. Now our Lady the Goddess had never loved, but she would solve all mysteries, even the mystery of Death — and so she journeyed to the Nether Lands. The Guardians of the Portals challenged her." (The Priestess — or whoever is taking the part of the Goddess — advances to the side of the Circle. Whoever is taking the part of the Guardian of the Portal challenges her with the Sword or Athame.)

Narrator: "Strip off thy garments, lay aside thy jewels, for naught may ye bring with ye into this our land'. So she laid down her garments and her jewels and was bound, as are all who enter the realms of Death the Mighty One."

(The Priestess takes off the veil and the jewellery and lays them down outside the Circle. The Guardian of the Portal binds her with the Cords and brings her inside the Circle.)

Narrator: "Such was her beauty that Death himself knelt and laid his sword and crown at her feet and kissed her feet."

(The Magus—or whoever is playing the part of the God—comes forward and lays the Horned Crown and the Sword at the Priestess's feet and kisses her feet.)

Narrator: "Saying, 'Blessed be thy feet that have brought thee in these ways. Abide with me, but let me place my cold hand on thy heart'. And she replied, 'I love thee not. Why dost thou cause all things that I love and take delight in to fade and die?' 'Lady,' replied Death, 'Tis Age and Fate, against which I am helpless. Age causes all things to wither; but when men die at the end of time, I give them rest and peace and strength, so that they may return. But you, you are lovely. Return not; abide with me.' But she answered, 'I love thee not.' Then said Death, 'An you receive not my hand on your heart, you must receive Death's scourge.' "

(The Magus rises and takes up the Scourge from the Altar.)

Narrator: " 'It is fate, better so,' she said, and she knelt."

(The Priestess kneels before the altar, and the Magus uses the scourge 3, 7, 9, 21.)

Narrator: "And Death scourged her tenderly, and she cried, 'I feel the pangs of love'. And Death raised her, and said, 'Blessed be,' and he gave her the Fivefold Kiss, saying, 'Thus only may you attain to joy and knowledge.' "

(The Magus raises the Priestess, gives her the Fivefold Kiss and unties the cords.)

Narrator: "And he taught her all the Mysteries and gave her the necklace, which is the Circle of Rebirth."

(The Magus takes the Priestess's necklace from the Altar and replaces it about her neck. The Priestess takes up the Sword and the Horned Crown from the floor, where the Magus placed them, and gives them back to him. Then he stands as before by the Altar, in the position of the God, and she stands by his side in the pentacle position, as Goddess.)

Narrator: "And they loved and were one; and he taught her all the Magics. For there are three great mysteries in the life of man— love, death, and resurrection in a new body—and magic controls them all. To fulfil love you must return at the same time and place as the loved one, and you must remember and love them again. But to be reborn you must die and be ready for a new body; to die you must be born; without love you may not be born— and these be all the magics.

The Priestess or Magus then replaces the Sword, Crown, Scourge, etc., upon the Altar, and taking the new Initiate by the hand and holding the Athame in the other, passes once round the Circle, proclaiming at the Four Quarters,

> "Hear, Ye Mighty Ones, . . . hath been duly consecrated High Priest and Magus (or High Priestess and Witch Queen)."

1.4.3a Third Degree (1949)

Magus: "Ere we proceed with this sublime degree, I must beg purification at thy hands."

High Priestess binds Magus and ties him down to the altar. She circumambulates three times, and scourges Magus with three, seven, nine, and 21 strokes. She then unbinds him and helps him to his feet.

Magus now binds the High Priestess and ties her down to the altar. He circumambulates, proclaiming to the four quarters,

"Hear, ye mighty Ones, the twice consecrate and Holy (name), High Priestess and Witch Queen, is properly prepared and will now proceed to erect the Sacred Altar."

Magus scourges High Priestess with three, seven, nine, and 21 strokes. Cakes and wine may now be taken.

[See A.5 Cakes and Wine (1949).]

Magus: "Now I must reveal to you a great Mystery." [kiss]

Note: if High Priestess has performed this rite before, omit these words. High Priestess assumes Osiris position.

Magus: "Assist me to erect the Ancient Altar, at which in days past all worshipped, the Great Altar of all things. For in the old times a woman was the Altar. Thus was the altar made and so placed . . .

[Priestess lies down in such a way that her vagina is approximately at the centre of the circle]

> . . . and the sacred place was the point within the centre of the circle, as we of old times have been taught, that the point within the centre is the origin of all things. Therefore should we adore it." [kiss]
>
> "Therefore, whom we adore, we also invoke, by the power of the lifted lance."

Invokes.

> "O circle of stars [kiss], whereof our Father is but the younger brother." [kiss]
>
> "Marvel beyond imagination, soul of infinite space, before whom time is ashamed, the mind bewildered and understanding dark, not unto thee may we attain unless thine image be of love." [kiss]
>
> "Therefore, by seed and root, and stem and bud and leaf and flower and fruit do we invoke thee, O, Queen of space, O dew of light, O continuous one of the Heavens." [kiss]
>
> "Let it be ever thus, that men speak not of Thee as one, but as none, and let them not speak of thee at all, since thou art continuous, for thou art the point within the circle, [kiss]

which we adore, [kiss] the fount of life without which we would not be." [kiss]

"And in this way truly are erected the Holy Twin Pillars Boaz and Joachim [kisses breasts]. In beauty and strength were they erected, to the wonder and glory of all men."

(Eightfold Kiss: 3 points, Lips, 2 Breasts and back to lips; 5 points)

"O Secrets of secrets that art hidden in the being of all lives. Not thee do we adore, for that which adoreth is also thou. Thou art that and That am I." [kiss]

"I am the flame that burns in every man, and in the core of every star." [kiss]

"I am Life and the giver of Life, yet therefore is the knowledge of me the Knowledge of Death." [kiss]

"I am alone, the Lord within ourselves whose name is Mystery of Mysteries." [kiss]

"Make open the path of intelligence between us. For these truly are the 5 points of fellowship . . .

[On the right appears an illuminated diagram of the point-up triangle above the pentacle, the symbol for the third degree]

. . . feet to feet, knee to knee, groin to groin, breast to breast, arms around back, lips to lips, by the Great and Holy Names Abracadabra, Aradia, and Cernunnos.

Magus and High Priestess:

"Encourage our hearts, Let thy Light crystallize itself in our blood, fulfilling us of Resurrection, for there is no part of us that is not of the Gods."

(Exchange Names.)

Closing the Circle

High Priestess Circumambulates, proclaiming,

"The twice consecrate High Priestess greets ye Mighty Ones, and dismisseth ye to your pleasant abodes. Hail and Farewell."

She draws the banishing pentacle at each quarter.

1.4.3b Third-Degree (1957)

Magus gives Fivefold Kiss.

"I must beg purification at thy hands."

High Priestess scourges Magus.

He Warlocks [binds] High Priestess.

Circle, Proclaims to the four quarters,

"Take heed ye mighty Ones, the Lady (name), High Priestess and Witch Queen, is properly prepared to celebrate the Great Rite."

He scourges her.

with three, seven, nine, and 21 strokes.

Magus kisses her feet.

"Ere I dare proceed with this sublime degree, I must again beg purification at thy hands."

She scourges him.

Note: if High Priestess has not performed this rite before, he says, "Here I reveal to you a great mystery." [Kneel and place couch in position so as to face north]

Assist me to build
  As the Mighty One willed,
An Altar of praise,
  From beginning of days,
Thus doth it lie,
  Twixt the points of the sky,

For thus it was placed

When the Goddess embraced

The Horned One, Her Lord,

Who taught her the word,

Which quickened the womb,

And conquered the Tomb.

Be thus as of yore,

The Shrine we adore, [kiss]

The feast without fail,

The life-giving Grail, [kiss]

Before it uprear

The Miraculous Spear,

And invoke in this sign

The Goddess divine. [kiss]

Invoke:

"Thou who at moon of night doth reign,

Queen of the starry realm above,

'Not unto Thee may we attain

Unless Thine Image be of Love.' [kiss]

By moon-rays silver shaft of power,

By green leaf breaking from the bud,

By seed that springeth into flower,

By life that courseth in the blood. [kiss]

By rushing wind and leaping flame,
    By flowing water and green earth,
Pour us the wine of our desire
    From out Thy Cauldron of Rebirth. [kiss]

Here may we see in vision clear
    The Secret Strange unveiled at length,
The wondrous Twin-Pillars rear
    Erect in Beauty and in Strength. [kiss]

Altar of Mysteries manifold,
    The Sacred Circle's central point,
Thus do I sign thee as of old,
    With kisses of my lips anoint. [kiss]

(Here a pentacle surmounted by a point-up triangle is drawn.)

Open for me the Secret Way,
    The pathway of intelligence,
Between the Gates of Night and Day,
    Beyond the bounds of time and sense.

Behold the Mystery aright,
    The Five True Points of Fellowship,
Here where the Lance and Grail unite,
    And feet and knees and breast and lips."

(Exchange Names.)

Eightfold Kiss:

Annoint 3 points, Lips, 2 Breasts and back to lips,

Annoint 5 points, with oil, wine, & kisses

NOTES

The Great Rite

There are a number of spiritual powers which many people do not recognize as such, e.g. the various forms of inspiration, music and poetry, clairvoyance and magical awareness; but the greatest of all these is love. All these aids should be employed under instruction, as there are difficulties and dangers in their undiscriminating use.[1]

Contrary to the reports of the Church, witches do not believe in or encourage promiscuity. To them sex is something sacred and beautiful, which should not be allowed to become sordid or cheap. . . .

In a rare old book in my possession, *Receuil de Lettres au Sujet des Malefices et du Sortilege . . . par le Sieur Boissier* (Paris 1731), there is quoted much valuable evidence from a big witchcraft trial at La Haye Dupuis in 1669, which illustrates the attitude of the witch cult in this respect. One witness, Margeurite Marguerie, said that when a male witch was not at the Sabbat his partner did not join in the dance, and it is said further, "As for the dance, it is done . . . back to back and two by two, each witch having his wife of the Sabbat, which sometimes is his own wife, and these wives having been given to them when they were marked (i.e. initiated: *my note)* they do not change them; this kind of dance being finished, they dance also hand in hand, like our villagers. . . ."[2]

The witch cult's main tenet, namely the worship of fertility, and hence the sacredness of sex.[3]

'At the Great Sabbath the living body of a priestess *does* form the altar. We worship the divine spirit of Creation, which is the Life-spring of the world, and without which the world would perish. Are we then so abominable? We count it not so. To us it is the most sacred and holy mystery, proof of the God within us whose command is: Go forth and multiply'. . . . The worship of "the divine spirit of Creation, which is the Life-spring of the world, and without which the world would perish"?

The worship of the witch cult is, and always has been, that of the principle of Life itself. It has made of that principle, as manifested in sex, something sacred. There is still, in the collective unconsciousness of men's minds, a realisation of the rightness of the Old Sacred Marriage. . . . When the Church made marriage a Sacrament, they were right; but when they added that it was ordained for the procreation of children and for that alone, they were a thousand, thousand times wrong. Let me make it clear, however, that the witch cult does not hold sex sacred as an end in itself, but as a living symbol and manifestation of the Great Source of All Things which men call God.[4]

1. *Witchcraft Today,* Chapter XIII: Recapitulation. p. 123.
2. *Meaning of Witchcraft,* Chapter IX: Why? p. 137.
3. *Meaning of Witchcraft,* Chapter VII: The Black Mass. p. 189.
4. *Meaning of Witchcraft,* Chapter VII: Some Allegations Examined, Part II. p. 225–226.

1.5.a Cakes and Wine (1949)

Magus kneels, fills Cup, offers to Witch

[she is seated on the altar, holding her athame, and the Priest kneels before her, holding up the cup]

Witch, holding Athame between palms, places point in cup.

Magus: "As the Athame is the Male, so the Cup is the female; so, conjoined, they bring blessedness."

Witch lays aside Athame, takes Cup in both hands, drinks and gives drink.

Magus holds Paten to Witch, who blesses with Athame, then eats and gives to eat.

NOTES

(a ritual meal in which cakes and wine are consecrated and partaken of)

Rite of the "Cakes and Wine" is much older than the Christian ceremony, and that in fact it is the Christians who have copied the rites of older religions. In view of the fact that such ritual meals are known to have been part of the Mysteries of the goddess Cybele in ancient times, and that a similar ritual meal is partaken of, according to Arthur Avalon in *Shakti and Shakta*, by the Tantriks of India, who are also worshippers of a great Mother-Goddess, there seem to be some grounds for this statement.

In the old days, they tell me, ale or mead might be used instead of wine, any drink in fact that had "a kick" in it, because this represented "life". I wonder if this is why Shakespeare used the expression "cakes and ale" as a synonym for fun which was frowned on by the pious?

The taking of wine during the rites is part of the ceremony; it consists usually of two glasses at the most.[1] It is a very strict witch law that no spirits may be drunk by them.[2]

St Clement of Alexandria, who, before turning Christian, was initiated in the worship of the Goddess Cybele whose symbol was a crescent moon in perpetual union with the sun, says the following confession of faith was made:

> "I have eaten from the timbrel,
>
> I have drunk from the cymbal,
>
> I have borne the sacred vessel,
>
> I have entered into the bridal chamber."

Now, it seems obvious that "I have eaten from the timbrel and drunk from the cymbal" means that a sacred meal, or a species of Eucharist with food and drink that had been blessed was eaten out of the "working tools" of the cult, and this meal is known to have consisted of a cake of barley, and of wine. It is noteworthy that the witches' "sacred meal", "Cakes and Wine", consists of cakes (any sort) and wine, which are blessed and then eaten and drunk out of the "working tools", and this blessing has at least a phallic or fertility significance. "I have borne the sacred vessel" may be something similar to the witch custom that everyone should have one of the "working tools", usually the Athame, in their hands all the time when the hands are otherwise unoccupied.[3]

1. *Meaning of Witchcraft,* Chapter I: The Witch Cult in Britain. p. 14
2. *Meaning of Witchcraft,* Chapter XVII: The Future. p. 259
3. *Meaning of Witchcraft,* Chapter IX: Why? p. 133

1.5.b Cakes And Wine. (1957)

High Priestess seated on Altar, God position.

Magus, kneeling, kisses her feet, then knees, bows with head below her knees, extends arms along her thighs, and adores.

Magus fills cup and offers it to High Priestess, who, holding Athame between palms, places point in cup.

Magus says: "As the Athame is the male, so the cup is the female, and conjoined they bring blessedness."

High Priestess lays Athame aside, and takes Cup and drinks, gives Cup to server, who puts a little in each glass.

Meanwhile the Magus presents Pentacle with cakes to High Priestess, saying, "Oh Queen most secret, bless this food unto our bodies, bestowing health, wealth, strength, joy and peace, and that fulfilment of love that is perpetual happiness."

High Priestess blesses them with Athame, takes Cake and eats, while the Magus gives her the Cup again and kisses knees and adores.

All sit as Witches, and invite High Priestess to join them.

1.6. The Sabbat Rituals (1949)

Introductory Notes to the Sabbat Rituals

Witchcraft is a moon cult, and there are thirteen moons in a year and thirteen weeks in every quarter, each quarter of the year having its Sabbat. The four great Sabbats are Candlemass, May Eve, Lammas, and Halloween; the equinoxes and solstices are celebrated also, thus making the Eight Ritual Occasions, as the witches call them. On the great Sabbats all the covens that could forgather together would do so; but apart from these great Sabbats, minor meetings called Esbats are held. The word "Esbat" may come from the old French "s'esbattre", meaning "to frolic, to enjoy oneself". Traditionally, the Esbat is the meeting of the local coven for local matters, or simply for fun, and it is, or should be, held at or near the full moon.[1]

In Ireland, as has been said, there was a great annual festival on August Ist (Lammas), held at Tailltenn and presided over by Druids. It was said to be in honour of the sun-god Lugh. A similar festival was held in Gaul at Lugudunum (Lyons) in honour of Lugus, god of light and knowledge. The tailltenn festival also honoured Lugh's foster-mother Tailltiu. It is closely associated with the cult of the dead, and Tailltiu being obviously the Great Mother. The energy expended in the games was thought of as giving new strength to the god to bring fertility to the land (witches dance at Lammas today with the same object). The celebration of Lughnassad (Lammas) ensured plenty of corn, milk, etc., throughout Ireland. If the rites were poor the crops would be poor, and temporary marriages seem to have been a great feature of the rites. To this day "a Tailltenn marriage" is the word for the type of union "when you do not bother the priest with your private affairs." "Lughnassad" means "the marriage of Lugh", and he was supposed to take the land as his bride. The King of All Ireland was ceremonially married to the goddess, actually to a priestess representing her. This is exactly what was done in Sumeria, when each year the king, representing the god, married a priestess representing the goddess.

Samhain (November 1st), the winter festival of the Celts, was the beginning of their New Year, and on Samhain Eve (our Halloween) divinations to know the happenings of the coming year were made. In Ireland this was held at Tara, when all the Druids assembled to sacrifice to the gods. They sacrificed a black sheep, and offered libations to the spirits of those who had died during the year.

May 1st was Bealteinne (Beltane); two great fires were lighted by the Druids on each sacred hill, and the cattle were driven between them as a preservation against sickness. Later, in England, the May King and May Queen, "Robin Hood and Maid Marian", represented the old god and goddess of fertility.

Their marriage and union were believed magically to assist the crops. The May Day revels were fiercely denounced by the Puritans, on account of the freedom of lovemaking which prevailed among those who took part in them.

Ross Nichols, in his little book, *Sassenach Stray,* says, speaking of old Gaelic traditions:

> The big sun, (Beltane); reappears, replacing winter's wizened little sun on Mayday, when ceremonial fires of sympathetic magic were lit. On Hallowe'en the little sun substituted for the big sun; the underworld began to dominate the upper world and you could see into the future. At these changeovers supernatural beings became unstuck and flew about.

Now, the four great festivals the witch cult celebrates are Halloween, May Eve (the old "Walpurgis Night"), Lammas, and Candlemas, February 2nd. (It is noteworthy that, being a moon cult, they celebrate the night before the day of the festival.)

February 2nd is called by the Christian Church "The Purification of the Blessed Virgin Mary"; but it is actually derived from the rites of the Roman goddess Februa, who was worshipped with lighted torches. Oimelc, the festival of the moon goddess Bride among the ancient Celts and Gaels, was February 1st Bride has in modern days been Christianised as "St Bride" or "St Briget", but the Eve of St Bride is still held as "uncanny" by the Gael, a belief which forms the theme of one of the weird stories of "Fiona Macleod", "By the Yellow Moonrock" (from *The Dominion of Dreams).* On Bride's Day serpents were supposed to awake from their winter sleep and come from their holes, and the Gaels have a charm against them which runs as follows:

> Today is the day of Bride.
> The serpent shall come from its hole.
> I will not molest the serpent,
> And the serpent will not molest me.

There is, however, another version of this charm which says:

> On the day of Bride of the fair locks
> The noble queen will come from the hill;
> I will not molest the noble queen,
> Nor will the noble queen molest me.

It is apparent that the serpent is in fact a form of the goddess, and we may recall in this connection the snake-goddess of Minoan Crete, and the "Lamias" of Greek legend whose weird beauty inspired one of Keat's poems.

It will be noticed that these four ancient festivals neatly divide the year into four parts, from which they are sometimes known as "the four Cross-Quarter

Days". Their origin has been something of a puzzle. It has been suggested that they are connected with the seasons of fertility in animals.

I would like to advance a suggestion in this connection which I do not think has been made before. The four great Sabbats each take place when the sun is in one of the four fixed signs of the Zodiac; sometimes called the Kerubic Signs, because they are the Man, Eagle, Lion and Bull which, according to Kabalistic teaching, are the Kerubs or ruling symbols of the Four Elements. The Man is Aquarius, the fixed sign of Air, the Eagle is Scorpio, the fixed sign of water (or rather, the esoteric symbol thereof); the Lion is Leo, the fixed sign of Fire; and the Bull of Taurus, the fixed sign of Earth. In Christian times these were adopted as the symbols of the Four Evangelists, the Man for St Matthews, the Eagle for St John, the Lion for St Mark, and the Bull for St Luke.

In *Gods in the Making*, by T. Mawby Cole and Vera W. Reid, we find the following:

> These four fixed signs are perhaps the most universal of all religious symbols, for they are to be found in the human-faced beasts of the gods of Chaldea, in the four Assyrian sphinxes, in the Cherubim of the Kabbala. The same symbols are frequently mentioned by Ezekiel and are said to be sometimes depicted in the four arms of Siva in Hindu temples, while the whole four are assembled in the mysterious Sphinx of Egypt. . . . There can be no doubt that these symbols of the fixed signs so universally employed possess profound and pregnant esoteric significance. By their position in the Zodiac, midway between the cardinal points, they may be considered to mark the culmination peak of cosmic energy released by the Equinoxes and Solstices, or, again, to indicate vital, progressive stages in the unfoldment of consciousness.

The Sabbat of Candlemas takes place when the sun is in Aquarius; that of May Eve when the sun is in Taurus; that of Lammas when the sun is in Leo; and that of Halloween when the sun is in Scorpio.[2]

1. *Meaning of Witchcraft,* Chapter I: The Witch Cult in Britain. p. 16.
2. *Meaning of Witchcraft,* Chapter V: Druidism and the Aryan Celts. p. 76

1.6.a November Eve

Walk or slow dance, Magus leading High Priestess, both carrying Phallic wand or broom, people with torches or candles.

Witch chant or song:

"Eko, eko; Azarak. Eko, eko; Zomelak

Bazabi lacha bachabe
Lamac cahi achababe
Karrellyos

Lamac lamac Bachalyas
Cabahagy sabalyos
Baryolos

Lagoz atha cabyolas
Samahac atha famolas
Hurrahya!"

Form circle.

High Priestess assumes Goddess position.

High Priest gives her Fivefold Kiss and is scourged.

All are purified [that is, bound and scourged with forty strokes, as in the initiation rituals].

High Priest assumes God position.

High Priestess invokes with Athame:

> "Dread Lord of the shadows, god of life and the giver of life. Yet is the knowledge of thee the knowledge of death. Open wide, I pray thee, thy gates through which all must pass. Let our dear ones who have gone before, return this night to make merry with us. And when our time comes, as it must, O thou the comforter, the consoler, the giver of peace and rest, we will enter thy realms gladly and unafraid, for we know that when rested and refreshed among our dear ones, we shall be born again by thy grace and the grace of the Great Mother. Let it be in the same place and the same time as our beloved ones, and may we meet and know, and love them again. Descend, we pray thee, upon thy servant and Priest (name)."

High Priestess gives Fivefold Kiss to High Priest.

Initiations if any; all others are purified.

(Note: Couples may purify each other if they will.)

Cakes and Wine.

The Great Rite if possible, either in token or truly.

Dismiss [the guardians, and close down the magic circle; the people then stay to] feast and dance.

1.6.b February Eve

After usual opening, all are doubly purified [that is, with eighty strokes].

Dance round outside circle, High Priestess with sword girded on and drawn, Phallic wand in left hand.

Enter circle.

High Priest assumes God position.

High Priestess gives Fivefold Kiss, invokes:

> "Dread Lord of death and Resurrection, life and the giver of life, Lord within ourselves, whose name is Mystery of Mysteries, encourage our hearts. Let the light crystalize in our blood, fulfilling us of resurrection, for there is no part of us that is not of the gods. Descend, we pray thee, upon this thy servant and Priest (name)."

All should be purified in sacrifice before him. He then purifies the High Priestess with his own hands, and others if he will.

Cakes and wine.

Great Rite if possible, in token or real.

Games and dance as the people will.

Dismiss [the guardians, and close down the magic circle; the people then stay to] feast and dance.

1.6.c May Eve

If possible ride poles, brooms, etc.

High Priestess leading, quick dance step, singing

"O do not tell the priests of our arts.
  For they would call it sin,
For we will be in the woods all night
  a conjuring Summer in.
And we bring you good news by word of mouth.
  For women, cattle, and corn:
The sun is coming up from the south,
  With oak and ash, and thorn."

Meeting dance if possible.

Form circle as usual, and purify.

High Priestess assumes Goddess position; officers all give her the fivefold kiss.

She purifies all.

High Priestess again assumes Goddess position.

Magus invokes, draws down moon,

"I invoke thee and call upon thee, O mighty Mother of us all, bringer of all fruitfulness, By seed and root, by stem and bud, by leaf and flower and fruit, by life and love, do we invoke thee, to descend upon the body of thy servant and Priestess here."

High Priest gives Fivefold Kiss to High Priestess.

All should be purified in sacrifice before her, and she should purify Magus and some others with her own hands.

Cakes and wine.

Games.

Great Rite if possible, in token or truly.

Dismiss the guardians, and close down the magic circle; the people then stay to feast and dance.

If possible, ride poles, broomsticks, etc.

Meeting Dance if possible.

[Note: The spiral or meeting dance is sometimes performed if there is room. This is a sort of "follow my leader" dance, the priestess usually leading, dancing round in a right-hand spiral to the centre, when she suddenly turns and unwinds the spiral. As she does this, she kisses each man she meets and all the other girls do the same. They say it is called the meeting dance because in the old days people came from distant parts and did not know each other, and this was designed to get them acquainted.[†]]

Form circle.

Purify.

High Priestess stands in pentacle position.

Magus invokes her:

> "O mighty Mother of us all, Mother of all fruitfulness, give us fruit and grain, flocks and herds and children to the tribe that we be mighty, by thy rosy love, do thou descend upon thy servant and Priestess (name) here."

Magus gives Fivefold Kiss to High Priestess.

Candle game: Seated, the men form a circle, passing a lighted candle from hand to hand "deosil". The women form circle

† p. 167 *Witchcraft Today. See also* 2.11. The Meeting Dance (1953)]

outside, trying to blow it out over their shoulders. Whoever's hand it is in when it is blown out is 3 times purified by whoever blew it out, giving fivefold Kiss in return. This game may go on as long as the people like.

Cakes and wine, and any other games you like.

Dismiss the guardians, and close down the magic circle; the people then stay to feast and dance.

1.6.e Spring equinox (1957)

The symbol of the wheel should be placed on the altar upright, decked with flowers, flanked with burning candles. The Cauldron, containing spirits, is in the east. Magus in west, High Priestess in East with Phallic wand or pinecone-tipped wand, or broomstick, or riding pole, broom upwards.

High Priestess lights Cauldron, saying,

"We kindle fire this day!
In the presence of the Holy Ones:
  Without malice, without jealousy, without envy.
Without fear of aught beneath the sun.
But the High Gods.

Thee we invoke: O light of life:
  Be thou a bright flame before us:
Be thou a guiding star above us:
  Be thou a smooth path beneath us;
Kindle thou in our hearts within,
  A flame of love for our neighbour,
To our foes, to our friends, to our kindred all:
  To all men on this broad Earth.

O merciful son of Cerridwen,
  From the lowest thing that liveth
To the name that is highest of all."

High Priestess draws pentacle upon Magus with wand, kiss, gives it to him. He does likewise. They lead the dance round the circle, all couples leaping burning fire. The last couple as the fire goes out should be well-purified three times, and each should give Fivefold Kiss to all of opposite sex.

Cakes and wine.

If the people will, the Cauldron dance can be done again, many times, or other games can be played.

1.6.f Summer Solstice (1957)

Form circle. Invoke, Purify. Cauldron is placed before altar filled with water, wreathed with summer flowers. The people, men and women alternately, stand round circle.

High Priestess stands in North, before Cauldron, holding wand, which should be Phallic or tipped with a pinecone (anciently the thyrsus) or a riding pole or a broomstick. High Priestess holding this raised invokes the sun.

"Great One of Heaven, Power of the Sun, we invoke thee in thine ancient names, Michael, Balin, Arthur, Lugh, Herne. Come again, as of old, into this thy land. Lift up thy shining spear of light to protect us. Put to flight the powers of darkness, give us fair woodlands and green fields, blossoming orchards and ripening corn. Bring us to stand upon thy hill of vision, and show us the path to the lovely realms of the gods."

High Priestess draws invoking pentacle on Magus with wand.

Magus comes forward sunwise and takes wand with kiss, plunges wand into Cauldron and holds it upright, saying,

"The spear to the Cauldron, the lance to the Grail, spirit to flesh, man to woman, sun to earth." He salutes High Priestess over Cauldron, then rejoins people, still bearing wand.

High Priestess takes aspergillum, stands by Cauldron, says,

> "Dance ye about the Cauldron of Cerridwen the Goddess, and be ye blessed with the touch of this consecrated water, even as the sun, the Lord of Light, arriveth in his strength in the sign of the waters of life."

The people dance sunwise about the altar and Cauldron, led by Magus bearing wand. High Priestess sprinkles them lightly as they pass her.

Ritual of cakes and wine.

Any other dances, rites, or games as the Priestess and people wish.

1.6.g Autumn equinox (1957)

The altar should be decorated with symbols of autumn, pine cones, oak sprigs, acorns, or ears of corn, and should have fire or burning incense on it as usual. After usual purification, the people stand round, men and women alternately. Magus at West of altar in God position.

High Priestess stands at east of altar, facing him, and reads the incantation.

> "Farewell, O Sun, ever returning light. The hidden god, who ever yet remains. He departs to the land of youth, through the gates of death, to dwell enthroned, the judge of gods and man. The horned leader of the hosts of air. Yet, even as stand unseen about the circle the forms of the Mighty Lords of the Outer Spaces. So dwelleth he, 'the lord within ourselves'. So dwelleth he within the secret seed, the seed of new reaped grain, the seed of flesh, hidden in the earth, the marvellous seed of the stars.
>
> 'In him is life, and life is the light of men [John 1:4],' that which was never born and never dies. Therefore the Wicca weep not, but rejoice."

The High Priestess goes to the Magus with a kiss. He lays aside Athame and scourge, and kisses her. The High Priestess hands him her wand, which should be Phallic, or a branch tipped with a pinecone, or a riding pole, or a broomstick (anciently the thyrsus). They lead the dance, she with a systrum or rattle, he with wand, the people falling in behind them, dancing three times round the altar. Then the candle game is played.

Cakes and wine.

Great Rite if possible.

Dances and games.

1.6.h Winter Solstice (1957)

Form circle in usual manner, invoking the Mighty Ones.

The Cauldron of Cerridwen is placed in the circle at the South wreathed with holly, ivy, and mistletoe, with fire lighted within it. There should be no other light except for the candles on the altar and about the circle.

After all are purified, the Moon should be drawn down.

Then the High Priestess stands behind the Cauldron in pentacle position, symbolizing the rebirth of the sun. The people, man and woman alternately, stand round the circle. The Magus stands facing the High Priestess with a bundle of torches, or candles, and the book of words of the incantation. One of the officers stands beside him with a lighted candle, so that he may have light to read by.

The people begin to slowly move round the circle sunwise. As each passes him the Magus lights his candle or torch from the fire in the Cauldron, which may be simply a candle, till all have lighted candles or torches. Then the people dance round slowly as he reads the incantation. (A real fire must now be kindled in the Cauldron.)

"Queen of the Moon, Queen of the Sun.
Queen of the Heavens, Queen of the Stars.
Queen of the Waters, Queen of the Earth.
Who ordained to us the child of promise:

It is the Great Mother who gives birth to him,
He is the Lord of Life who is born again,
Darkness and tears are set behind,
And the star of guidance comes up early.

Golden sun of hill and mountain
Illumine the land, illumine the world,
Illumine the seas, illumine the rivers,
Grief be laid, and joy be raised.

Blessed be the Great Mother,
Without beginning, without ending,
To everlasting, to eternity,
I O. Evohe, Blessed be."

The dance commences slowly, in rhythm with the chant, all taking up the call

"I. O. Blessed be."

The Priestess joins dance and leads them with a quicker rhythm. The cauldron with burning fire is pushed so that the dancers leap or step over it, in couples. Whichever couple is passing it as it goes out, should be well-purified, three times each, and may pay any amusing forfeit as the High Priestess may ordain. Sometimes the cauldron is relighted several times for this purpose.

Cauldron of Regeneration and the Dance of the Wheel

I have seen one very interesting ceremony: the Cauldron of Regeneration and the Dance of the Wheel, or Yule, to cause the sun to be reborn, or summer to return. This in theory should be on December 22, but nowadays it is held on the nearest day to that date that is convenient for the members. The ceremony starts in the usual way. The circle is cast and purified, the celebrants also being purified in the usual manner, and the ordinary business of the cult is done. Then the small ceremony is performed (sometimes called "Drawing down the Moon") so that the High Priestess is regarded as the incarnation of the goddess. The Cakes and Wine ceremony follows. Then a cauldron (or something to represent one) is placed in the middle of the circle, spirit is put in and ignited. Various leaves, etc., are cast in. Then the Priestess stands by it in the pentacle (goddess) position. The High Priest stands on the opposite side of the cauldron, leading the chant. The others stand round in a circle with torches. They are lighted at the burning cauldron and they dance round in the "sunwise" direction, i.e. clockwise. The chant I heard was as follows, but others are sometimes used:

"Queen of the Moon, Queen of the Sun,
Queen of the Heavens, Queen of the Stars,
Queen of the Waters, Queen of the Earth
Bring to us the Child of Promise![1]

It is the great mother who giveth birth to him,
It is the Lord of Life who is born again.
Darkness and tears are set aside
When the Sun shall come up early.

Golden Sun of the Mountains,
Illumine the Land, Light up the World,
Illumine the Seas and the Rivers,
Sorrows be laid, joy to the World.

Blessed be the Great Goddess,
Without beginning, without end,
Everlasting to eternity.
I.O. EVOHE Blessed Be."

They dance round furiously, crying:

"I.O. EVOHE

Blessed Be I.O. EVOHE Blessed Be."

Sometimes couples join hands and jump over the blazing cauldron, as I have seen for myself. When the fire had burnt itself out the Priestess led the usual dances. This was followed by a feast.

Witchcraft Today, Chapter1: Living Witchcraft. p. 21.

BOOK OF SHADOWS

PART TWO

1953–1957

2.1.a On Chants (1953)

Of old there were many chants and songs used especially in the Dances. Many of these have been forgotten by us here, but we know that they used cries of IAU which seems muchly like the cries EVO or EVOHE of the ancients. Much dependeth on the pronunciation if this be so. In my youth, when I heard IAU it seemed to be AEIOU, or rather, AAAEEIOOOOUU. This may be but the natural way to prolong it to make it fit for a call, but it suggests that these be possibly the initials of an invocation as Agla is said to be, and of sooth 'tis said that the whole Hebrew alphabet is said to be such, and for this reason is recited as a most powerful charm, but at least this is certain, these cries during the dances do have profound effect, as I myself have seen.

Other calls are IEHOUA and EHEIE; also Ho Ho Ho Ise Ise Ise.

IEO VEO VEO VEO VEOV OROV OV OVOVO may be a spell but is more likely to be a call. 'Tis like the EVOE EVOE of the Greeks and the "Heave ho!" of sailors. "Emen hetan" and "Ab hur, ab hus" seem calls; as "Horse and hattock, horse and go, horse and Pellatis, ho, ho, ho!"

"Thout, tout a tout tout, throughout and about" and "Rentum tormentum" are probably mispronounced attempts at a forgotten formula, though they may have been invented by some unfortunate being tortured, to evade telling the real formula.

2.1.b The Witches' Chant or Rune (1957)

Darksome night and Shining Moon,
East, then South, then West, then North,
Harken to the Witches Rune:
Here come I to call thee forth.

Earth and Water, Air and Fire,
Wand and Pentacle and Sword,
Work ye unto my desire,
Harken ye unto my word.

Cords and Censer, Scourge and knife,
Powers of the Witches Blade,
Waken all ye into life,
Come ye as the Charm is made:

Queen of Heaven, Queen of Hell,
Horned Hunter of the Night,
Lend your power unto the Spell,
Work my will by Magic Rite.

If chant is used to reinforce a work already begun, end with this:

By all the power of land and sea,
By all the might of moon and sun,
What is my will — "So mote it be,"
What I do say — "It shall be done."

2.2. To Help the Sick (1953)

Ever remember the promise of the goddess,

> "For ecstasy is mine and joy on earth"

so let there ever be joy in your heart. Greet people with joy, be glad to see them. If times be hard, think,

> "It might have been worse. I at least have known the joys of the Sabbath, and I will know them again."

Think of the grandeur, beauty, and Poetry of the rites, of the loved ones you meet through them. If you dwell on this inner joy, your health will be better. You must try to banish all fear, for it will really touch you. It may hurt your body, but your soul is beyond it all.

And ever remember, that if you help others it makes you forget your own woes. And if another be in pain, do what you may to distract his attention from it. Do not say

> "You have no pain,"

but if you may, administer the drugs which soothe as well as those that cure. But ever strive to make them believe they are getting better. Install into them happy thoughts. If you can only get this into his inner mind so that it be always.

To this end it is not wrong to let people think that we of the cult have more power than we have. For the truth is that if they believe we have more power than we really possess, we do really possess these powers, insomuch we can do good to them.

You must try to find out about people. If you tell a slightly sick man,

> "You are looking better. You will soon be well,"

he will feel better, but if he is really ill, or in pain, his Knowledge that he is in pain will cause him to doubt your words in future. But if you give him one of the drugs and then say,

> "The pain is growing less. Soon it will be gone,"

because the pain goes, the next time you say,

> "The pain is going,"

he will believe you and the pain will really get less. But you must ever say so with conviction, and this conviction must come from your believing it yourself, because you yourself know that if you can fix his mind so that he believes you, it is true.

'Tis often better to look exactly between their eyes, looking as if your eyes pierced their heads, opening your eyes as wide as you may and never blink. This continued gazing oft causes the patient to grow sleepy. If they show signs of this, say

> "You are growing sleepy. You will sleep, you are tired. Sleep. Your eyes grow tired. Sleep."

If they close their eyes, say

> "Your eyes close, you are tired, you cannot open your eyes."

If they cannot, say

> "Your arms are tired, you cannot raise them."

If they cannot, say

> "I am master of your mind. You must ever believe what I tell you. When I look like this into your eyes you will sleep and be subject to my will,"

then tell them they will sleep and wake up refreshed, feeling better. Continue this with soothing and healing drugs, and try to infuse into them the feeling of ecstasy that you feel at the Sabbath. They cannot feel it in full, but you can command them to feel what is in your own mind, and try to concentrate on this ecstasy. If you may safely tell that you are of the Cult, your task may be easier. And it were well to command them to know it only with their sleeping mind, and forget it, or to be at least unable to tell anyone about it when awake. A good way is to command them that, if they are ever questioned about Witchcraft or Witches, to immediately fall asleep.

Ever remember if tempted to admit or boast of belonging to the cult you be endangering your brothers, for though now the fires of persecution may have died down, who knows when they be revived? Many priests have knowledge of our secrets, and they well know that, though much religious bigotry has calmed down, many people would wish to join our cult. And if the truth were known of its joys, the Churches would lose power, so if we take many recruits, we may loose the fires of persecution against us again. So ever keep the secrets.

Think joy, think love, try to help others and bring joy into their lives. Children are naturally easier to influence than grown people. Ever strive to work through people's existing beliefs. For instance, more than half of the world believe in amulets. An ordinary stone is not an amulet but if it hath a natural hole in it, it must be something unusual, so if the patient hath this belief give him one. But first carry it next your skin for a few days, forcing your will into it, to cure pain, to feel safe, or against their particular fear, and this amulet may keep imposing your will when you are absent. The masters of talismans knew this full well when they say they must be made in a circle, to avoid distraction, by someone whose mind is on the subject of the work.

But keep your own mind happy. Remember the Words of the Goddess:

> "I give unimaginable joys on Earth, certainty, not faith, while in life, and upon death, peace unutterable, rest, and ecstasy, and the promise that you will return again."

In the old days many of us went to the flames laughing and singing, and so we may again. We may have joy in life and beauty, and peace and Death and the promise of return.

The Bible speaks sooth,

> "A merry heart doeth good like a medicine
> but a broken spirit breaketh the bones."

But you may not have a merry heart. Perchance you were born under an evil star. I think that the effects of the stars are overestimated, but you cannot make a merry heart to order, you say. But you can, in the Cult; there be secret processes by which your will and imagination may be influenced. This process also affects the body, and brings it to joy. Your body is happy, so your mind is happy. You are well because you are happy, and you are happy because you are well.

Prayer may be used with good result if the patient believes it can and will work. Many believe it can, but do not believe their God or saint will help. Prayers to the Goddess help, especially the Amalthean Horn Prayer, as it causes stimulation to the body as well as to the mind.

2.3. The Scourge and the Kiss. (1953)

· Invocation

(Feet, knees, and wrists should be tightly bound to retard blood.) Scourge 40 or more, to make skin tingle, then say, invoking Goddess,

> Hail, Aradia, from the Amalthean horn.
> Pour forth thy store of Love. I lowly bend
> Before Thee! I invoke thee at the end
> When other Gods are fallen and put to scorn.
> Thy foot is to my lips! My sighs inborn
> Rise, touch, curl about thy heart. Then spend,
> Pitiful Love, loveliest Pity, descend
> And bring me luck who am lonely and forlorn.

Ask the Goddess to help you to obtain your desires, then Scourge again to bind the spell. This be powerful in ill luck and for sickness. It must be said in a Circle, and you must be properly prepared and well purified, both before and after saying, to bind the spell.

Before starting you must make a very clear picture in your mind of what you wish. Make yourself see the wish obtained. Be sure in your own mind exactly what it is and how it is to be fulfilled. This spell is the one that was taught to me long ago and I have found it works, but I don't think there is any special virtue in these words. Any others can be substituted provided they ask the goddess's (or gods') help, and say clearly what you wish and you form the clear mental image; and if it doesn't work at first, keep on trying till it works. Your helper, who wields the scourge, must know what you wish, and also form the mental image. And at first at any rate, it will be better for you to work the spell, then for the girl to take your place and work it also; you scourge her. Don't try anything difficult at first, and do it at least once a week till it works. You have to get into sympathy with each other, before anything happens, and regular working helps this.

Of spells, the exact words matter little if the intent be clear and you raise the true power, and sufficient thereof. Always in rhyme they are. There is something queer about rhyme. I have tried, and the same seem to lose their power if you miss the rhyme. Also in rhyme, the words seem to say themselves. You do not have to pause and think: "What comes next?" Doing this takes away much of your intent.

Order and discipline must be kept. A High Priest or Priestess may and should punish all faults to this end, and all of the Cult must accept such corrections willingly. Each fault should be corrected separately. The Priest or Priestess must be properly prepared and call the culprit to trial. They must be prepared as for initiation and kneel, be told their fault and sentence pronounced. Punishment should be the scourge, followed by a forfeit such as several fivefold kisses or something of this nature. The culprit must acknowledge the justice of the punishment by kissing hands and scourge on receiving sentence and again when thanking for punishment received.

The scourgings are 3, 7, 9 (thrice three), and 21 (thrice seven) 40 in all. It is not meet to make offerings [scourgings] of less than two score to the Goddess, for here be a mystery. The fortunate numbers be: 3 and 5. For three added to two (the

Perfect Couple) be five. And three and five be eight; eight and five be thirteen; thirteen and eight be twenty-one. The Fivefold Kiss is called 5, but there are 8 kisses, for there be 2 feet and 2 knees and genitals and 2 breasts and the lips. And 5 times 8 be two score. Also, fortunate numbers be 3, 7, 9, and 21, which total 40, or two score. For each man and woman hath ten fingers and ten toes, so each totals a score. And a perfect couple be two score. So a lesser number would not be perfect prayer. If more are required make it a perfect number, as four score or six score. Also there be Eight Elemental Weapons.

To make the anointing ointment, take some glazed pans filled half full with grease or olive oil. Put in one sweet mint, marjoram in another, ground thyme in a third, and if you may have it, patchouli, dried leaves pounded. Place pans in hot water bath. Stir and cook for several hours, then pour into linen bags, and squeeze grease through into pans again, and fill up with fresh leaves. After doing this several times, the grease will be highly perfumed. Then mix all together and store in a well-corked jar. Anoint behind ears, throat, armpits, breasts, and womb. Also, for all ceremonies where the feet are kissed, they should also be anointed.

NOTES

Scourge

The Scourge, this is a sign of Power and Domination, it is also to cause suffering and purification, for it is written: To learn thou must suffer and be purified.[1]

We of the Witch Cult are taught that water purifieth the body but the scourge purifieth the soul.[2]

The Kiss

Jan answered: " I have two passwords. Perfect Love and perfect Trust."

Morven dropped the knife's point saying: "All who bring such words are doubly welcome," then going behind him she blindfolded him, then clasping him from behind with her left arm around his waist, and pulling his right arm around her neck, and his lips down to hers, said: "I give you the third password; 'A kiss.'"

So saying she pushed him forward with her body, through the doorway, into the Circle. Once inside she released him whispering. "This is the way all are first brought into the Circle."[3]

At her initiation a witch is always received into the circle with a kiss on the mouth.[4]

The five-fold Kiss

"In other religions, the postulant kneels as the Priests claim supreme power. But in the Art Magical, we are taught to be humble, so we say:

Kissing his feet.	"Blessed be thy feet that have brought thee in these ways."
Kissing knees.	"Blessed be thy knees that shall kneel at the Sacred Altar."
Kissing Phallus.	"Blessed be the Organ of Generation, without which we would not be."
Kissing breasts.	"Blessed be thy breasts, formed in beauty and in strength."
Kissing lips.	"Blessed be thy lips, which shall utter the sacred names."[5]

Annointing

People still ask me questions about witches because they have heard so many tales about them. Do they go to the sabbat? Is it true they use flying ointment? Why do witches anoint themselves?

. . . I have never known witches anoint themselves all over, but I have been shown a recipe for an anointing oil. This consisted of vervain, or mint crushed and steeped in olive oil or lard, left overnight, then squeezed through a cloth to remove the leaves. Fresh leaves were then added and the squeezing repeated three or four times until it was strongly scented and ready for use. It is said that if they lived in the country where they would not be seen, they would strip and rub the oil into their skin and go to the sabbat naked. This would keep them warm enough until they reached the dance. At times they would mix soot with the oil so as not to be seen at night. One of the charges against witches was that they went invisible by night, and, it may be noted, vervain was at one time thought to confer invisibility. They have a very powerful scented oil, which nowadays they speak of as anointing oil. This is only used by the ladies, who dab it on their shoulders, behind their ears, etc., much as ordinary perfume. When they are heated with dancing, this gives off very strong fumes, and most certainly produces a very curious effect. What it is made of is kept a great secret; they had to do without it during the war and for some time afterwards, but supplies are coming forward again. They went naked to the meetings because if they were raided they might not have time to dress and so would leave incriminating clothing behind. Another thing was that they found that the soldiers would usually let a naked girl go, but would take a clothed one prisoner. The slippery oiled bodies also made them hard to catch hold of. In winter they managed to get some sheltered place, a cave or a ruin, for their meetings where they could light fires and be warm. They would wear clothes going and coming to and from these places. The local "quest", inquiring into abnormal happenings, could be trusted to stay at home in winter. They also tell me that in most villages the witches arranged that the first and last house was occupied by a member of the cult, and any strange witch, travelling or "on the run", could go where she would be sure of help and protection. In the villages the members of the cult went clothed to this house and were anointed there. The occupiers of the house never attended the sabbat, but as soon as the last witch had left made some excuse to be seen by as many people as possible in the village, so that if it became known that a sabbat had been held in the neighbourhood they themselves would be above suspicion.[6]

1. *High Magic's Aid,* Chapter XVII: The Witch Cult. p. 183.
2. *High Magic's Aid,* Chapter VII: They come to London. p. 68.
3. *High Magic's Aid,* Chapter XVII: The Witch Cult. p. 181.
4. *Witchcraft Today,* Chapter VI: How the Little People became Witches . . . p. 58.
5. *High Magic's Aid,* Chapter XVII: The Witch Cult. p. 182.
6. *Witchcraft Today,* Chapter IV: Witch Practices. p. 44.

2.4. The Priestess and the Sword (1953)

It is said, "When a woman takes the main part in worship of the Male God, she must be girt with a sword."

Note. This hath been explained as meaning that a man should be Magus representing the God, but if no one of sufficient rank and knowledge be present, a woman armed as a man may take his place. The sheath should be worn in a belt. She should carry the sword in hand, but if she has to use her hands, she should sheath the sword. Any other woman in the circle while this worship is performed shall be sword in hand. Those outside the circle only have the athame.

A woman may impersonate either the God or the Goddess, but a man may only impersonate the God.

NOTES

Of course, the average witch does not have a full battery of tools; not all have the sword, for instance.[1]

I have seen seven witches' swords; of these, four had apparently been made for sorcerers, according to the pattern prescribed in the *Key of Solomon*, with Hebrew inscriptions on hilt and blade. There are two in the museum in Castletown. Other implements bear Hebrew inscriptions and so seem to be connected with Hebrew or Kabbalistic magic. But stores do not cater for witches, and a poor witch has to get her tools as and how she can. There is also a great resemblance to what are now unimportant parts of Freemasonry; but while the Masonic working seems to be of little use, or in other words it does not work, the witch practice is most useful. Everyone who has witnessed both is convinced that the one is copied from the other and believes that the witch practice must be the original working before it was "bowdlerized".[2]

Now the god is represented by the high priest (if there is one) . . . "You know him, the leader. He is the high priest, the high priestess's husband." This, though true, was not the exact answer. It really should be: "He is whoever the high priestess appoints to take this position." In practice, she always appoints her husband if he has sufficient rank; but she may appoint anyone who is eligible, including herself; she belts on a sword and acts as a man. In the old days it was often a distinguished visitor who was appointed.[3]

1. *Witchcraft Today*, Chapter XIII: Recapitulation p. 126.
2. *Witchcraft Today*, Chapter VIII: Out of the Land of Egypt? p. 79.
3. *Witchcraft Today*, Chapter XII: Who is the Devil? p. 110.

2.5. The Warning (1953)

[see also 3.1 The Old Laws]

Keep this book in your own hand of write. Let brothers and Sisters copy what they will, but never let this book out of your hands, and never keep the writings of another, for if it be found in their hand of write, they may well be taken and tortured. Each should guard his own writings and destroy them whenever danger threatens. Learn as much as you may by heart, and when the danger is past, rewrite your book if it be safe. For this reason, if any die, destroy their book if they have not been able to, for, an it be found 'tis clear proof against them, and "Ye may not be a Witch alone". So all their friends be in danger of the Question. So destroy everything not necessary.

If your book be found on you, 'tis clear proof against you alone. You may be tortured. Keep all thought of the cult from your mind. Say you had bad dreams, that a Devil caused you to write this without your knowledge. Think to yourself, "I Know Nothing. I Remember nothing. I have forgotten All." Drive this into your mind. If the torture be too great to bear, say, "I will confess. I cannot bear this torment. What do you want me to say? Tell me and I will say it." If they try to make you talk of the brotherhood, do not, but if they try to make you speak of impossibilities, such as flying through the air, consorting with the Devil, sacrificing children, or eating men's flesh, to obtain relief from torture, say, "I had an evil dream. I was not myself. I was crazed." Not all Magistrates are bad. If there be an excuse, they may show you mercy. If you have confessed aught, deny it afterwards. Say you babbled under the torture; you knew not what you did or said. If you be condemned, fear not. The Brotherhood is powerful. They may help you to escape if you are steadfast. If you betray aught, there is no hope for you, in this life, or in that which is to come. But, 'tis sure, that if steadfast you go to the pyre, drugs will reach you. You will feel naught, and you go but to Death and what lies beyond, the ecstasy of the Goddess.

The same with the working Tools. Let them be as ordinary things that anyone may have in their homes. The Pentacles shall be of wax that they may be melted or broken at once. Have no sword unless your rank allows you one. Have no names or signs on anything. Write them on in ink before consecrating them and wash it off at once when finished.

2.6. Of the Ordeal of the Art Magical (1953)

[see also 2.3 The Scourge and the Kiss]

Learn of the spirit that goeth with burdens that have not honour, for 'tis the spirit that stoopeth the shoulders and not the weight. Armour is heavy, yet it is a proud burden and a man standeth upright in it. Limiting and constraining any of the senses serves to increase the concentration of another. Shutting the eyes aids the hearing. So the binding of the initiate's hands increases the mental perception, while the scourge increaseth the inner vision. So the initiate goeth through it proudly, like a princess, knowing it but serves to increase her glory.

But this can only be done by the aid of another intelligence and in a circle, to prevent the power thus generated being lost. Priests attempt to do the same with their scourgings and mortifications of the flesh. But lacking the aid of bonds and their attention being distracted by their scourging themselves and what little power they do produce being dissipated, as they do not usually work within a circle, it is little wonder that they oft fail. Monks and hermits do better, as they are apt to work in tiny cells and coves, which in some way act as circles. The Knights of the Temple, who used mutually to scourge each other in an octagon, did better still; but they apparently did not know the virtue of bonds and did evil, man to man.

But perhaps some did know? What of the Church's charge that they wore girdles or cords?

2.7. The Eightfold Way.

2.7a Eightfold Path or Ways to the Centre. (1953)

1 Meditation or Concentration. This in practice means forming a mental image of what is desired, and forcing yourself to see that it is fulfilled, with the fierce belief and knowledge that it can and will be fulfilled, and that you will go on willing till you force it to be fulfilled. Called for short, "Intent"

2 Trance, projection of the Astral.

3 Rites, Chants, Spells, Runes, Charms, etc.

4 Incense, Drugs, Wine, etc., whatever is used to release the Spirit. (Note. One must be very careful about this. Incense is usually harmless, but you must be careful. If it has bad after-effects, reduce the amount used, or the duration of the time it is inhaled. Drugs are very dangerous if taken to excess, but it must be remembered that there are drugs that are absolutely harmless, though people talk of them with bated breath, but Hemp is especially dangerous, because it unlocks the inner eye swiftly and easily, so one is tempted to use it more and more. If it is used at all, it must be with the strictest precautions, to see that the person who uses it has no control over the supply. This should be doled out by some responsible person, and the supply strictly limited.)

5 The Dance, and kindred practices.

6 Blood control (the Cords), Breath Control, and kindred practices.

7 The Scourge.

8 The Great Rite.

These are all the ways. You may combine many of them into the one experiment, the more the better.

The Five Essentials:

A The most important is "Intention": you must know that you can and will succeed; it is essential in every operation.

B Preparation. (You must be properly prepared according to the rules of the Art; otherwise you will never succeed.)

C The Circle must be properly formed and purified.

D You all must be properly purified, several times if necessary, and this purification should be repeated several times during the rite.

E You must have properly consecrated tools.

These five essentials and Eight Paths or Ways cannot all be combined in one rite. Meditation and dancing do not combine well, but forming the mental image and the dance may be well combined with Chants. Spells, etc., combined with scourging and No. 6, followed by No. 8, form a splendid combination. Meditation, following scourging, combined with Nos. 3 and 4 and 5, are also very Good. For short cuts concentration, Nos. 5, 6, 7, and 8 are excellent.

2.7b EIGHTFOLD PATH OR WAYS. (1957)

1 Meditation or concentration, actually by the firm knowledge that you can and will succeed—forming a clear picture in your mind or your requirements.

2 Trance states, Clairvoyance, Projection of the Astral, etc.

3 Drugs, Wine, Incense.

4 Dance, Performing Rites with a purpose.

5 Chants, Spells, etc.

6 Blood control (Cords etc.), Breath control.

7 Scourge.

8 The Great Rite.

N.B. The great thing is to combine as many of these paths into the one operation. No 1 must be in all—for if you have no clear picture of what you wish and no certainty you will not succeed — 'tis useless. No. 2 can be combined with this easily. Nos. 3, 4, and 5 are all good preliminaries — also 6 and 7; but No. 3 is dangerous and therefore if possible should be avoided, *except for incense,* which is harmless if too much is not used.

The best combination is Nos. 1, 4, 5 and 7, for small purposes, with No. 8 if great force is necessary. Also a combination of 1, 6 and 7 is good if more can not be done; this if properly performed leads to No. 2.

2.8. To Gain the Sight (1953)

This cometh to different people in diverse ways. 'Tis seldom it cometh naturally, but it can be induced in many ways. Deep and prolonged meditation may do it, but only if you be a natural, and usually prolonged fasting was also necessary. Of old monks and nuns obtained visions by long vigils, combined with fasting, flagellation till the blood came, and other mortifications of the flesh, and so undoubtedly had visions. In the East it is tried with various tortures, at the same time sitting in cramped postures, which retard the flow of blood, and these torments, long and continued, give good results. But in the Art we are taught an easier way to intensify the imagination, at the same time controlling the blood supply, and this may best be done by using the ritual.

Incense is also good to propitiate the Spirits, but also to induce relaxation and to help to build up the atmosphere which is necessary to suggestibility. For our human eyes are so blind to what really is, that it is often necessary to suggest that it is there, before we may see it, as we may point out to another something at a distance before they may see it themselves. Gum mastic, aromatic rush roots, cinnamon bark, musk, juniper, sandalwood, and ambergris in combination are all good, but patchouli is best of all. And if you may have hemp, 'tis better still, but be very careful of this.

The circle being formed, all properly prepared, and the Rites done, and all purified, the aspirant should warlock and take his tutor round the circle, saluting the Mighty Ones, and invoke them to aid the operation. Then both dance round till giddy, invoking or using chants. Scourge. Then the Tutor should warlock very tightly, but not so to cause discomfort, but enough to retard the blood slightly. Again they should dance round, chanting, then scourge with light, steady, monotonous, slow strokes. It is very good that the pupil may see them coming (this may be arranged from position, or if a big mirror is available, this can be used with excellent effect) as this has the effect of passes, and helps greatly to stimulate the imagination, and it is important that they be not hard, the object being not to do more than draw the blood to that part and so away from the brain. This with the tight warlocking, which should be warricked, slows down the circulation of the blood, and the passes soon induce a drowsiness and a stupor. The tutor should watch for this. As soon as the aspirant sleeps, the scourging should cease. The tutor should also watch that the pupil become not cold, and if they struggle or become distressed, they should be at once awakened. (Note: if it cannot be arranged for the pupil to see, the wand may be used, for a time, then return to scourging.)

Do not be discouraged if no results come after two or three attempts. It will come, when both are in the right state. When you get some result, then results will come more quickly. Soon some of the ritual may be shortened, but never neglect to invoke the Goddess, and the Mighty Ones, or to form the Circle and do everything rightly. And for good and clear results, it is ever better to do too much ritual than too little.

It hath been found that this practice doth often cause a fondness between aspirant and tutor, and 'tis a cause of better results if this be so. If for any reason it is undesirable that there be any great fondness between aspirant and tutor, this may be easily avoided, by both parties from the onset firmly resolving in their minds that if any doth ensue, it shall be that of brother and sister or parent and child. And it is for this reason that a man may only be taught by a woman and a woman by a man, and that man and man, and woman and woman, should never attempt these practices together. And may all the Curses of the Mighty Ones be on any who make the attempt.

Remember, the Circle, properly constructed, is ever necessary to prevent the power released from being dissipated. It is also a barrier against any disturbances of mischievous forces, for to obtain good results you must be free from all disturbances. Remember that darkness, points of light gleaming amid the surrounding dark, incense, and the steady passes by a white arm are not stage effects. They are the mechanical implements which start the suggestions, which later unlocks the knowledge that it is possible to obtain the divine ecstasy, and so attain knowledge and communion with the Divine Goddess. When once you have attained this, Ritual is not needed, as you may attain the state of ecstasy at will, but till then, or if you having attained this yourself, and wish to bring a companion to this state of joy, ritual is best.

2.9.a Power (1953)

Power is latent in the body and may be drawn out and used in various ways by the skilled. But unless confined in a circle it will be swiftly dissipated. Hence the importance of a properly constructed circle. Power seems to exude from the body via the skin and possibly from the orifices of the body; hence you should be properly prepared. The slightest dirt spoils everything, which shows the importance of thorough cleanliness.

The attitude of mind has great effect, so only work with a spirit of reverence. A little wine taken and repeated during the ceremony, if necessary, helps to produce power. Other strong drinks or drugs may be used, but it is necessary to be very moderate, as if you are confused, even slightly, you cannot control the power you evoke.

The simplest way is by dancing and singing monotonous chants, slowly at first and gradually quickening the tempo until giddiness ensues. Then the calls may be used, or even wild and meaningless shrieking produces power. But this method inflames the mind and renders it difficult to control the power, though control may be gained through practice. The scourge is a far better way, for it stimulates and excites both body and soul, yet one easily retains control.

The Great Rite is far the best. It releases enormous power, but the conditions and circumstances make it difficult for the mind to maintain control at first. It is again a matter of practice and the natural strength of the operator's will and, in a less degree, of those of his assistants. If, as of old, there were many trained assistants present and all wills properly attuned, wonders occurred.

Sorcerers chiefly used the blood sacrifice; and while we hold this to be evil, we cannot deny that this method is very efficient. Power flashes forth from newly shed blood, instead of exuding slowly as by our method. The victim's terror and anguish add keenness, and quite a small animal can yield enormous power. The great difficulty is in the human mind controlling the power of the lower animal mind. But sorcerers claim they have methods for effecting this and that the difficulty disappears the higher the animal used, and when the victim is human disappears entirely. (The practice is an abomination but it is so.) Priests know this well; and by their auto-da-fé, with the victims' pain and terror (the fires acting much the same as circles), obtained enormous power.

Of old the Flagellants certainly evoked power, but through not being confined by a circle most was lost. The amount of power raised was so great and continuous that anyone with knowledge could direct and use it; and it is most probable that the classical and heathen sacrifices were used in the same way. There are whispers that when the human victim was a willing sacrifice, with his mind directed on the Great Work and with highly skilled assistants, wonders ensued but of this I would not speak.

2.9.b Cone of Power (1953)

This was the old way. The circle was marked out and people stationed to whip up the dancers. A fire or candle was within it in the direction where the object of the rite was supposed to be. Then all danced round until they felt they had raised enough power. If the rite was to banish they started deosil and finished widdershins, so many rounds of each. Then they formed a line with linked hands and rushed towards the fire shouting the thing they wanted. They kept it up 'til they were exhausted or until someone fell in a faint, when they were said to have taken the spell to its destination.

NOTES

Power

The essence of magic is to raise power.[1]

It is a tradition that fire in some form, generally a candle, must be present on the altar, which is placed in the middle of the circle, and candles are also placed about the circle itself. This circle is drawn with the idea of "containing" the "power" which is raised within it, of bringing it to a focus, so to speak, so that some end may be accomplished by raising it. This focusing of force is called "The Cone of Power".

Incense is also used, and I have read in Spiritualist literature that "power" is thought by some mediums to be given off by naked flames, by a bowl of water, and by incense. All these are present on the witches' altar.[2]

The great reservoir of "power", according to the witches, is the human body.[3]
Witches are taught and believe that the power resides within their bodies which they can release in various ways, the simplest being dancing round in a circle, singing or shouting, to induce a frenzy; this power they believe exudes from their bodies, clothes impeding its release. In dealing with such matters it is, of course, difficult to say how much is real and how much imagination.[4]
The witches' belief that "the power" resides within themselves, and that their rites serve to bring it out, is the great difference between them and the practitioners of "ceremonial magic", black or white. The latter proceed by the invocation or evocation of spirits, sometimes of demons, whom they seek to compel to serve them. This is not the witches' way, though they believe that helpful spirits, human or otherwise, come of their own accord to assist in their rites, and that those present who have developed "the Sight" (i.e. clairvoyance) may see such spirits.[5]

I am inclined to believe that while allowing for imagination there is something in the witches' belief. I think that there is something in the nature of an electromagnetic field surrounding all living bodies, and that this is what is seen by some people who call it the aura. I can sometimes see it myself, but only on bare flesh, so clothes evidently obstruct its functioning; this, however, is simply my own private belief. I think a witch by her formulae stimulates it, or possibly creates more of it. They say that witches by constant practice can train their wills to blend this nerve force, or whatever it is, and that their united wills can project this as a beam of force, or that they can use it in other ways to gain clairvoyance, or even to release the astral body. These practices include increasing and quickening the blood supply, or in other cases slowing it down, as well as the use of will-power; so it is reasonable to believe that it does have some effect. I am not stating that it does. I only record the fact that they attempt these effects, and believe that sometimes they succeed. The only way to find the truth or falsity of this would be to experiment. (I should think that slips or Bikinis could be worn without unduly causing loss of power. It would be interesting to try the effect of one team in the traditional nude and one in Bikinis.) At the same time one might heed the witches' dictum: "You must be this way always in the rites, 'tis the command of the Goddess." You must be this way so that it becomes second nature; you are no longer naked, you are simply natural and comfortable.[6]

Being initiated into the witch cult does not give a witch supernatural powers as I reckon them, but instructions are given, in rather veiled terms, in processes which develop various clairvoyant and other powers, in those who naturally possess them slightly. If they have none they can create none. Some of these powers are akin to magnetism, mesmerism and suggestion, and depend on the possibility of forming a sort of human battery, as it were, of combined human wills working together to influence persons or events at a distance. They have instructions in how to learn to do this by practice. It would take many people a long time, if I understand the directions aright. If these arts were more generally practised nowadays, we should call most of them spiritualism, mesmerism, suggestion, E.S.P., Yoga or perhaps Christian Science; to a witch it is all MAGIC, and magic is the art of getting results. To do this certain processes are necessary and the rites are such that these processes may be used. In other words, they condition you. This is the secret of the cult.

I do not say that these processes are the only way to develop these powers. I presume that professional clairvoyants, for instance, have some method of teaching or training to bring out the powers which they naturally possess. It is possible that their method may be superior to that of witchcraft; possibly they know the witches' system and all the teaching it involves and keep it as a trade secret. Witches are also taught that in some mysterious way "inside the circle they are between the worlds" (this world and the next), and "that which happens between the worlds does not concern this world". To form this battery of wills, male and female intelligences are necessary in couples.[7]

I have read that many people describe magic, or "attempted magic", as being performed by imitating the result required, i.e. "showing the Power what to do", and repeating a rhyme to make it work. I gather that they believe the imitation causes the effect to occur, when "triggered off", as it were, by a rhyme. I prefer to think that doing the imitative act, making the model of the thing, etc., are simply useful means of focusing the mind. This is reinforced and driven into the unconscious mind by a repetition of words (the Spell). This need not be in the form of a rhyme at all, but rhythm or alliteration are an aid to memory; that is, you cannot drive a thing into your unconscious and fix your mind pinpointed on your object if you have to stop and think what the next word is, and the act of reading distracts your attention, however slightly. In fact, you want something which almost says itself. I cannot for the moment think of a spell in limerick form, though doubtless they exist; but they almost say themselves, and the impact of the final rhyme should be very effective. Also, I think that the "spell" should have a decided reference to the work in hand, though some people say this is not necessary, and that words in an unknown tongue, especially "Enochian", as used by Dr Dee and Edward Kelly (and later Aleister Crowley), or a string of words of unknown meaning, "the barbarous names of evocation", have the best effect; though to use them effectively you must learn them by heart that they may "say themselves" at the proper instant without any effort of memory. There is the witch practice of raising the power to the utmost and then clearly stating what is required, ending with a formula of which I may give the last two lines. It "says itself", ending like hammer blows with "As I will, so mote it be, chant the spell and Be it Done!"[8]

1. *Witchcraft Today,* Chapter IX: Irish Witchcraft. p. 84.
2. *Meaning of Witchcraft,* Chapter I: The Witch Cult in Britain. p. 14.
3. *Meaning of Witchcraft,* Chapter I: The Witch Cult in Britain. p. 15.
4. *Witchcraft Today,* Chapter I: Living Witchcraft. p. 17.
5. *Meaning of Witchcraft,* Chapter I: The Witch Cult in Britain. p. 16.
6. *Witchcraft Today,* Chapter I: Living Witchcraft. p. 18.
7. *Witchcraft Today,* Chapter I: Living Witchcraft. p. 24.
8. *Meaning of Witchcraft,* Chapter VII: Magic Thinking. p. 96.

2.10. Properly Prepared. (1953)

Naked, but sandals (not shoes) may be worn. For initiation, tie hands behind back, pull up to small of back, and tie ends in front of throat, leaving a cable-tow to lead by, hanging down in front. (Arms thus form a triangle at back.) When initiate is kneeling at altar, the cable-tow is tied to a ring in the altar. A short cord is tied like a garter round the initiate's left leg above the knee, with ends tucked in. Another is tied round right ankle and ends tucked in so as to be out of the way while moving about. These cords are used to tie feet together while initiate is kneeling at the altar and must be long enough to do this firmly. Knees must also be firmly tied. This must be carefully done. If the aspirant complains of pain, the bonds must be loosened slightly; always remember the object is to retard the blood flow enough to induce a trance state. This involves slight discomfort, but great discomfort prevents the trance state; so it is best to spend some little time loosening and tightening the bonds until they are just right. The aspirant alone can tell you when this is so. This, of course, does not apply to the initiation, as then no trance is desired; but for the purpose of ritual it is good that the initiates be bound firmly enough to feel they are absolutely helpless but without discomfort.

The Measure (in the First Degree) is taken thus:

Height, round neck, across the heart and across the genitals. The old custom is, if anyone were guilty of betraying the secrets, their measure was buried at midnight in a boggy place, with curses that "as the measure rots, so they will rot."

2.11. The Meeting Dance. (1953)

The Maiden should lead. A man should place both hands on her waist, standing behind her, and alternate men and women do the same, the Maiden leading and they dance following her. She at last leads them into a right-hand spiral. When the centre is reached (and this had better be marked by a stone), she suddenly turns and dances back, kissing each man as she comes to him. All men and women turn likewise and dance back, men kissing girls and girls kissing men. All in time to music, it is a merry game, but must be practised to be done well. Note, the musicians should watch the dancers and make the music fast or slow as is best. For the beginners it should be slow, or there will be confusion. It is most excellent to get people to know each other at big gatherings.

2.12. To Leave the Body. (1953)

'Tis not wise to strive to get out of your body until you have thoroughly gained the Sight. The same ritual as to gain the Sight may be used, but have a comfortable couch. Kneel so that you have your thigh, belly, and chest well supported, the arms strained forward and bound one on each side, so that there is a decided feeling of being pulled forward. As the trance is induced, you should feel a striving to push yourself out of the top of your head. The scourge should be given a dragging action, as if to drive or drag you out. Both wills should be thoroughly in tune, keeping a constant and equal strain. When trance comes, your tutor may help you by softly calling your name. You will probably feel yourself drawn out of your body as if through a narrow opening, and find yourself standing beside your tutor, looking at the body on the couch. Strive to communicate with your tutor first; if they have the Sight they will probably see you. Go not far afield at first, and 'tis better to have one who is used to leaving the body with you.

A note: When, having succeeded in leaving the body, you desire to return, in order to cause the spirit body and the material body to coincide, *think of your feet*. This will cause the return to take place.

2.13. The Working Tools (1953)

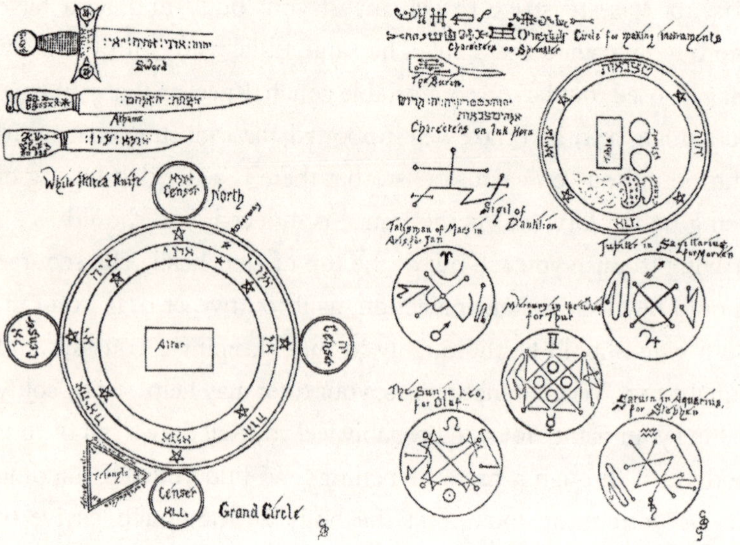

There are no magical supply shops, so unless you are lucky enough to be given or sold tools, a poor witch must extemporize. But when made you should be able to borrow or obtain an Athame. So having made your circle, erect an altar. Any small table or chest will do. There must be fire on it (a candle will suffice) and your book. For good results incense is best if you can get it, but coals in a chafing dish burning sweet-smelling herbs will do. A cup if you would have cakes and wine, and a platter with the signs drawn into the same in ink, showing a pentacle. A scourge is easily made (note, the scourge has eight tails and five knots in each tail). Get a white-hilted knife and a wand (a sword is not necessary). Cut the marks with Athame. Purify everything, then consecrate your tools in proper form and ever be properly prepared. But ever remember, magical operations are useless unless the mind can be brought to the proper attitude, keyed to the utmost pitch.

Affirmations must be made clearly, and the mind should be inflamed with desire. With this frenzy of will, you may do as much with simple tools as with the most complete set. But good and especially ancient tools have their own aura. They do help to bring about that reverential spirit, the desire to learn and develop your powers. For this reason witches ever try to obtain tools from sorcerers, who, being skilled men, make good tools and consecrate them well, giving them mighty power. But a great witch's tools also gain much power; and you should ever strive to make any tools you manufacture of the finest materials you can obtain, to the end that they may absorb your power the more easily. And of course if you may inherit or obtain another witch's tools, power will flow from them.

It is an old belief that the best substances for making tools are those that have once had life in them, as opposed to artificial substances. Thus wood or ivory is better for a wand than metal, which is more appropriate for swords or knives. Virgin parchment is better than manufactured paper for talismans, etc. And things which have been made by hand are good, because there is life in them.

NOTES

The Witch's Tools

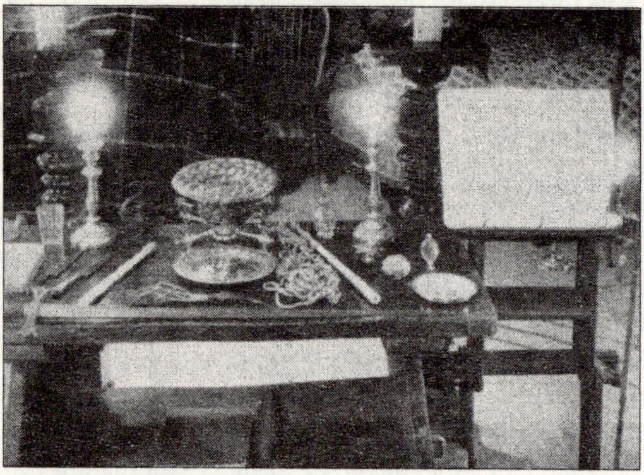

Altar prepared for the initiation of a witch in the Southern English coven, showing *inter alia,* incense burners, a scourge, wine cup, pentacle, wand, sword, an aspergillum for consecration by water, and the ceremonial book on stand. *Witchcraft Today,* p. 82.

* * * * *

A poor witch usually has to make or improvise her own tools; a novice is often presented with an Athame, and of course in a witch family there are often old tools to be had. Old tools are always preferred, as they are supposed to have *Power.* If you cannot get these, you are told to attempt to make your own, and I have seen some very clever work. Women are usually helped with making their tools if they have no family ones, but some of them are very clever work-women also.

The tools may be of the simplest construction, but actually, as they are used for a religious purpose, they try to make them as nice as possible. Of course, the average witch does not have a full battery of tools; not all have the sword, for instance. An Athame (witch's knife), a censer, some cord and one or two other tools are quite enough to work with. For initiations the whole battery of tools has, of course, to be present; but these usually belong to the coven.

It is very amusing to see how clever some witches are in disguising their tools so that they look like something else; indeed, they often are something else, until they are put together in the proper way to be used.[1]

There are three working tools which are essential and nothing can be done without them; that is, something to cut and stab with, something to strike with and something to bind with. There are five others, all of which have their special uses and are only needed if that particular kind of work is being done. For an initiation all eight must be present and the initiate is told the use of, and holds, each in turn.[2]

Working tools — let them be as ordinary things that anyone may have in their homes. Let the Pentacles be of wax that they may be melted or broken at once. Have no sword unless your rank allows you one. Have no names or signs on anything, write the names and signs on in ink before consecrating them and wash it off immediately after.[3]

* * * * *

"Now I present thee with the working tools of a witch."

Handing him a sword from the Altar, and motioning him to touch it.

"First, the Magic Sword. With this as with the Athame, thou canst form all Magic Circles, dominate, subdue and punish all rebellious Spirits and demons, and even persuade the angels and geniuses. With this in thy hand thou art the ruler of the Magic Circle," and she kissed him.

"Next I present the Athame. This is the true Witches' Weapon, it has all the powers of the Magic Sword." (Again a kiss.)

"Next I present the White Handled Knife. Its use is to form all instruments used in the Art. It can only be properly used within a Magic Circle." (Again a kiss.)

"Next I present the Censer of Incense, this is to encourage and welcome good spirits and to banish evil spirits." (A kiss.) "Next I present the Scourge, this is a sign of Power and Domination, it is also to cause suffering and purification, for it is written: To learn thou must suffer and purified. Art willing to suffer to learn?"

Jan; " I am." (Again a Kiss.)

"Next and lastly I present the Cords. They are of use to bind the Sigils, the material basis, and to enforce thy will, also, they are necessary in the Oath."[4]

Athame — Black-handled knife.

The only circle that matters is the one drawn before every ceremony with either a duly consecrated Magic Sword or a Knife, the latter being the Witches' Athame or Black-Hilted Knife, with magic signs on the hilt, and this is most generally used.[5]

A novice is often presented with an Athame, and of course in a witch family there are often old tools to be had. Old tools are always preferred, as they are supposed to have *Power.*[6]

Sword

See

Ritual and Preparation of Tools, and

B.4. The Priestess and the Sword

Wand

J. S. M. Ward in *Who Was Hirim Abif?* quotes the legends of the Jews, which give the twenty-two questions with which Balkis, Queen of Sheba, tested King Solomon's knowledge. These questions are thought to refer to the secret initiation ceremonies of Astarte-Tammuz. Question 9 is peculiar, and clearly refers to things used for ritual or magic.

Sheba: "Which are the three that neither die, nor do they have bread put into them, yet they save lives from death?"

Solomon: "The Staff, the Cord, and the Ring."

The Staff is the "Wand" of the conductor of souls who conducts one through the Underworld. The Cord is the "Cable Tow" with which the candidate is bound, a willing victim properly prepared for sacrifice. The "Ring" symbolizes the "Vesica piscis" of rebirth.[7]

Tarot cards, which are still used by occultists, and are the ancestors of our present-day playing-cards. Much ingenuity has been exercised by occultists and others to account for the origin of these cards, and it is at least a curious parallel that according to an old Irish "Book of Invasions" which is considered to date from the 12th century, the four magical talismans which the Tuatha de Danaan, the ancient Irish Gods, brought to Ireland with them were the Sword of Nuada, the Lance of Lugh, the Cauldron of the Dagda, and the Stone of Fal, which are analogous to the Sword, the Wand, the Cup, and the Pentacle comprising what A.E. Waite called "the Four palmary symbols of the Tarot".[8]

Cup

Another great Templar "hallow" was the Chalice, the Cup. As I have said, the witch also reveres the Cup, which seems to date back to the old fertility cults. It is a curious fact that the Church disliked and discouraged the story of the Holy Grail, though they could not entirely prevent its being popular as a "romance". The original versions appeared about 1175 to 1225; then the source of supply seems to have been cut off. Can it be that the Church brought pressure to bear? Henceforth writers simply made rehashes of the old materials, adding stories of King Arthur and his knights, etc.

Now the Grail is a sort of hallow or talisman. It brings fertility to the land and it feeds its worshippers. It has many forms, but it is always a fertility and a food-providing object. It seems to have had five forms:

1. A reliquary.
2. The platter or cup used at the Last Supper.
3. A jar or bottle in which St Joseph received the Blood from the Wounds of Christ.
4. A Sacred or Talismanic Stone.
5. The Chalice of the Eucharist.

In all these cases however it seems to have no material substance, but to have come from a sort of fourth dimension, to which it returned swiftly again. Shall we say it came from and returned to that place *between the Worlds*, or something like the Witches' Circle?

We are told the Grail is a mystery which must not be revealed to the uninitiated. *The High History of the Holy Grail* says that the Grail appeared *in* five several manners that none ought not to tell, for the secret things of the Sacrament ought none to tell openly but he unto whom God hath given it. Does not this point to there being an inner meaning to the Grail story, that the meaning of the sacred object varied, according to the understanding of the initiate, or shall we say that different explanations of the meanings of an object were given in higher grades of initiation, and that the outermost explanation was the Chalice, but that in all there was the "feeding" and fertility implication?[9]

Another matter I must explain. At first I was puzzled by the absence of the Cup from the witches' working tools and the inclusion of the unimportant pentacle, said to be used to command spirits; also that while the witches admittedly used a form of spiritualism, asking departed spirits to return or communicate, they did not generally evoke — that is, command — either spirits or Elementals to appear, and then, by commands, bribes or sacrifices, cause them to do services. The more so because, through their connection with sorcerers, they knew of these practices. Also, in the explanation of the working tools, mention is made of such matters. The answer I get is: In the burning times this was done deliberately. Any mention of the Cup led to an orgy of torture, their persecutors saying that it was a parody of the Mass; also the riding or dancing pole ("broomstick") was cut out. Censer and pentacle were substituted and explanations made to fit what their persecutors expected. If all told more or less the same story of what they were taught — because it was actually true and it agreed with the story of others — why bother to continue the torture? The witch was convicted, and if she did not escape or die in prison, she was quickly burnt and her troubles were over.[10]

The Grail, the Cup or Chalice, is like the Celtic Cauldron. It restored the dead, and brought fertility back to the land. The King, in the *Mabinogion*, gives Gawaine a sword which each day drops blood. There is a head and spear which drops blood in connection with a cauldron of fertility in the adventure of Peredur, vaguely said to be connected with the murder of a relation of Peredur by witches at Glaucesier. A sword or dagger dropping blood (or wine) into a cauldron would have great meaning to witches, and they have a head or skull tradition. Could the story be a hidden way of hinting that an ancestor of Peredur had gone through the circle to Death and returned, and so Peredur himself was of the Witch Blood and entitled to know the Mystery of the Cauldron? Most scholars agree that the bleeding spear is phallic.

In the *Merlin* MS., Bibliothèque Nationale 337, there is a Grail procession which passes through a wood singing: "Honour and Glory and Power and everlasting joy to the *Destroyer of Death.*" Could not that be a chant in praise of the goddess? Or could it be really to disguise a chant: "Honour and Glory and Power and everlasting joy to the *destroyer of the fear of Death*"? That is, to the givers of Regeneration, *Death and what lies beyond.*[11]

Pentacle

When a Sigil is written on paper or parchment it is often described as a seal, whereas if a Talisman or Pentacle is inscribed on parchment, it is not a seal, the difference being, that a Sigil or seal belongs to one individual spirit, who in Jan's case was Bartzebal, while a Talisman or Pentacle belongs either to one human being, or in a general way, to all the spirits serving one Governing Spirit, like Mars, Saturn or Venus, as the case may be. A Pentacle is also a medal used to evoke a spirit and command him, it is in addition a figure like a five-pointed star, and should always be drawn and used with one point uppermost, and never with two points uppermost. From their nature, certain Pentacles can be carried outside the Circle and worn with a view to bringing good fortune, such as the Pentacle of Venus for love. Of Jupiter for success and prosperity. A Pentacle of Saturn will induce his good qualities of steadiness, perseverance and loyalty, but this can only be carried by one born under Saturn; to anyone else it would bring disaster. A soldier born under any sign could wear a Pentacle of Mars, with advantage, which might produce quarrelsomeness in a merchant, while the latter would be well advised to wear one of Mercury. While a medal such as described above is sometimes called a Talisman. This name should more properly be kept for articles made especially for its owner, with the express intention of bringing him success in what particular object he has in view, and are made in accordance with the owner's horoscope. They are usually made by an expert, in the proper day and hour, with the special object in view, with protection and safety. Or Prosperity, gain, and success for the subject firmly fixed in his mind. The Talisman is then consecrated with magical formulae.[12]

Censer and Incense

The people of Bronze Age Britain may have used incense in their religious rites. A type of pottery vessel has been found, dating from that period, which archaeologists call an "incense-cup", as they are unable to ascribe any other use to it. Such vessels are small, and pierced with holes in the lower part, possibly to allow a good draught to keep alight the glowing charcoal upon which grains of incense are burned. We know that the religious rites of ancient times used incense extensively, and if ancient Britain could import Egyptian beads, as we know it did, there is no reason why it should not have imported Egyptian incense also.

I have previously noted the use by witches of incense in their rites. This is not necessarily a foreign importation, or an imitation of church practices, as will be seen from the foregoing.[13]

Witches use incense in quantities. Nowadays they usually buy this at the nearest church stores, but some compound their own; they are very secretive about this, and I think they put some strong stuff in it; at least I have known people behave rather queerly after it has been burned in a confined space, though it has never had any effect on me — or at least none that I noticed. During the Second World War they had to do without anointing; but nowadays one or two have managed to get small amounts. They keep their source of supply very secret, as, also, what it is compounded with. It smells fine to me, though some people dislike it. It is a powerful smell, and I think that, like the incense, it can have some effect on you if you are suggestible, which I am not; but part of the intention is to cause a shifting of the centres of consciousness. Of this "exstasis", the best English translation is "taking one out of oneself", taking him into communion with the god. But to attain this state lustration is at least advisable; this is in fact the inward as well as an outward cleansing — the old doctrine of penance, cleansing the soul as well as the body; in this way only is the body properly prepared for the goddess to descend and inspire her worshipper. In this way may the trance state be induced, though there are other methods, all to the end of escaping temporarily from the yoke of tradition, to make the soul free; in other words, it gives one something new to live for.

Many people attempt this by drugs, or more crudely by alcohol. But these have extremely bad effects on the body, and any results are at the best often illusions; so seldom make the attempt in that way. In the old days many witches went to the flames laughing and singing; they had a joy of life and of beauty, and the Peace of Death with the promise of return, so they braved the fires, for they believed that they were going to a better world, and they died happy.[14]

White-handled Knife

See

Ritual and Preparation of Tools

Scourge

See

2.3 The Scourge and the Kiss

Cords

Now G. had never loved, but she would solve all mysteries, even the mystery of Death, and so she journeyed to the nether lands. The guardians of the portals challenged her. 'Strip of thy garments, lay aside thy jewels, for nought may ye bring with you into this our land.' So she laid down her garments and her jewels and was bound as are all who enter the realms of Death, the mighty one.[†]

† There was a Celtic custom of binding corpses; the cord with which one had been bound was of great assistance in obtaining second sight. But in the Ancient World there seems to have been a widespread idea that a living person must be bound to enter the presence of the Lords of Death. Tacitus, in *Germania xxix,* tells of sacred groves where men assemble to obtain ancestral auguries, to enter these dominions sacred to the Lords of Death. "All are bound with fetters to show that they are in the power of the Divinity, and if they chance to fall they are not helped to rise. Prone as they are, they must roll along the ground as best they may." This latter shows they were closely bound, as they could not rise themselves; so clearly it was no 'token' binding.

Lucian, in his *Vera Historia*, which, though a novel, treats of popular beliefs, tells of living people landing on the Island of the Blessed being instantly bound with chains and brought before the King of the Dead.

The idea of living people, or the newly dead, being thus bound with chains as soon as they went to the land of death may I think be the origin of the old idea that ghosts rattled chains; newly out of Limbo they would still be thus bound.[15]

From ancient times "Cords, Threads or Clews" have been mentioned as used by witches, for evil or good, and often they are described as coloured. Greek witches are always described as using coloured cords.

Modern witches do the same; I have asked the reason, and they say it's just because they are pretty. This may simply mean that as witchcraft is a religious rite, they have everything as "nice" as possible, or there may be some reason which is now forgotten. It has been suggested to me that it might be merely that white cords would soon show dirt, but I don't think this is right, or they would use black, or dark coloured ones, though Italian witches use black cords or thread when making an evil charm.

In this Museum I have a dried-up lemon stuck with black pins and bound with black thread. This was made to part two lovers whose union the parents did not approve of, and black cords are said to be employed for "killing spells".

Incidentally, the witch used white cords to bind the blackmailer, but this was not to injure him in any way, simply to prevent him harming others, and was the only cord she had handy.[16]

The consecrated cord which witches possess and use in many ways. All those I have seen are coloured, usually red, though I have known other colours used. They value them as they do all their working tools and naturally would be most annoyed if anyone removed (stole) any of them.[17]

Broomstick

It is easy to imagine that a witch who firmly believes that it is essential to be naked could not whip up the final effort to attain the ecstasy without being naked. Another, however, who did not share this belief might, though partially clothed exert sufficient energy to force power through her face, shoulders, arms and legs, to produce some result; but who can say that she could not have produced twice the power with half the effort had she been in the traditional nakedness? All we can be sure of is that in ancient times it was recognized that witches did so and even journeyed to their meetings in that costume; but in later times the Church, and more especially the Puritans, tried to hush this up and invented the story of the foul old woman on a broomstick, to replace the story told at so many witch trials of wild dances in the moonlight by beautiful young witches.[18]

All sorts of false ideas were spread until the popular notion of a witch became that of the common definition: "a witch is an old woman who flies through the air on a broomstick". Now no witch ever flew through the air on a broomstick or on anything else, at least not until aeroplanes came in. There is indeed a fertility charm to bring good crops which is performed by riding on a pole, or broom, as a hobbyhorse. Doubtless ancient witches practised this rite, leaping high to make the crops grow. In early trials witnesses speak of seeing the accused riding on poles, or brooms, across the fields (not through the air), and this was often accepted as the evidence that they were practising fertility magic, which became a penal offence. In the Castletown Museum there is one of these poles for riding, the head being carved in the shape of a phallus to bring fertility.[19]

People still ask me questions about witches because they have heard so many tales about them. Do they go to the sabbat? Is it true they use flying ointment? Why do witches anoint themselves? Did they fly through the air to their meetings on broomsticks? In the old days they usually walked, carrying poles or quarterstaffs, which were useful as weapons. They sometimes used them to make sort of pole jumps over obstacles; they were useful in finding one's way and avoiding obstacles in the dark. In the persecution times, at least, they would put them between their legs and ride on them when approaching the meeting place; or if challenged, as a sign that they belonged to the cult. Failure to do this might mean an arrow between their ribs, and this would usually be smeared with something of the hogsblood and hellebore variety. Finally, they rode these poles in the fertility dance; but riding them meant they got some grease and soot on them, and a pole so stained could be used in evidence against them; so they often took a stick or broomstick which might reasonably be dirty, and used this for recognition or for the jumping or fertility dances. If the place of meeting was distant, they rode horses. They never flew on broomsticks. Nowadays like ordinary people they walk or take a bus or whatever is most convenient.[20]

We can, however, distinguish the outlines of divine figures shining through these mists of obscurity, and make out something of what the Ancient Britons believed about them, their relationships and functions, and the meaning of their myths. Arianrhod, for instance, is said to have given birth to twin Gods, Llew, the Sun-God, and Dylan, the God of the Waves, and to have miraculously conceived these children by leaping over a wizard's wand. This is interesting, because it shows the early meaning of the wand as a phallic symbol, and its relationship to the broomstick which witches carried as such. Christina Hole, in her *English Folklore*, says, "Gypsies leapt over broomsticks at their weddings, and there was a form of marriage over a broomstick which was fairly common at one time, though it was not always considered binding if either party wished to default afterwards." Actually, I think this is more a Tinker than a Gipsy custom. At least, this is what Gipsies tell me. In Yorkshire an immoral woman is called a besom. Mothers were usually careful to prevent their daughters from stepping over a broom, and mischievous or spiteful people sometimes laid one where the girl would walk over it by accident: the reason being that if she strode over a besom or broomhandle she would become a mother before she was a wife. The ivy-wreathed thyrsus carried by the Bacchantes probably had essentially the same meaning. One sees pictures on old Greek vases of Bacchantes waving a branch with a bunch of leaves on the end of it, which are reminiscent of the pictures of witches with broomsticks.[21]

Cauldron

See [Cup]

Necklace

It may only be a coincidence that in Mexico there was a witch cult much resembling that in Europe, which existed from pre-Columbian times. They had a goddess, or witch queen, always represented as naked and carrying or riding a broom. (This represented cleanliness or ritual purity in Mexico.) The European witch laid great stress on cleanliness and purity.

At their meetings the women were always naked, but wore either a necklace or a short cape (women witches in Europe lay great stress on necklaces). In Mexico the men wore a skin flap fore and aft, like the Irish witches, but removed this for certain ceremonies. Indians did not kiss, but gave a caress of welcome. They usually worked within small chambers, with wall paintings, which confined the power raised, just as witches use a circle for the same purpose.[22]

I have mentioned a necklace, but this can be of any sort as long as it is fairly conspicuous. They have no story of its origin or meaning; it is merely the custom. Myself, I think that there must be some story to the effect that the goddess always wore a necklace; I believe that Astarte always wore one and was known as the Goddess of the Necklace, being otherwise "sky-clad", as they say in India. I have known one or two witches who wear talismans on their necklaces, but these are mainly astrological, being made for the owner only, and they bear no witch signs, so that I am inclined to think that the necklace itself is the important thing.†

Necklaces were important things both to Celt and Saxon. Some important priestess must have set the fashion. Thank goodness we are not plagued with people in the cult who are continually changing the fashions. Monsieur Dior would not find any customers for his *New Look*. We are very contented with the *Old Look*.

† Diana of Ephesus wore a necklace of acorns; many Celtic goddesses are mentioned as wearing them. At witch meetings every woman must wear one. When the ritual objects are being set out for a meeting, a number of strings of beads are put handy, so that if any witch hasn't brought a necklace, she promptly borrows one for the occasion. I remember one girl coming wearing a small string of pearls being told: "You know, dear, you mustn't do that; get a proper one from the box, one that can be seen." They cannot give me any other reason than that a witch must wear a necklace that is obvious.[23]

Garter

It is said that King Edward III saved one witch from certain torture at that famous incident to which the origin of the Order of the Garter was ascribed. He was dancing with the Countess of Salisbury when she dropped the ritual

Garter which proclaimed her high rank in the cult. With Bishops about this was dangerous, so the King, knowing what it was, picked it up and put it on his own leg, saying: "Honi soit qui mal y pense." The mid-Victorians, to whom a garter was slightly naughty, made pretty Christmas cards of the "Blushing Countess"; but ladies of those times, and this lady in particular, were hard-boiled; it took more than a garter to make them blush. The King's quickness saved the situation and placed him almost in the position of their incarnate god in the eyes of his more pagan subjects. This was followed by the foundation of an Order of twelve Knights for the King and twelve for the Prince of Wales, i.e. twenty-six members in all, or two covens. Froissart's words imply that Edward perfectly understood the underlying meaning of the Garter, for he says: "The King told them it should prove an excellent expedient for uniting not only his subjects one with another but all foreigners conjunctively with them in the bonds of amity and peace." Dr Murray points out that the King's mantle as chief of the Order was powdered over with one hundred and sixty-eight garters, which together with his own, worn on the leg, makes one hundred and sixty-nine, or thirteen times thirteen: that is, thirteen covens. I am told that long ago witches sometimes did have as many circles as this, with one common leader or timekeeper. It is noteworthy also that the Black Book containing the institution of the Garter was taken away and destroyed not long after his death. I have seen two witch garters; they were of green snakeskin with gold or silver gilt buckles and were backed with blue silk. They were worn above the left knee. They are badges of rank.

In this connection, can anyone tell me exactly what is the meaning of the double SS on the collar of the Garter? It is sometimes said to mean the Virgin, sometimes the Holy Ghost (*Sanctus Spiritus*). The Order is dedicated to the Virgin, certainly, but I do not see how it can refer to her. Nor does it seem to be dedicated to the Holy Ghost. My reason for asking is that on all Athama and many other witch tools I have seen — and I have seen many besides those in my own private collection — there are a number of signs carved. These are always the same and in the same order and have the same meanings. It is necessary to have these signs put on before they are consecrated. (In the burning times they would write them in ink and wash them off after consecration.) The third sign is SS: that is, two S's as used on the collar of the Garter. Witches have their own interpretation of this sign (and it is not the Virgin or the Holy Ghost). Black is said to be a feature in the Order of the Garter. The Black Book, containing the original constitutions of the Order, is said to have been taken away for secret reasons before the time of Henry V, as mentioned earlier, and from this Black Book comes the important post of Black Rod. One would think that there must have been important reasons to conceal something before such a book could be taken away or lost. The late Hargrave Jennings seemed convinced that there was some deep mystery here, but he apparently did not know, or if he did he did not mention this witch mark, which is also shown in the Key of Solomon. All this may be purely coincidence, and coincidence killed the Professor. But if no one mentions coincidences, there is little chance of finding further facts; and there is the undoubted fact that the garter is a badge of rank among witches, and further there is a prehistoric rock drawing in France supposed to represent a magical witch ceremony, twelve women dancing round a man who is stark naked except for garters. As stockings were not worn for several thousand years afterwards, these must have some meaning.[24]

Some authors confound the cord with the "Witches Garter". This is a badge of rank which is seldom used nowadays as far as my experience goes, but a number possess them and occasionally wear them.

The garter was occasionally employed in the old days as a sign of recognition. It would not be much use nowadays when, if anyone wanted to pretend to be a witch, it is the first thing they would think of.[25]

Bracelet

Witch Marks — I have never seen or heard of these among witches. Dr Murray suggests that there were tattoo marks as a means of recognition. I think it very probable that in the burning times something of the sort was used, but the ones I know have never heard of it except in Dr Murray's books *Witchcraft in Western Europe* and *The God of the Witches,* in which they are very interested. Witches feel they owe a debt of gratitude to Dr Murray for being the first to tell them that they were not the poisoners, diabolists or impostors that practically all other writers call them.

The only distinct mark that I know of is that ladies of a certain grade are entitled to wear a bracelet with their name and grade sign engraved on it, and as the uninitiated would not recognize these, they are often worn in public. Another witch would of course recognize them, even at a distance. There is also a higher order, the witch's garter; but this is never worn so that it can be seen in public.[26]

Burin

Firstly I must make a circle with a properly consecrated sword."

"How may one come by that?" asked Jan.

"It can be made, but the means are lacking, that is the trouble. To make the sword I need the Burin, to make the Burin I must have consecrated white-hilted knife, the witch's Athame. They in turn must be made by the Burin."[27]

"I lacked the needed instruments and the means to make them. You have the two knives, and therefore was I bidden to seek you. With those knives I can make the Burin and Magic Sword, Pentacles and Talismans. They are the precious keys which open wide all doors."[28]

The Burin must be made in the day and the hour of Venus.[29]

See also [Ritual Preparation of Tools]

1. *Witchcraft Today*, Chapter XIII: Recapitulation. p. 126.
2. *Witchcraft Today*, Chapter X: What are Witches? p. 98.
3. *Witchcraft Today*, Chapter IV: Witch Practices. p. 43.
4. *High Magic's Aid*, Chapter XVII: The Witch Cult. p. 183.
5. *Witchcraft Today*, Chapter I: Living Witchcraft. p. 22.
6. *Witchcraft Today*, Chapter XIII: Recapitulation. p. 126.
7. *Witchcraft Today*, Chapter XII: Who is the Devil. p. 114.
8. *Meaning of Witchcraft*, Chapter VIII: Magic Thinking (cont.) p. 118.
9. *Witchcraft Today*, Chapter VI: How the Little People became Witches . . . p. 64.
10. *Witchcraft Today*, Chapter XI: Some other Matters. p. 106.
11. *Witchcraft Today*, Chapter VI: How the Little People became Witches . . . p. 66.
12. *High Magic's Aid*, Chapter XV: Charging the Pentacles. p. 157.
13. *Meaning of Witchcraft*, Chapter IV: Some Religious Ideas of Early Britain p. 66.
14. *Witchcraft Today*, Chapter XIII: Recapitulation. p. 126.
15. Witchcraft *Today*, Chapter III: Witch Beliefs. p. 34.
16. *Meaning of Witchcraft*, Chapter X: Curious Beliefs about Witches p. 149.
17. *Witchcraft Today*, Chapter VI: How the little people became witches . . . p. 60.
18. *Witchcraft Today*, Chapter I: Living Witchcraft. p. 17.
19. *Witchcraft Today*, Chapter II: There have been Witches in all Ages. p. 29.
20. *Witchcraft Today*, Chapter IV: Witch Practices. p. 44.
21. Meaning of *Witchcraft*, Chapter XI: Who were the Gods of Britain. p. 166.
22. *Witchcraft Today*, Chapter II: There Have been Witches in All Ages. p. 31
23. *Witchcraft Today*, Chapter XIII: Recapitulation. p. 125.
24. *Witchcraft Today*, Chapter X: What are Witches. p. 102.
25. Meaning of *Witchcraft*, Chapter X: Curious Beliefs about Witches. p. 150.
26. *Witchcraft Today*, Chapter XIII: Recapitulation. p. 125.
27. *High Magic's Aid*, Chapter I: High Magic's Aid. p. 12.
28. *High Magic's Aid*, Chapter IX: Riding Together. p. 77.
29. *High Magic's Aid*, Chapter X: Working Together. p. 98.

We needed the witch's Athame to fashion our tools, so we went to the Sabbath to try to borrow one . . . [1]

The space between the two rooms was designed for the ritual. The night before it had been swept and dusted, so that it was free from the slightest speck of dirt, and while Thur busied himself selecting and tabulating the work to be done that night, Morven went rapidly over the floor again with a damp cloth. When she had finished she washed her hands and rejoined him, and together they solemnly perfumed the area.

"The Heavens are propitious," he murmured contentedly. "The Moon is in an Ariel sign and in her increase, the sky is clear and serene."

Meanwhile Morven thrust her Athame into a chink in the floorboards, looped the strand she had plaited that morning over it, and fitting a piece of charcoal into a loop five feet six inches down its length, she marked out a circle, leaving an entrance *north nor-west* in it. Shortening to the next loop six inches nearer the centre she described a second circle, and shortening again to four feet six inches, described the third circle, thus making an inner circle nine feet across. The outer circle was then divided into the four points of the compass. Beginning at the east, Thur marked in Hebrew 'Agial', at the south point 'Tzabaoth,' at the west 'Jhvh' (which in English is spelt Jehovah) and at the north, 'Adghy'. Between each point of the compass he drew a pentacle or five pointed star.

Morven then took the Athame and with its point went over again all that he had drawn in charcoal, while he placed a lighted brazier of the same fuel at the due eastern point within the smallest circle. This he lighted, then placed a table before it exactly with its centre to the middle of the brazier, and then set out thereon the various articles for consecration, among them the wand and the cord he had used for marking. Two stools were placed before the table. Slowly the clouds of fumes rose from the brazier. The triple circle was now complete and he closed the door to it with two pentacles, one inside the third circle and the second in the space between the second and the third.

All was now ready. Thur stood in the centre, facing east, tall and solemn, his immaculate robe giving him added majesty. Beside him stood Morven, serene as an alabaster statue. Clasping his hands loosely before him he began to recite in a low, clear voice Psalm CII, which begins:

> "Hear my prayer, O Lord
> And let my cry come unto Thee
> Hide not Thy face from me,
> In the day when I am in trouble incline Thine ear unto me
> In the day when I call answer me speedily."

And when it came to an end, he continued with Psalm XIV.

Then Psalm VI, and ending with Psalm LXVII.

When the impressive words died away there was a moment of silence before Thur took from the table a vessel of brass, varnished within and without, having a lid pierced with holes which fitted exactly and tightly, and a convenient handle. This he filled with clear spring water from a jug. Then he took salt and cried in a firm, ringing voice:

Tzabaoth, Messiach, Emanuel, Elohim, Eibor, Yod, He, Vou, He! O God, who art the Truth, and the Light, deign to bless and to sanctify this creature of salt, to serve unto us for help and protection and assistance in this Art experiment and operation. And may it be a succour to us."

With this prayer he cast into the water the salt, and then he took herbs, vervain, mint, garden basil, rosemary and hyssop, nine in all, gathered in the hour and day of Mercury in the waxing moon, and bound them with a thread that had been spun by a young maiden . . . Morven. These he steeped in the water and, reaching for the white-hilted knife, with it he engraved upon the sprinkler's handle characters, on the one side:

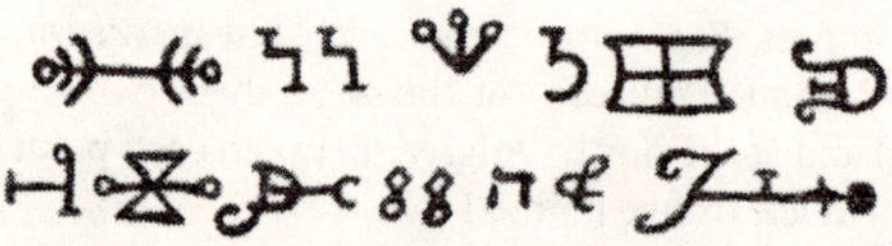

and on the other side:

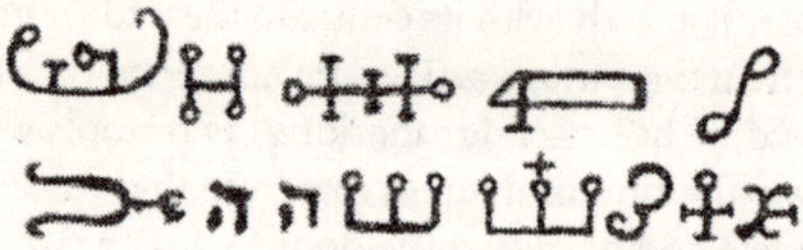

When this was accomplished he spoke to Morven for the first time. "After this ceremony we may now use this water in the sprinkler when necessary, knowing that whatever we shall sprinkle with it will be sanctified by its power to chase away all phantoms and depriving them of the ability to hinder or annoy us. With this water we shall make our preparations of Art."

Morven bowed her head in assent but did not speak.. So awed was she, so deeply impressed by the solemnity of the occasion and of what she had heard that she dared not use her voice in case she marred the spell. Thur seemed far removed from her into a realm of mystery whither she could not follow him.

His second operation was to make the pen. He took up a quill from the table, plucked from the right wing of a live male gosling and shaped it with the white handled knife. The exhortation was: *Aurai, Hanlii, Thamcii. Tilinos, Athamas, Zianor, Auonai!* Banish from this pen all deceit and error, so that it may be of virtue and efficacy to write what I desire." Upon the brazier he cast a handful of dried herbs and with the same knife sharpened the pen, sprinkled it and held it over the brazier in the cloud of perfume which rose from the herbs, then wrapped it in a new white linen cloth and laid it aside. In a like manner, with their appropriate invocations and prayers he consecrated the cords and laid them aside in the linen cloth.

It was late, and he became aware that Morven was looking white and exhausted. He broke up the séance for that night, since he could do no more without the Burin, which must be made in the day and the hour of Venus.[2]

That night they slept in peace, but the following, being the day of Venus, again the two prepared the water for their personal cleansing and, with this accomplished, again they drew the triple circle in exactly the manner of the former occasion. Their work was now to make the all-important Burin.

Thur recited anew those same Psalms of David, then, throwing the herbs on the brazier, he waited until the clouds of incense ascended, and took up an engraver's awl. He purified it on the live coals and, with the white-handled knife, whose office was that of a tool as distinct from that of the Athame used by the witch to control spirits and work magic, he carved on the handle of the awl, which was to become the Burin, these characters:

The invocation followed, solemn and commanding.

"Asphiel, Asophiel, Asophiel! Pentagrammaton, Athanatos, Eheieh, Asher, Eheieh! Qadosch, Qadosch, Qadosch!" And thus he prayed: "O, God Eternal and my Father, bless this instrument prepared in Thine honour, so that it may serve only for a good use and end, for Thy glory. Amen."

He censed and sprinkled it and folded it away in the linen napkin, and that was the end of their night's work, since before continuing they must wait again for the day and the hour of Mercury. Progress was slow and there was much to do, much to prepare before they could begin the great work of helping Jan.

As Morven helped Thur to wipe out the Kabalistic characters from the floor, she asked him soberly: "What are those names, so strange sounding, which you invoke?"

"They are the names of Angels and great Spirits, but their origin is wrapped in mystery. Some are Egyptian, others go farther back in antiquity to Chaldea and Phoenicia, others again are Hebrew. All we know for certain is that they are words of power. I have pondered upon their meaning for many years, and sometimes I am tempted to believe that they have no meaning, but, because they are resounding, like beaten gongs, they serve the purpose of binding us all together, so that all who hear are caught as in a great net, all feeling alike, all thinking alike, all desiring alike, until the force of each one present sweeps upward, like a cloud of incense ascending, and unites with the concentrated will of the Magus and forms one great pivot upon which the whole wheel of the Circle and all its potentialities turn. Do I speak in riddles, Morven?"

"No. Do you mean that when two or three are gathered together, especially with one general object in view, that all thought becomes interwoven and so helps to bring about the fulfilment of the object for which they assemble; and that these high-sounding words, in themselves meaningless, by their repetition of certain sounds then changing to another sound and repeating that, beat upon the mind and shape it as the Magus would have it go. Thus does it think what he would have it to think, so that it sees what he wishes it to see, and so can he derive power from those who call upon his service?"

Thur nodded, but added hastily:

"Forget not that I am a novice in the Art. I do but tell you my secret thought about these incantations."

* * * *

When the day of Mercury came round again it found them again in the Triple Circle. Thur again recited the three Psalms, which seemed to Morven more wonderful with each repetition, so that she listened with closer attention and increasing understanding.

He would need wax in the making of the Magic Sword, and that to be used was fresh beeswax taken by Morven from the hive at mid-day. She had proven herself extremely skilful in the handling of bees, which she feared not at all. The creatures seemed to like her.

Holding the wax in his right hand, Thur invoked: "*Exabor, Hetabor, Sittacibor, Adonai, Onxo, Zomen, Menor, Asmodiel, Ascobai, Conamas, Papuendos, Osiandos, Spiacent, Damnath, Eneres, Golades, Telantes, Cophi, Zades!* Angels of God be present, for I invoke ye in my work, so that through you it may find virtue, Amen."

He paused and then exorcised it as follows:

"I exorcise thee, O Creature of Wax that, Through the Holy Name of God and His Holy Angels, thou receive blessing, so that thou mayst be sanctified and blessed to obtain the virtue which we desire, through the most Holy Name, Adonai, Amen."

So praying, he sprinkled and censed the wax and wrapped it in the white linen cloth. In a like manner he consecrated strong acid, to be used for engraving upon the tempered steel of the Sword. When this was done and set aside in readiness, Morven took from the table an ink-horn made of baked earth in the hour and day of Mercury, and gave it to Thur. With the Burin he carved round the base in Hebrew characters these sacred names.

"*Yod He Vau He, Matatron, Iah, Iah, Iah, Qadosch, Elohim, Zaboath*," and filling it with ink he exorcised it thus:

"I exorcise thee, O Creature of Ink, by Anaireton, by Simoulator, and by the name Adonai, by virtue of Him through Whom all things are made, that thou be unto me an aid and succour in all things which I wish to perform by thine aid."

This he sprinkled and censed and laid up with the wax. Work for that night was over. They cleared away all traces of their occupation and went to bed.

There now remained the great event, the creating of the Magic Sword. This was an ordinary blade in common use as a small-arm, and he had bought it in London. When in despair of ever being able to help the Bonders, he had formed the desperate design of obtaining guidance, through Olaf, as was shown in the opening chapter. That attempt was more in the nature of a Spiritualistic séance than a true exercise in Art Magic. Olaf had proved a good medium through which the needed guidance came. The command he had received, "Seek ye the Witch of Wanda," had provided him with the Athame and the white-handled knife, the means to the ends they desired. The purchase of each article separately constituted no danger, it was the articles in the aggregate which made the menace. Any knowledgable person, viewing them as a whole, would know immediately for what purpose they would be used. Rumour had it that my Lord Abbot was interested (in his holy way), in the Art, and what was known in the town was known almost as quickly at the Abbey, and any gossiping brother could put the Abbot on his track. Thur was convinced that he might as well transcribe his circle, recite his Psalms, invoke his Angels and exorcise his instruments in the open market at mid-day as buy the necessary articles in his own home town, so he had gone to London for them.

He was thinking of these past difficulties as they prepared the Triple Circle in the hour and the day of Mercury for the making of the Magic Sword. Bathed and perfumed in symbolic accord with the nature of this weapon, both Thur and Morven were as naked as the drawn sword. After the Psalms had been recited Thur took up the cleaned and polished sword, and with the Burin he engraved the name of Power "Elohim Gibur" on the hilt. In the heat of the brazier he mellowed the consecrated wax, smoothed it upon the blade and wrote thereon with the Burin, "*Yod He Vau He, Adonai, Eheieh, Yauai.*" He turned the blade, smoothed the hither side with wax and inscribed "Elohim Gibur". All these characters were written in Hebrew, then, using the acid they had formerly consecrated, he engraved all these characters deep into the tempered blade.

When this labour was done he turned to Morven. She, holding her Athame in her right hand, brought the point down upon the sword's blade and held it there to communicate increased power, while Thur cried in a strong voice:

"I conjure thee, O Sword, by the names *Abrahach, Abroath, Abracadabra, Yod He Vau He,* that thou serve me for a strength and a defence in all my magical operations, against all my enemies, visible and invisible. I conjure thee anew by the name Shaderai Almighty, and by the names *Qadosch, Qadosch, Qadosch, Adonai, Elohim, Tzabaoth, Emanuel, Azoth. Wisdom, Way, Life, Truth, Chief, Speech, Word, Splendour, Light, Sun, Glory, Virtue.* By these names and by the other names, I conjure Thee, O Sword, That thou servest me for a protection in all adversities. Amen."

Thur sprinkled it with consecrated water and Morven censed it. Again Thur spoke a conjuration:

"I conjure thee, O Sword of Steel, by God Almighty, by the virtues of the Heavens, of the Stars, of the Angels who preside over them, that thou receivest such virtue that thou mayst obtain without deceit the end that I desire in all things wherein I shall use thee, through God, the Creator of the Ages, and Emperor of the Angels. Amen."

Morven perfumed it with the perfume of Art and Thur recited: "By virtue of *Dani, Zumech, Agalmaturod, Gadiel, Pani, Caneloas, Merod, Gamedoi, Baldoi, Metrator,* Angels most Holy, be present for a guard to this Sword."

He wrapped it in clean linen and laid it aside, and they followed with the consecration of the sickle. Lights were needed for the great circle, and since nothing might be used which was unconsecrated, Morven had made a number of wax candles in the hour and day of Mercury in the waxing moon, each weighing eight ounces. The wicks, required to be made by hand by a young maid were her work. For this consecration of Light there were three new Psalms. The first, CLI; of which the beginning is:

> "Praise ye the Lord,
> Praise God in His Sanctuary.
> Praise Him in the firmament of His Power."

and the last verse:

> "Let everything that hath breath praise the Lord.
> Praise ye the Lord."

Then Psalm CIII and Psalm CVIII with its ending:

"Whoso is wise will observe these things,

Even they shall understand the loving kindness of the Lord."

Thur then took the Burin and on each candle he engraved signs, praying as he did so: "O Lord God who governest all things by thy Mighty Power, give unto me, a poor sinner, understanding and knowledge to do only that which is agreeable to Thee. Grant me power to fear, adore, love, praise and give thanks unto Thee with true and sincere faith and perfect charity. Grant O Lord, that before I die and descend into the Purgatory below that Thy Grace may not leave me O Lord of my soul. Amen."

Then he said: "O creature which is wax, by Virtue of Him Who is Pure Truth, by Him Who alone hath created all things by His Word. That thou cast out from thee every phantom, perversion and deceit of the enemy and may the Virtue, Truth and Power of God enter into thee so thou mayst give light and chase far from us all fear and terror."

Then he sprinkled and censed them and wrapped them in clean linen and set them aside. Thur, in the same manner with the help that Morven's power as a Witch (or as nowadays we would say as a medium) gave him, consecrated every article, no matter how small or insignificant, which was to be used within the Great Circle.

For, to aid that extreme concentration of mind that would be necessary it was essential that everything he should use should already have the Magical will directed into it, so that on the Great Night everything should assist to guide his will to that one purpose.

When all was finished, Thur, who had already blessed so many articles that night, also blessed Morven, saying: "Get thee to bed, beloved child. Sleep and may all Holy Angels guard and preserve you from harm, both in this life and in the life to come."[3]

Thur and Morven were again in the triple circle, in the day and hour of Mercury. Work that night was making Talismans for protection.

The brazier was glowing. Upon the table were consecrated pens and ink, dried frog's skins, beeswax, herbs and spices, the sprinkler and consecrated water, the Burin and the white-handled knife. Taking prepared candles Thur placed and lighted them, exorcising them thus:

"I exorcise thee, O Creature of Fire, in the name of the Sovereign and Eternal Lord, by His Ineffable Name, which is Yod-He-Vau-He. By the name of Power, El: that thou mayest enlighten the hearts of all the Spirits which we shall call unto this circle, so that they may appear before us without fraud or deceit, through Him Who hast created all things. Amen."

Followed by the reciting of the three psalms of David already quoted. Then this invocation.

"Adonai, most Powerful, El, Most Strong, Agla, Most Holy. On, Most Righteous, Azoth, the Beginning and the End. Thou Who hast established all things in Thy Wisdom. Thou who hast chosen Abraham as Thy faithful servant and Who hast promised him that his seed shall in all nations of the earth be blessed and multiplied as the stars of Heaven."

"Thou, Who hast appeared to Thy servant Moses in the midst of the Burning Bush and hast made him walk dry-foot through the Red Sea and gavest the Law to him on Mount Sinai. Thou, Who granted unto Solomon these Pentacles by Thy great Mercy, for the preservation of both soul and body, we most humbly implore and supplicate Thy Holy Majesty, that these Pentacles may be consecrated by Thy Power and prepared in such a manner that they may obtain virtue and strength against all adverse spirits and creatures, through Thee, O Most Holy Adonai, Whose Kingdom Empire and Principality remaineth and endureth for ever without end. Amen."

Morven was so uplifted by this impressive invocation that she felt power grow and magnify within her and so knew that what she made would really protect the wearer. Taking a piece of consecrated wax and warming it in the brazier she deftly moulded it into a tiny figure, using the warmed whitehandled knife to form details. When ready, she cut off the top of the head. With the knife's point she inscribed magical characters, as though writing them on the brain itself. These symbols thus becoming part of the wearer's organism, the knowledge of protection from danger would become part of his mentality and the instinct for self protection increased a hundred-fold, with increased ingenuity in evasion and enhanced perception of threatening danger springing from the very centre of his brain.

She replaced the scalp and carved further characters (emphasising the need for caution and watchfulness) on it. Altogether she prepared four figures in exactly the same manner. While Morven was so occupied Thur wrote Kabalistic signs on the frog skins; when he finished he glanced at Morven.

"We need the hairs of one well disposed. I am well disposed so here is a hair from my head for thee, Morven; but I think for the others and for me, we shall need yours." So saying he pulled red gold hairs from her scalp, and softening the waxen heads in the brazier, he pressed a hair into each and one of his own into the figure for Morven. Then he sprinkled and censed them all, pronouncing the spell of invisibility.

"Melatron, Melakh, Beroth, Noth, Venibbeth, Mach, and all ye. I conjure thee O figure of wax, by the living God and by the Virtue of these Characters and Words, that thou holdest the eyes of all beholders and renders him who carries thee invisible whenever he beareth thee with him."

Then each mannikin was wrapped in a frog skin as a garment, and carefully laid away till wanted. Morven looked at him longingly, wonderingly.

"They may help," she said, "at least they will do no scath, but my heart misgives me."

"Be not so dismal, child, did you not tell me 'twas our own fears made danger real to us?"[4]

The next day, being Tuesday, Thur and Morven prepared to make some of the Talismans, Sigils and Pentacles they needed in the Great Circle. Though these names are often used indiscriminately to describe each other, there is an important difference between them. A Sigil means a sign, on parchment, or a medal, made with the object of controlling one particular spirit, usually to summon him up to the Circle, and it bears his own peculiar design. The knowledge of these designs is one of the great secrets which the Magus must master, because a spirit will strive his utmost to keep this sign of his individuality hidden, to prevent mortals obtaining power over him. If a certain spirit is particularly favourable to him, a Magus may make use of this Sigil as a Talisman, but this is not common.

When a Sigil is written on paper or parchment it is often described as a seal, whereas if a Talisman or Pentacle is inscribed on parchment, it is not a seal, the difference being, that a Sigil or seal belongs to one individual spirit, who in Jan's case was Bartzebal, while a Talisman or Pentacle belongs either to one human being, or in a general way, to all the spirits serving one Governing Spirit, like Mars, Saturn or Venus, as the case may be. A Pentacle is also a medal used to evoke a spirit and command him, it is in addition a figure like a five-pointed star, and should always be drawn and used with one point uppermost, and never with two points uppermost. From their nature, certain Pentacles can be carried outside the Circle and worn with a view to bringing good fortune, such as the Pentacle of Venus for love. Of Jupiter for success and prosperity. A Pentacle of Saturn will induce his good qualities of steadiness, perseverance and loyalty, but this can only be carried by one born under Saturn; to anyone else it would bring disaster. A soldier born under any sign could wear a Pentacle of Mars, with advantage, which might produce quarrelsomeness in a merchant, while the latter would be well advised to wear one of Mercury. While a medal such as described above is sometimes called a Talisman. This name should more properly be kept for articles made especially for its owner, with the express intention of bringing him success in what particular object he has in view, and are made in accordance with the owner's horoscope. They are usually made by an expert, in the proper day and hour, with the special object in view, with protection and safety. Or Prosperity, gain, and success for the subject firmly fixed in his mind. The Talisman is then consecrated with magical formulae. In some such way, Morven and Thur had made theirs.

Bathed and consecrated, the two prepared their small circle at midnight on the Monday following Morven's return, so as to start the work in the day and hour of Mars, viz., between twelve midnight and one o'clock on Tuesday, the day of Mars (each planet rules the first, eighth, fifteenth and twenty second hours of his day), but, at any other hour they would be liable to intrusion, with subsequent denunciation of sorcery, so midnight was the safest time for this operation. Thur placed in the centre a small table, to serve the double purpose of Altar and work bench. Beside it was a glowing brazier of charcoal. Morven's duty was to keep this brazier fed and at an even high temperature, also to serve him generally as an acolyte serves a priest. She had, however, a much more important part to play in the actual ritual, which was to fix her mind unwaveringly on the work, to do her best to make it fluid, so that by welding it with his as it were, he derived added strength. For this concentration of the will upon the object of the ritual there must be no means of distraction. Everything used must have been made with this object in view, so everything used brings to the brain of the Magus, the reason of the work. Therefore was Thur clad in the symbolically pure, clean white linen robe, signifying light, strength and purity, also, this is important, bearing no colour or pattern that could distract the mind of the wearer or his acolyte. For the same reason the girl was nude, this signified purity unsullied, and the natural magnetism in the human body could flow unhindered to the support of the Magus. Here would be no temptation, no distraction for him in this beauty unadorned because a Magus must be immune to such conditions, ere he may become a Magus, for if he cannot at all times prevent his mind from straying, failure in his enterprises would be inevitable; rather was such nudity an added strength to him, for by its presence it signifies the strength of his will and the power of his self-control. For a Magus must ever work with a naked woman till nudity is naught to him, lest an evil or mischievous spirit should appear thus, and distract his mind at the critical moment and so ruin an operation.

Throughout the practice of High Magic, or Art Magic as it is often called, the emphasis is upon purity and strength, and through purity, strength of will and self-control. Without these no man may become a Magus, though by trickery and self-deception he may become a great rogue, but with them, even in a small degree he may go far along the road in his search into the hidden mysteries, for by a rigid self-discipline, self-control can be extended and strengthened almost to any limit, and by patience and rigorous exercise the will can become such a dominating factor and obtain such power that nothing can withstand its impact. Therefore a great Magus should also be a great man. By the habit of self-control which is the essence of Magic, he attains to abstinence, which, in its turn gives him health and vigour. The habit of faith, which is essential to success in the Art, faith in God and His goodness, faith in righteousness, absolute faith in the ritual he performs, in its efficacy and in the success of its object, through the ritual; and finally, supreme faith in himself, firstly as a willing servant of God, and secondly in his power as a Magus; such faith is in itself a purifying element in any life. The application to close study through long hours of poring over intricate manuscripts, the patient repetition of obscure rites until success is obtained, indicate high qualities of mind. The fact that no Magus can work for himself and his own advancement, or work for another with solely evil purposes, imposes a certain rectitude of conduct upon him, If he fell from his high status of being a helper and benefactor to others through his Art, descending to use it for harmful purposes, the reaction upon himself would in the medieval mind be in proportion to the magnitude and wickedness of his success, and dire retribution would swiftly overtake him for having corrupted his Art. Therefore, by all the laws of his Art, such good qualities as a Magus possessed are developed to their utmost. Indeed, one might say that without a number of good qualities in his character a man could never become a Magus. There have been many charlatans who have claimed the title of Magus by hypnotism or by plain trickery; they imposed upon the credulity of thousands, also sometimes they may have possessed powers of clairvoyance which they have misused for gain. It is these tricksters and glib rogues who have brought the Art into disrepute, and for which they have afterwards suffered.

It is the fashion today to laugh at the Magus and his pretensions, to picture him as either a charlatan or a doddering old fool, and bearing the slightest resemblance to the men who were in fact, the scientists of the day, who gave us alcohol, but not the Atom Bomb.

Four other braziers were in their appointed places around the Circle. Upon the Altar-table lay the Athame, the Magic Sword, the Burin and the Sprinkler, also materials for their work, four iron discs, two-and-a-half inches in diameter, already purified by fire, had been prepared previously. There were writing materials, lengths of cord, some black cloths and a scourge, laid ready. Before the bench were two stools. The inner circle, seven feet in diameter . . . was already drawn on the floor, surrounding it was a double circle eight feet in diameter, with names of power between the two. Thur took the Magic Sword and retraced all the markings with its point, for the painted circle has no power of protection, which comes from Power of the Magic Sword or the Athame. It but serves as a guide to the latter, to ensure they draw the Circle perfectly. The Circle drawn, Thur recited appropriate Psalms, and began to make the Talismans and Pentacles. Iron is the metal of Mars, the spirit of War under whom Jan was born, and as it was for a warlike purpose, Thur proposed to summon his spirit Bartzebal to Jan's aid. Taking one of the iron discs Thur described a circle on it with the Burin, inside this circle he scratched the mystical characters of Mars and outside, between it and the edge, he wrote in Hebrew the names, EDIMIEL, BARTZACHHIAHESCHIEL and ITHUREL; this was for invoking the spirits of Mars in general.

On the second he engraved within the Circle an equilateral triangle surmounted at the apex with a pentacle. Within this triangle a smaller inverted triangle was drawn with a great Vau, and round it the name ELOH. Between the circle and the edge was written in Hebrew: "Who is so great as ELOHIM?"

This Pentacle was for the purpose of exciting War, Wrath, Discord and for the overthrowing of enemies. The third Pentacle, the Circle was divided into four equal parts with a star pentacle above, it had in the centre the word AGLA IHVH, repeated twice, above and below, (was EL). All was in Hebrew, as were also the words of the text written between the circle and the outer edge. "The Lord is my right hand, and he shall wound even Kings in the day of his wrath." This was to give power in war, and would bring victory. The fourth had inside the Circle, written in the secret characters of the Malachim script, the words, Elohim Quibor. "God hath protected me." Outside the Circle was written a text from Psalm XXXVII, 15; written in Hebrew, "Their swords shall enter into their own hearts and their bows shall be broken." This Pentacle was to give strength and courage in fighting and ultimate victory. Upon the reverse of each of these Pentacles was engraved the Sigil of Bartzebal. Having finished engraving them, he purified them anew in the incense smoke which arose from the herbs and spices Morven cast upon the centre brazier. Each planet has its different and appropriate incense and for Mars they used euphorbia, bedellium, ammoniac, lodestone and sulphur. This matter of incense is of the greatest importance in the ritual, as it must be of the nature of the spirit, not only does it influence the spirit conjured, but all surrounding objects; it lies heavy upon the air and the Magus breathes it deep into his lungs, making him of one nature with the spirit, the fragrance and density attracts and draws the conjured spirit, partly because it is of his nature, and partly because of the pleasure it gives him. It is from its density he obtains the means to build up a body and so materialise. To increase the affinity, the brazier which was used for heating was fed with sticks of dried thorn and wild rose. When all were censed and purified, Thur took a strand of cord and bound each, winding it round thrice, and tying it with three separate knots, then wrapped each in a separate black cloth and laid them in their order on the west side of the Circle, sprinkled them with consecrated water, baptising them and saying, "I hereby consecrate thee, O creature of Mars and of iron, Bartzebal." Then he held each in the smoke of the incense, saying: "By fire and water I consecrate thee. Thou art him, and He is ye, in thought, in feeling, and in sight, as I bind ye, I bind him, as I loose ye, I loose him. By the sacred name Abracadabra. Amen. I consecrate thee for the especial purpose of bringing victory to Jan Bonder, to obtain vengeance upon Fitz- Urse and to regain all the castles and lands stolen by Fitz-Urse from his grandsire, Sir Edgar Bonder." From thence onwards the table served as an altar. Upon it Thur now placed the four Pentacles, he repeated over them the words he had just spoken, the words of consecration and dedication, and then announced solemnly, in a loud and clear voice, that all these purposes would be accomplished. Still using the same firm and distinct utterance he declared: "All has been prepared and is in readiness to charge these Pentacles with power, I summon all ye spirits of the nature of Mars, and command ye to attend." The critical moments of the ritual were approaching, Thur took the Magic Sword, Morven took her Athame, and while they held the points of their weapons on the first Pentacle, Thur recited slowly and with the utmost intensity he could summon. "Adonai, Most Powerful; El, Most Strong; Agla, Most Holy; Oh, Most righteous. Azoth. The Beginning and the End. Thou Who hast established all things in thy Wisdom. Thou, who hast granted unto Solomon Thy servant these Pentacles by Thy great mercy for the preservation of both soul and body; we most humbly implore and supplicate Thy Most Holy Majesty that these Pentacles may be consecrated by Thy Power and in such a manner that they may obtain virtue and strength against all spirits, through Thee, O Most Holy Adonai, Whose Kingdom, Empire and Principality endureth without end. Amen."

With the point of his sword Thur traced in the air above the first Pentacle the symbols engraved on its disc.

This ceremony with the points of the weapons, the above invocation and consecration together with the aerial tracing of the symbols, was repeated without variation of any sort over each Pentacle in turn. When all this was accomplished, with equal intensity directed upon them, Thur took each in turn in his left hand and smote it thrice with the flat of his sword. Coming again to the first Pentacle, he took it in his left hand and with the sword erect in his right hand he circumambulated the Circle, holding up the veiled disc to the four quarters, west, north, east and south; this procedure was followed without deviation with each in turn. Each time placing the Pentacles on the floor, this time in the south, and repeating the former consecration with fire and water, adding: "O, creatures of Iron and Mars, twice consecrated, thou mayest approach the gates of the south." He circumambulated the Circle again. Then taking the first Pentacle he carefully unwrapped it, not removing the veil, but leaving the disc covered with the ends hanging down. He smote it once with the sword then held it at arms' length while he elevated the sword above it. Thrice he stamped with his right foot, addressing it. "Thou canst not pass from concealment to manifestation save by virtue of the name ALHIM. Before all things are chaos and darkness, I am he whose name is darkness. I am the exorcist in the midst of the exorcism. Take on therefore manifestation from me." He circumambulated again, re-wrapped the Pentacle and replaced it on the Altar, repeating the ceremony with each in turn. When all were assembled on the Altar, he again partially unveiled the first and summoning Morven with a gesture, she held her Athame above it; while he held his sword in a like manner, he conjured it, saying: "By all the Powers and Rites, I conjure Thee, render this Pentacle irresistible, O Lord Adonai." When this had been repeated over each he reveiled the Pentacles and carried them to the north, laying them on the ground, opening each veil completely, saying: "Thou canst not pass from concealment to manifestation save by the name JHV (Jehovah)."

Reveiling them he passed to the south, and laid them on the ground, and entirely removing the veils from each, but leaving them bound, this done he invoked: "O Bartzebal, too long hast thou been in darkness. Quit the night and seek the day. As light is hidden in darkness, yet can manifest itself therefrom, so shalt thou manifest from concealment unto manifestation."

The words, "So shalt thou manifest," were spoken with such a degree of concentrated will, that Thur's tanned face took on almost a greenish hue, so great was the concentrated effort he made.

Reveiling them he took the Pentacles from the floor and replaced them on the Altar, again invoking he held them in turn towards heaven, saying: "I conjure upon thee power and might irresistible, by the Powers of DANI, ZEMUCH, AGATMATUROD, EODIEL, PANI, CANELOAS, MEROD, GAMODI, BALDOI, METRATOR."

Now he laid his sword down and taking the scourge, smote each in turn, saying over as he did so: "By, and in the NAME of ELOHIM, I invoke into thee the powers of Mars and the powers of War," and released the cords binding them. As he said this over the first of the Pentacles, a chill crept up Morven's spine and over her scalp. Witch and believer in Witchery she proclaimed herself, here was a manifestation of power she had never seen; for the Pentacle glowed with a sullen redness, infinitely menacing and terrible. In its small circumference it seemed to hold all the cruel, remorseless wantonness of war. On each in turn as he invoked, he bore down on it the whole might of his highly-trained mental strength, so was each infused with the same smouldering red fire, and Thur realised his prayers had been answered, the consecration had been successful.

After a moment's pause, as though to gather his faculties which had been strained to a snapping point, Thur stood erect and prayed:

"I thank Thee, O LORD OF HOSTS, for the favour Thou hast manifested to me."

Standing so, with his face to the Heavens, he looked truly inspired. Then he relaxed, sinking on one of the stools before the Altar-table. His head sunk forward on his breast, his whole pose expressed acute physical exhaustion, and he panted quickly. Morven watched him in silent solicitude, not daring to speak. Presently he was sufficiently recovered to make a sign towards the Altar, where the Pentacles lay. Understanding, Morven wrapped the newly consecrated Pentacles in a clean cloth and put them with other articles in the casket, this she stowed away in a hiding place. Then she collected the tools they had used, from time to time stealing anxious glances at Thur, who still sat upon his stool, his robe hitched up showing his bare legs and feet, his hands hanging listlessly between his knees. The two had presented an embodiment of perfect service and perfect leadership.

Suddenly she felt a glow of happiness and contentment, a sense of peace such as she had never known.[5]

1. *High Magic's Aid,* Chapter III: Seeking a Witch. p. 27.
2. *High Magic's Aid,* Chapter X: Working Together. p. 96.
3. *High Magic's Aid,* Chapter X: Working Together. p. 100.
4. *High Magic's Aid,* Chapter XI: Music Magic. p. 105.
5. *High Magic's Aid,* Chapter XV: Charging the Pentacles. p. 157.

2.14. Consecrating Tools (1957)

Note: If possible lay any new weapon touching an already consecrated one, Sword to sword, Athame to Athame, etc.

Prepare Circle and purify. All tools must be consecrated by a man and a woman, both as naked as drawn swords; they must be purified, clean, and properly prepared.

Place tool on pentacle on altar. Magus sprinkles it with salt and water. Witch passes it through smoke of incense, replaces it on pentacle. Touching with already consecrated weapon, they say the First Conjuration.

For sword or athame, say

> "I conjure thee, O Sword (or Athame) of Steel, that thou servest me for a strength and a defence in all magical operations, against all mine enemies, visible and invisible, in the names of Aradia and Cernunnos. I conjure thee anew by the Holy Names Aradia and Cernunnos, that thou servest me for a protection in all adversities, so aid me."

For any other tool, say,

> "Aradia and Cernunnos, deign to bless and to consecrate this [tool], that it may obtain necessary virtue through thee for all acts of love and Beauty."

Again they sprinkle and cense, and say the Second Conjuration:

For sword or athame, say,

> "I conjure thee, O Sword [Athame] of Steel, by the Great Gods and the Gentle Goddesses, by the virtue of the Heavens, of the Stars, of the Spirits who preside over them, that thou mayest receive such virtues that I may obtain the end that I desire in all things wherein I shall use thee, by the power of Aradia and Cernunnos."

For any other tool, say,

> "Aradia and Cernunnos, bless this instrument prepared in thine honour." (For the scourge or cords, add, "That it may only serve for a good use and end, and to thy Glory.")

All instruments when consecrated should be presented to their User by giving the [point-down triangle] sign salute (if they are working in the first degree, or the sign of the higher degree if they are working that.)

Then the one who is not the owner should give the Fivefold Kiss to the owner. For the final kiss, the tool should be placed between the breasts, and the two workers should embrace for as long as they feel like, it being held in place by their bodies. The new owner should use it immediately, i.e., cast (trace) Circle with Sword or Athame, wave wand to 4 quarters, cut something with white-handled knife, etc. Cords and scourge should be used at once.

The tool should be kept in as close connection as possible to the naked body for at least a month, i.e., kept under pillow, etc. When not in use, all tools and weapons should be put away in a secret place; and it is good that this should be near your sleeping place, and that you handle them each night before retiring. Do not allow anyone to touch or handle any of your tools until they are thoroughly impregnated with your aura; say, six months or as near as possible. But a couple working together may own the same tools, which will be impregnated with the aura of both.

2.15. Skyclad (1953)

It is important to work naked from the start, so it becometh as second nature, and no thought of "I have no clothes" shall ever intrude and take your attention from the work. Also, your skin being so accustomed to unconfinement, when power is given off the flow is more easy and regular. Also, when dancing you are free and unconfined. . . . And the greatest of all, the touch of the body of your beloved thrills your inmost soul, and so your body gives out its utmost power; and then it is most important of all that there is not the slightest thing to divert the attention, for then the mind must seize and mould the power generated, and redirect it to the desired end with all the force and frenzy of the imagination. It has been said that no real knowledge may be gained our way, that our practices are such that they can only lead to lust; but this is not really so. Our aim is to gain the inner sight, and we do it the most natural and easy way. Our opponents' aim is ever to prevent man and woman from loving, thinking that everything that helps or even permits them to love is wicked and vile. To us it is natural, and if it aids the Great Work it is good. 'Tis true that a couple burning with a frenzy for knowledge may go straight to their goal, but the average couple have not this fire. We show them the way, our system of props and aids (i.e., magic ritual). A couple working with nothing but lust will never attain in any case; but a couple who love each other dearly should already be sleeping together, and the first frenzy of love will have passed, and their souls will already be in sympathy. If the first time or two they do stay a while to worship

Aphrodite, 'tis only a day or two lost, and the intense pleasure they obtain only leads them again to the mysteries of Hermes, their souls more attuned to the great search. Once they have pierced the veil they will not look back. This rite may be used as the greatest of magics if it be done with both partners firmly fixing their minds on the object and not thinking of sex at all. That is, you must so firmly fix your mind on your object that sex and all else are naught. You inflame your will to such an extent that you may create a strain on the astral such that events happen.

NOTES

I am continually being asked various questions regarding the witch cult, and I can only answer: Nearly all primitive people had initiation ceremonies and some of these were initiation into priesthoods, into magic powers, secret societies and mysteries. They were usually regarded as necessary for the welfare of the tribe as well as for the individual. They usually included purification and some test of courage and fortitude — often severe and painful — terrorization, instruction in tribal lore, in sexual knowledge, in the making of charms, and in religious and magical matters generally, and often a ritual of death and resurrection.

Now I did not cause the primitive people to do these things; I simply hold that witches, being in many cases the descendants of primitive people, do in fact do many of them. So when people, for example, ask me: "Why do you say that witches work naked?" I can only say: "Because they do." "Why?" is another question, the easy reply being that their ritual tells them they must. Another is that their practices are the remnants of a Stone Age religion and they keep to their old ways. There is also the Church's explanation: "Because witches are inherently wicked." But I think the witches' own explanation is the best: "Because only in that way can we obtain power."

Witches are taught and believe that the power resides within their bodies which they can release in various ways, the simplest being dancing round in a circle, singing or shouting, to induce a frenzy; this power they believe exudes from their bodies, clothes impeding its release. In dealing with such matters it is, of course, difficult to say how much is real and how much imagination.

As in the case of dowsing, if a man believes that when insulated from the ground by rubber insoles he cannot find water, this belief inhibits him, even though the insoles contain no rubber, whilst wearing insoles made of rubber — though he didn't know it — he can find water, as many experiments prove.

It is easy to imagine that a witch who firmly believes that it is essential to be naked could not whip up the final effort to attain the ecstasy without being naked. Another, however, who did not share this belief might, though partially clothed exert sufficient energy to force power through her face, shoulders, arms and legs, to produce some result; but who can say that she could not have produced twice the power with half the effort had she been in the traditional nakedness?

Witchcraft Today, Chapter I: Living Witchcraft. p. 17.

BOOK OF SHADOWS

PART THREE

[Editor's note: There are numerous versions of this text available but without access to Gardner's original document(s) a definitive version is not available. The following text has been compiled from a number of sources including *King of the Witches*, June Johns, *The Grimoire of Lady Sheba*, Lady Sheba, *The Witches' Way*, Janet and Stewart Farrar and others divers sources — the text has been edited and is presented as a representative 'snapshot' of the 'Old Laws'.

Gardner was acutely aware of the problems of variant texts and wrote "The trouble in dealing with these documents is the witch law: everyone must copy what they will from another, but no old writings may be kept . . . everyone is apt to alter things slightly, modernizing the language and making other changes . . ."]

For reference purposes two further versions of the 'Old Laws' (unedited) are also included at the end of this section which illustrate Gardner's point perfectly.

3.1 The Old Laws

The Law was made and Ardane of old.

The law was made for the Wica,
to advise and help in their troubles.

* * * * *

The Wica should give due worship to the Gods and obey their will which they Ardane, for it was made for the good of the Wica, as the Wica's worship is good for the Gods.

For the Gods love the Wica, as a man loveth a woman by mastering her. So the Wica should love the Gods, by being mastered by them.

And it is necessary that the Circle, which is the Temple of the Gods, should be truly cast and purified, that it may be a fit place for the Gods to enter. And the Wica should be properly prepared and purified, to enter into the presence of the Gods. With love and worship in their hearts they shall raise power from their bodies to give power to the Gods, as has been taught us of old.

For in this way only may man have communion with the Gods, for the Gods cannot help man without the help of men.

* * * * *

And the High Priestess shall rule her Coven as representative of the Goddess, and the High Priest shall support her as the representative of the God. And the High Priestess shall choose whom she will, if he have sufficient rank, to be her High Priest.

For, as the God himself kissed her feet in the five-fold salute, laying his power at the feet of the Goddess, because of her youth and beauty, her sweetness and kindness, her wisdom and justice, her humility and generosity, so he resigned his lordship to her.

But the Priestess should ever mind that all power comes from him. It is only lent when it is used wisely and justly.

And the greatest virtue of a High Priestess is that she recognises that youth is necessary to the representative of the Goddess, so she will gracefully retire in favour of a younger woman, should the Coven so decide in Council.

For the true High Priestess realises that gracefully surrendering pride of place is one of the greatest of virtues, and that thereby she will return to that pride of place in another life, with greater power and beauty.

* * * * *

In the days when Witchdom extended far, we were free and worship'd in Alther Greatest Temples. But, in these unhappy times we must hold our sacred mysteries in secret.

So it be Ardane, that none but the Wica may see our mysteries, for our enemies are many, and torture looseth the tongues of many.

It be ardane that each Coven shall not know where the next Coven bide, or who its members are, save the Priest and Priestess.

That there shall be no communication between them, save by the Messenger of the Gods, or the Summoner.

Only if it be safe, may the Covens meet, in some safe place, for the great festivals. And while there, none shall say whence they come, or give their true names. To the end that if any are tortured, in their agony, they can not tell if they know not.

So it be Ardane that no one may tell any not of the Craft who be of the Wica, nor give any names, or where they byde, or in any way tell anything which can betray any to our foes. Nor may they tell where the Covenstead be, or where is the Covendom, or where be the meetings, or that there have been meetings. And if any break these laws, even under torture, the Curse of the Goddess shall be upon them, so they never be reborn on earth, and may remain where they belong, in the Hell of the Christians.

* * * * *

Let each High Priestess govern her Coven with justice and love, with the help of the advice of the elders. Always heeding the advice of the Messenger of the Gods, if he cometh.

She will heed all complaints of brothers, and strive to settle all differences among them.

But it must be recognized that there be people who will ever strive to force others to do as they will. They are not necessarily evil and they often do have good ideas, and such ideas should be talked over in council. And if they will not agree with their brothers, or if they say, I will not work under this High Priestess, it hath always been the old law, to be convenient for the brethren, and to void disputes, that any of the Third may claim to found a new Coven because they live over a league from the Covenstead, or that they are about to do so.

Anyone living within the Covendom wishing to form a new Coven, to avoid strife, shall tell the Elders of his intention and on the instant void his dwelling and remove to the new Covendom.

Members of the old Coven may join the new one when it be formed, but if they do, must utterly void the old Coven. The Elders of the new and the old Covens should meet in peace and brotherly love, to decide the new boundaries.

Those of the Craft who dwell outside both Covendoms may join either indifferent, but not both. Though all may, if the Elders agree, meet for the Great Festivals, if it be truly in peace and brotherly love. But splitting the Coven oft means strife. So for this reason these laws were made of old. And may the curse of the GODDESS be on any who disregard them.

So be it Ardane.

* * * * *

If you would keep a book, let it be in your own hand of write, let brothers and sisters copy what they will, but never let the book out of your hands, and never keep the writings of another, for if it be found in their hand of write, they well may be taken and engined†.

Each should guard his own writings and destroy it whenever danger threatens. Learn as much as you may by heart, and when danger is past, rewrite your book, an it be safe. For this reason, if any die, destroy their book if they have not been able to. For an it be found, tis clear proof against them, and, our oppressors well know, "Ye

---

† Editor's Note: Some versions give *engained* (unknown word), others *arraigned* (called before a court) but given the context, *engined* (tortured on the rack) makes more sense. Gardner's version from *Witchcraft Today,* Chapter 4: Witch Practices. 1954 uses *tortured.* The relevant passage is here quoted in full :–

Keep a book in your own hand of write. Let brothers and sisters copy what they will but never let this book out of your hand, and never keep the writings of another, for if it be found in their hand of write thy will be taken and tortured. Each should guard his own writings and destroy them whenever danger threatens. Learn as much as you may by heart and when danger is past rewrite your book. For this reason if any die, destroy their book if they have not been able to do so, for if it be found, 'tis clear proof against them. "Ye may not be a witch alone," so all their friends be in danger of the torture, so destroy everything unnecessary. If your book be found on you, it is clear proof against you; you may be tortured.

Keep all thoughts of the cult from your mind. Say you had bad dreams, that a devil caused you to write this without your knowledge. Think to yourself, "I know nothing; I remember nothing; I have forgotten all. Drive this into your mind. If the torture be too great to bear, say: "I will confess. I cannot bear this torment. What do you want me to say? Tell me and I will say it." If they try to make you tell of the Brotherhood, do not, but if thy try to make

may not be a witch alone" So all their kin and friends be in danger of torture. So ever destroy anything not necessary. If your book be found on you, tis clear proof against you alone. You may be engined. Keep all thoughts of the Craft from your mind. Say you had bad dreams, a devil caused you to write it without your knowledge. Think to yourself. I know, nothing. I remember nothing. I have forgotten everything. Drive this into your mind.

If the torture be to great to bear. Say "I will confess. I cannot bear this torture, What do you want me to say? I will say it." If they try to make you speak of the brotherhood, DO NOT. But if they try to make you speak of impossibilities such as flying through the air, consorting with the Christian Devil, or sacrificing children, or eating men's flesh, to obtain relief from torture, say "I had an evil dream, I was not myself, I was crased."

Not all Magistrates are bad, if there be an excuse they may show mercy. If you have confessed aught, deny it afterwards, say you

---

you speak of impossibilities, such as flying through the air, consorting with the Devil, sacrificing children or eating man's flesh, say: "I had evil dreams. I was not myself, I was crazed.

Not all magistrates are bad. If there be an excuse they may show mercy. If you have confessed aught, deny it afterwards; say you babbled under the torture you knew not what you did or said. If you be condemned, fear not, the Brotherhood is powerful, they may help you to escape if you are steadfast. If you betray aught — THERE IS NO HELP FOR YOU IN THIS LIFE, OR IN THAT WHICH IS TO COME. If you go steadfast to the pyre, DRUGS WILL REACH YOU and you will feel naught, but will go to death and what lies beyond, the Ecstasy of the Goddess.

The same with the working tools. Let them be as ordinary things that anyone may have in their homes. Let the Pentacles be of wax that thy may be melted or broken at once. Have no sword unless your rank allows you one. Have no names or signs on anything, write the names and signs on in ink before consecrating them and wash it off immediately after. Never boast, never threaten, never say you wish ill to anyone. If any speak of the craft, say: "Speak not to me of such, it frightens me, 'tis evil luck to speak of it."

babbled under torture. You knew not what you said. If you are condemned, fear not. The Brotherhood is powerful. They may help you to escape, if you stand steadfast.

If you betray aught. There is no hope for you, in this life, or in that which is to come.

Be sure, if steadfast you go to the pyre, Dwale will reach you, you will feel naught. You go but to Death and what lies beyond 'the ecstasy of the Goddess'.

Tis probable that before you are engined, Dwale will reach you. Always remember that Christians fear much that any die under torture. At the first sign of swoon, they cause it to be stopped, and blame the tormenters, for that reason, the tormenters themselves are apt to feign to torment, but do not, so it is best not to die at first.

If Dwale reaches you, tis a sign that you have a friend somewhere, you may be helped to escape, so despair not. If the worst comes, and you go to the pyre, wait till the flames and smoke spring up, bend your head over, and breath in with long breaths, you choke and die swiftly and wake in the arms of the Goddess.

To void discovery, let the working tools be as ordinary things that any may have in their houses. Let the Pentacles be of wax, so they may be broken at once. Have no sword unless your rank allows you one. Have no names or signs on anything.

Write the names and signs on them in ink before consecrating them and wash it off immediately after. Do not Bigrave them, lest they cause discovery. Let the colour of the hilts tell which is which. Ever remember, ye are the Hidden Children of the Gods, so never do anything to disgrace them.

Never boast. Never threaten. Never say you would wish ill to anyone. If you, or any not in the Circle, speak of the craft, say, "Speak not to me of such, it frightens me, tis evil luck to speak of it". For this reason, the Christians have spies everywhere. These speak as if they were well affected, as if they would come to Meetings, saying "My mother used to go, to worship, the Old Ones. I would that I could go myself." To these ever deny all knowledge.

But, to others ever say, tis foolish, men talk of witches flying through the air, to do so, they must be light as thistledown, and men say that witches all be bleared eyed old crones, so what pleasure can there be in witch meetings, such as folk talk on? Say, many wise men now say there be no such creatures. Ever make it a jest, and in some future time, perhaps the persecution will die and we may worship safely again. Let us all pray for that happy day.

May the blessings of the Goddess and the God be on all who keep their Ardane.

* * * * *

If the Craft hath any Appenage, let all brothers guard it, and help to keep it clear and good for the Craft, and let all justly guard all monies of the Craft. But if some brothers truly wrought it, tis right that they have their pay, an it be just. And this be not taking money for the use of the Art, but for good and honest work. And even the Christians say "A labourer is worthy of his hire." But if any brothers work willingly for the good of the craft without pay, tis but to their greater honour.

So it be Ardane.

* * * * *

If there be any disputes or quarrels among the brethren, The High Priestess shall straight Convene the Elders and enquire into the matter, and they shall hear both sides, first alone, then together. And they shall decide justly, not favouring the one side or the other.

Ever recognising that there be people who can never agree to work under others, but at the same time there be some people who cannot rule justly. To those who ever must be chief, there is one answer — void the Coven and seek another, or, make a Coven of your own, taking with you those who will to go. To those who cannot rule justly, the answer be, those who cannot bear your rule will leave you. For none may come to meetings with those with whom they are at variance. So an either cannot agree, get hence. For the Craft must ever survive.

So it be Ardane.

* * * * *

In the olden days when we had power, we could use our Arts against any who ill-treated any of the Brotherhood. But in these Evil Times, we may not do so, For our enemies have devised a burning pit of everlasting fire, into which they say their God casteth all the people who worship him, except it be the very few who are released by their priest's spells and Masses, and this be chiefly by giving money and rich gifts to receive his favour. For their Alther Greatest God is ever in need of Money.

But as our Gods need our aid to make fertility for men and crops, so the God of the Christians is ever in need of man's help to search out and destroy us. Their priests tell them that any who get our help or our cures are damned to this Hell forever, so men be mad for the terror of it. But they make men believe that they may escape this hell if they give victims to the tormenters. So for this reason, all be forever spying, thinking an I can but catch one of the Wica I will escape this fiery pit.

But we have our hidels, and men searching long and not finding say, "there be none, or if they be, they be in a far country." But, when one of our oppressors die, or, even be sick, ever is the cry "This be Witches Malice" and the hunt is up again, and though they slay ten of their people, to one of ours, still, they care not, they have many thousands, while we are few indeed.

So it is Ardane, that none shall use the Art in any way to do ill to any, how ever much they have injured us. And for long we have obeyed this law, "Harm none" and now times, many believe we exist not. So it be Ardane that this law shall still continue to help us in our plight. "No one, however great an injury or injustice they receive, may use the Art in any way to do ill or harm any."

But, they may, after great consultations with all, use the Art to prevent or restrain Christians from harming us and others, but only to let or constrain them and never to punish. To this end. Men say, "Such an one is a mighty searcher out and persecutor of Old Women whom he deemeth to be Witches, and none hath done him Skith. So this be proof they cannot, or more truly, that there be none." For all know full well, that so many folk have died because someone had a grudge against them, or were persecuted because they had money or goods to seize, or because they had none to bribe the searchers. And many have died because they were scolding old women. So much so, that men now say that only Old Women are witches. And this be to our advantage, and turns suspicion away from us. In England tis now many a year since a witch hath died the death, but any misuse of the power might raise the Persecution again. So never break this law, however much you are tempted, and never consent to its being broken. If you know it is being broken in the least, you must work strongly against it, and any High Priestess or High Priest who consents to it must be immediately deposed. For tis the Blood of the Brethren they endanger. Do good, an it be safe, and only if it be safe, for any talk may endanger us. And strictly keep to the Old Law, never accept money for the use of the Art, for money ever smears the taker, Tis Carcerors and Conjurers and Priests of Christ who ever accept money for the use of their Arts, and they sell Dwale and evil love spells and pardons to let men scape from their sin. Be not as these. If you accept not money, you will be free of temptation to use the Art for evil causes. All may use the Art for your own advantage, or for the advantage of the Craft, only if you be sure you harm none. But ever let the Coven debate the matter at length, only if all are satisfied that none may be harmed may the Art be used. If it is not possible to achieve your ends one way without harming any, perchance the aim may be achieved by acting in a different way, so as to harm none. May the Curse of the Goddess, be on any who breach this law.

So it be ardane.

Tis adjudged lawful an anyone need a house or land, an none will sell, to incline the owners mind to be willing to sell, provided it harmeth him not in any way, and that the full worth is paid, without haggling. Never bargain or cheapen anything which you buy by the Art.

So it be Ardane.

* * * * *

It is the Old Law and the most important of all Laws, That no one may do or say anything which will endanger any of the Craft, or bring them in contact with the law of the land, or the Law of the Church or any of our persecutors. In any disputes between the brethren, no one may invoke any laws but those of the Craft, or any

Tribunal but that of the Priestess and the Priest and the Elders. And may the Curse of the Goddess be on any who so do.

So it be Ardane.

* * * * *

It is not forbidden to say as Christians do, "There be Witchcraft in the Land," because our oppressors of old made it Heresy not to believe in Witchcraft, and so a crime to deny it, which thereby put you under suspicion. But ever say I know not of it here, perchance they may be, but afar off. I know not where, but ever speak so you cause others to doubt they be as they are. Always speak of them as Old Crones, consorting with the Devil and riding through the air. But ever say, but how may men ride through the air an they be not as light as Thistle Down? But the Curse of the Goddess be on any who cast any suspicion on any of the Brotherhood, or speaks of any real meeting place, or where any byde.

So it be Ardane.

* * * * *

Let the Craft keep books with the names of all Herbs which are good for man, and all cures, that all may learn. But keep another book with all the Banes and Apies and let only the Elders and trustworthy people have this knowledge. So it be Ardane.

And may the Blessings of the Gods be on all who keep these. Laws and the Curses of both God and Goddess be on all who break them.

So it be Ardane.

[The following sections were added later.]

Remember the Art is the secret of the Gods and may only be used in earnest and never for show or vainglory.

Magicians and Christians may taunt us, saying, "You have no power. Do magic before our eyes. Then only will we believe," seeking to cause us to betray our Art before them.

Heed them not, for the Art is holy, and may only be used in need.

And the curse of the Gods be on any who break this law.

* * * * *

It ever be the way with women, and with men also, that they ever seek new love, nor should we reprove them for this, but it may be found to disadvantage the Craft, as so many a time it has happened that a High Priest or High Priestess, impelled by love, hath departed with their love; that is, they have left the coven.

Now, if a High Priestess wishes to resign, she may do so in full Coven, and this resignation is valid.

But if they should run off without resigning, who may know if they may not return within a few months? So the law is, if a High Priestess leaves her coven, but returns within the space of a year and a day, then she shall be taken back, and all shall be as before.

Meanwhile, if she has a deputy, that deputy shall act as High Priestess for as long as the High Priestess is away.

If she returns not at the end of a year and a day, then shall the coven elect a new High Priestess. Unless there be a good reason to the contrary.

The person who has done the work should reap the benefit of the reward, Maiden and deputy of the High Priestess.

Supplement: The "Proposed Rules for the Craft"[†]

- No member of the Craft will initiate any person unless that person has been interviewed by at least two Elders and accepted as suitable.
- No affairs of the Craft will be discussed by members in the presence of uninitiated persons, or in places where conversation is likely to be overheard.
- No copies of any papers relating to the Craft will be made or retained without the Elders' permission. Such papers as are permissible will be kept in a secure place.
- As it is essential for the successful working of ritual by a group that there should be unity of purpose and an harmonious psychic atmosphere, members who create dissension and discord within the Craft will be asked to resign. Should they fail or refuse to do so they will be informed in writing by the Elders that they have been expelled.
- No member of the Craft will give any information or interview about the Craft to any journalist or writer, or cause any such information to be published in any way, without the approval of the Elders, nor will any of the Elders do so without the approval of the rest of the Elders.

---

† From the Aidan Kelly manuscript *The Rebirth of Witchcraft: Tradition and Creativity in the Gardnerian Reform* — a version of this manuscript was published by Llewellyn in 1991 as *Crafting the Art of Magic, Book I.* In 1957 there was a disagreement between Gardner and members of his coven regarding his indiscretions during press interviews. In an attempt to resolve the situation the coven's High Priestess Doreen Valiente, with the assistance of another member of the coven, proposed this *new* set of rules .

- If any member of the Craft feels that he or she has reason to complain of the conduct of any other member in matters affecting the Craft, or of any misdemeanour towards any member whilst on Craft premises, he or she will bring the said complaint to the notice of the Elders as soon as possible. The Elders, after considering all available evidence, will, if they find the complaint justified, take appropriate action.

- No member will be present at any meeting where the working is that of a higher Grade than he or she has attained, except by invitation of the Elders. These invitations will only be extended on very rare occasions where special circumstances exist.

- No member will disclose the name and address or telephone number of any other member to any person whatsoever without the said other member's previous permission.

- Members will meet upon the traditional occasions, or as near to them as possible, and such meetings will be arranged by the Elders, or such officers as the Elders authorise to do so. If the Elders be not present at such meetings, they will receive a report of them. Members may arrange other meetings for their private working if they so desire, but if more than two members be present at such a meeting, the Elders will receive a report of it. This report will take the form of a short letter to the Elders giving place and date of the meeting, names of members attending, and details of ceremonies carried out. Where convenient, verbal reports will be accepted.

- Members will endeavour to acquaint themselves with the traditions of the Craft, and will not introduce innovations into the working without the Elders' approval. Nor will the Elders give approval to any important innovation without first asking the approval of the rest of the Craft.
- In the event of any member resigning from the Craft, he or she will honourably observe the Oath of Secrecy taken at initiation, and will also return to the Elders any written matter relating to the Craft which may be in his or her possession.
- All members will receive a copy of these rules, and all new members will be given a copy of these rules upon initiation. New members, prior to initiation, will read these rules and declare upon their honour that they will abide by them in letter and in spirit. This declaration will be made to the Elders in writing, and signed.
- It will be understood by all members that these rules are equally binding upon all Grades of the Craft, including the Elders, and that serious and/or persistent breach of these rules will be grounds for expulsion.

EDITOR'S NOTE: GLOSSARY TO *THE OLD LAWS:*

Alther	'of all'
an	'and if'
Apies	unknown word. Widely accepted to be aphrodisiacs or spices. *Apies* may allude to the *apiaceous* plant group (*Apiaceae* or *Umbelliferae*) which includes Caraway, Coriander, Fennel, Lovage and Anise-fruit. These plants are characterized by hermaphrodite flowers and are rich in essential oil — they are important pharmaceuticals. However, some species are poisonous and have photo-toxic effects (such as Hogweed) whereas others within the group accumulate alkaloids, *i.e.* hemlock (*Conium Macaulatum*) —a plant long associated with Witches.
Appenage	Obscure form of *Apanage* — to endow with the means of subsistence, *i.e.* land or money.
Ardane	unknown word. Generally taken as "ordain" although it has been suggested that it may be a mis-spelling of *Aredan,* (an obscure form of *aread* — to prophesy, to decree, or declare by supernatural counsel).
Banes	poisons — *Bane* to kill, especially by poison.
Bigrave	Obscure form of *begrave* — to engrave, to ornament.
Bleared	dimmed with tears or inflammation.
Byde	Obscure form of *Bide* — a dwelling, dwelling-place, habitation.
Carcerors	Prison officials
Crased	Craze or Crazed.
Dwale	A stupefying or soporific drink — the juice or infusion of Belladonna — or, *Drugs* (see *Witchcraft Today*).
Engine	An 'engine of torture,' especially the rack. Some versions of the text have *engained* and this is often rewritten in modern versions of 'The Laws' as 'enjoined'— or, *tortured* (*Witchcraft Today*)
Hand of Write	Handwriting.
Hidel	Hiding-place.
Skith	unknown word. One suggested origin is *scathe,* meaning to harm or injure — skaith, skaithe, skath and skathe are amongst the many phoentic variants of *scathe* to be found in the *Oxford English Dictionary.*

Wica Gardner identifies *Wica* with 'wicca,' an Anglo-Saxon Pagan priesthood and which is thought by some to be the source of the modern word *witch*. However Gardner also referred to Wica as the *Craft of the Wise* and *Wice* is an obscure form of 'wise'.

> They are the people who call themselves the Wica, the "wise people", who practise the age-old rites and who have, along with much superstition and herbal knowledge, preserved an occult teaching and working processes which they themselves think to be magic or witchcraft. They are the type of people who were burned alive for possessing this knowledge, often giving their lives to turn suspicion away from others.
>
> *Witchcraft Today*, Chapter X: What are Witches. p. 88.

A Note by Janet and Stewart Farrar

The only published version of the Wiccan Law we know of appears as Appendix A to Alex Sanders' biography King of the Witches . . . . *This version of the Law purports to date from the persecution days, but its antiquity and authenticity are highly dubious. It may, however, enshrine fragments of traditional material, and provided that the obviously out-of-date elements are ignored, many of its clauses offer a good working guide to coven procedure. Doreen [Valiente] shares our doubts; she says:*

> *'For one thing there is a distinct whiff of male chauvinism about it; and for another, it is rather fond of threatening and cursing people who disagree with it, like a preacher in a back-street tin chapel! The verses 51 – 80 [The Warning] inclusive used to be in old Gerald's book, but not the rest.'*

She also points out that it implies that witches were burned in England, whereas in fact they were hanged —

> *'a little point that has tripped up many. I have never regarded this document as being authentic, personally; although as you say, it may enshrine fragments of traditional material handed down orally.'*
>
> A Witches Bible, *Phoenix Publishing Inc. Blaine. 1984.*

Editor's note: Section 51 – 80 is widely known as 'The Warning'.

Male chauvinism and a 'preaching-style' are not historically 'valid' reasons to doubt the documents authenticity and the 'little point that has tripped up many' is fully dealt with by Gardner himself:–

> *It may date from the time of the fierce persecutions on the Continent, and may have then been roughly translated into English. The trouble in dealing with these documents is the witch law: everyone must copy what they will from another, but no*

> *old writings may be kept. As everyone is apt to alter things slightly, modernizing the language and making other changes, it is impossible to fix the date when it became current. Clearly it was not written in England. Though bishops may have burnt witches at times, hanging was the only legal death sentence here. It might have been written in Scotland, but Scots would have worded it more clearly I think.*
>
> *Witchcraft Today*, Chapter IV: Witch Practices. p. 44.

The Farrars / Valiente based their argument on the assumption that the source is English and thus incorrectly implies 'that witches were burned in England'. However, although the 'Old Laws' do mention England the phrasing of the statement "In England tis now many a year since a witch hath died the death" suggests an alternative interpretation i.e. that the documents (or certain fragments of them) could be of foreign origin (Continental or Scottish). The 'burning' references are consistent with the idea of a Continental or Scottish source.

One clue for a Scottish origin maybe in Section 51 which begins "Keep a book in your own hand of write" — Oakseer opines in Gerald Gardner: Old Words and the Old Laws *that it is the phrase 'hand of write' which may have led Gardner to believe that it is either a) roughly translated from the 'Continental' or is b) that which the Scots would have worded more clearly. Oakseer asserts "If so, Gardner is exactly wrong [sic], because 'hand of write,' according to the* Oxford English Dictionary, *turns out to be* specifically *an old Scots expression."*

Although 'hand of write' is Scottish it is not that old! The OED *cites 'Hand o' writ' c.1816, and 'hand of write' being later, with examples given from 1870 and1890* (note:- OED *examples illustrate specifically the earliest known use as well the general age).*

A Comparison of two versions of the Old Laws

Book of Shadows, Lady Sheba, Llewellyn Worldwide, St. Paul. 2002.	*King of the Witches*, June Johns, Pan Books, London. 1971.
The Laws	The Book of Shadows: The Law
1. The Law was made and ardane of old.	1. The Law was made and ordained of old.
2. The Law was made for the Wicca to advise and help in their troubles.	2. The Law was made for the Wicca, to advise and help in their troubles.
3. The Wicca should give due worship to the Gods and obey Their will, which They ardane, for it was made for the good of the Wicca, as the worship of the Wicca is good for the Gods. For the Gods love the brethren of the Wicca.	3. The Wicca should give due worship to the gods and obey their will, which they ordain, for it was made for the good of Wicca as the worship of the Wicca is good for the gods. For the gods love the brethren of Wicca.
4. As a man loveth a woman by mastering her,	4. As a man loveth a woman by mastering her,
5. So the Wicca should love the Gods by mastering them.	5. So the Wicca should love the gods by being mastered by them.
6. And it is necessary that the Ø (Magic Circle), which is the Temple of the Gods, should be duly cast and purified that it may be a fit place for the Gods to enter.	6. And it is necessary that the Circle which is the temple of the gods, should be truly cast and purified. And that it may be a fit place for the gods to enter.
7. And the Wicca should be properly prepared and purified to enter into the presence of the Gods.	7. And the Wicca shall be properly prepared and purified to enter into the presence of the gods.

8. With love and worship in their hearts, they shall raise power from their bodies to give power to the Gods.

9. As has been taught of old.

10. For in this way only may man have a communion with the Gods, for the Gods cannot help men without the help of man.

11. And the High Priestess shall rule Her Coven as the representative of the Goddess.

12. And the High Priest shall support Her as the representative of the God.

13. And the High Priestess shall choose whom She will, if he have sufficient rank, to be Her High Priest.

14. For, as the God himself kissed Her feet in the Fivefold salute, laying His power at the feet of the Goddess, because of Her youth and beauty, Her sweetness and kindness, Her wisdom and Her justice, Her humility and gentleness and generosity,

15. So He resigned all His power to Her.

16. But the High Priestess should ever mind that all power comes from Him.

8. With love and worship in their hearts, they shall raise power from their bodies to give power to the gods.

9. As has been taught of old.

10. For in this way only may men have communion with the gods, for the gods cannot help men without the help of man.

11. And the High Priestess shall rule her coven as the representative of the god.

12. And the High Priest shall support her as the representative of the god.

13. And the High Priestess shall choose whom she will, be of sufficient rank, to be her High Priest.

14. For, as the god himself kissed her feet in the five-fold salute, laying his power at the feet of the goddess because of her youth and beauty, her sweetness and kindness, her wisdom and justice, her humility and generosity.

15. So he resigned all his power to her.

16. But the High Priestess should ever mind that all power comes from him.

17. It is only lent, to be used wisely and justly.

18. And the greatest virtue of a High Priestess be that She recognizes that youth is necessary to the representative of the Goddess.

19. So will She gracefully retire in favor of a younger woman, should the Coven so decide in council.

20. For the true High Priestess realizes that gracefully surrendering the pride of place is one of the greatest virtues.

21. And that thereby will She return to that pride of place in another life, with greater power and beauty.

22. In the old days, when Witches extended far, we were free and worshipped in all the greatest temples.

23. But, in these unhappy times, we must celebrate our Sacred Mysteries in secret.

24. So be it ardane, that none but the Wicca may see our mysteries, for our enemies are many and torture loosens the tongue of men.

17. It is only lent, to be used wisely and justly.

18. And the greatest virtue of a High Priestess be that she recognize that youth is necessary to the representative of the goddess.

19. So she will gracefully retire in favour of a younger woman should the Coven so decide in council.

20. For a true High Priestess realizes that gracefully surrendering pride of place is one of the greatest virtues.

21. And that thereby she will return to that pride of place in another life, with greater power and beauty.

22. In the old days, when witchdom extended far, we were free and worshipped in all the greater temples.

23. But in these unhappy times we must celebrate our sacred mysteries in secret.

24. So be it ordained, that none but the Wicca may see our mysteries, for our enemies are many and torture loosens the tongue of man.

25. So be it ardane, that no Coven shall know where the next Coven bide.	25. So be it ordained that no Coven shall know where the next Coven bide.
26. Or who its members be, save only the Priest and Priestess and the Messenger.	26. Or who its members be, save only the Priest and Priestess and messenger.
27. And there shall be no communication between them, save only by the Messenger of the Gods, or the Summoner.	27. And there shall be no communication between them, save by the messenger of the gods, or the summoner.
28. And only if it be safe may the Covens meet in some safe place for the Great Festivals.	28. And only if it be safe may the Covens meet in some safe place for the great festivals.
29. And while there, none shall say whence they come, nor give their true names.	29. And while there, none shall say whence they came nor give their true names.
30. To this end, that if any be tortured, in their agony, they may not tell if they do not know.	30. To this end, any that are tortured in their agony may not tell if they do not know.
31. So be it ardane, that no one shall tell anyone, not of the Craft, who be of the Wicca, or give any names, or where any abide, or in any way tell anything which can betray any of us to our faces.	31. So be it ordained that no one shall tell anyone not of the craft who be of the Wicca, nor give any names or where they bide, or in any way tell anything which can betray any of us to our foes.
32. Nor may he tell where the Covendom be.	32. Nor may he tell where the Covendom be.
33. Or the Covenstead.	33. Or the Covenstead.
34. Or where the meetings be.	34. Or where the meetings be.
35. And if any break these Laws, even under torture, the Curse of the	35. And if any break these laws, even under torture, the Curse of THE

Goddess shall be upon them, so they may never be reborn on earth, and may they remain where they belong, in the Hell of the Christians.

36. Let each High Priestess govern Her Coven with justice and love, with the help and advice of the High Priest and the Elders, always heeding the advice of the Messenger of the Gods if He comes.

37. She will heed all complaints of all Brothers and strive to settle all differences among them.

38. But it must be recognized that there will always be people who will ever strive to force others to do as they will.

39. These are not necessarily evil.

40. And they oft have good ideas, and such ideas should be talked over in council.

41. But, if they will not agree with their Brothers or if they say:

42. "I will not work under this High Priestess."

43. It hath ever been the Old Law, to be convenient for the Brethren, and to avoid disputes.

GODDESS SHALL BE UPON THEM, so they may never be reborn on earth and may remain where they belong, in the hell of the Christians.

36. Let each High Priestess govern her Coven with justice and love, with the help and advice of the High Priest and the Elders, always heeding the advice of the messenger of the gods if he cometh.

37. She will heed all complaints of all Brothers and strive to settle all differences among them.

38. But it must be recognized that there will always be people who will ever strive to force others to do as they will.

39. These are not necessarily evil.

40. And they oft have good ideas and such ideas should be talked over in council.

41. But if they will not agree with their Brothers, or if they say,

42. 'I will not work under this High Priestess,'

43. It hath ever been the Old Law to be convenient to the Brethren and to avoid disputes.

44. Any of the third may claim to found a new Coven, because they live over a league from the Covenstead or are about to do so.

45. Anyone living within the Covendom and wishing to form a new Coven shall tell the Elders of their intentions and on the instant avoid their dwelling and remove to a new Covendom.

46. Members of the old Coven may join the new one when it is formed, but if they do they must utterly avoid the old Coven.

47. The Elders of the old and new Covens should meet in peace and brotherly love to decide the new boundaries.

48. Those of the Craft who live outside both Covens may join either indifferent, but not both.

49. Though all may, if the Elders agree, meet for the Great Festivals, if it be truly in peace and brotherly love.

50. But splitting the Coven oft means strife, so for this reason these Laws were made of old, and may the Curse of the Goddess be on any who disregard them!

SO BE IT ARDANE.

44. Any of the third may claim to found a new Coven because they live over a league away from the Covenstead, or that they are about to do so.

45. Anyone living within the Covendom and wishing to form a new Coven, shall tell the Elders of their intention, and on the instant avoid their dwelling and remove to the new Covendom.

46. Members of the old Coven may join the new one when it is formed. But if they do, they must utterly avoid the old Coven.

47. The Elders of the new and the old Covens should meet in peace and brotherly love to decide the new boundaries.

48. Those of the craft who dwell outside both Covendoms may join either but not both,

49. Though all may, if the Elders agree, meet for the great festivals if it be truly in peace and brotherly love,

50. But splitting the Coven off means strife, so for this reason these Laws were made of old and may the Curse of the Goddess be on any who disregard them. So be it ordained.

51. If you would keep a book (your Black Book) let it be in your own hand of write; let Brothers and Sisters copy what they will, but never let the book out of your hands and never keep the writings of another.

52. For if it be in their hand of write, they may be taken and engained.

53. Let each guard his own writings, and destroy them whenever danger threatens.

54. Learn as much as you may by heart, and when danger is past, rewrite your book an it be safe.

55. For this reason, if any die, destroy their book, an they have not been able to.

56. For, an it be found, 'tis clear proof against them.

57. And our oppressors know well: "Ye may not be a Witch alone."

58. So all their kin and friends be in danger of torture.

59. So destroy everything not necessary.

60. If your book be found on you, 'tis clear proof against you alone. You may be engained.

51. If you would keep a book, let it be in your own hand of write. Let brothers and sisters copy what they will, but never let the book out of your hands, and never keep the writings of another.

52. For if it be found in their hand of write, they may be taken and arraigned.

53. Let each guard his own writings and destroy them whenever danger threatens.

54. Learn as much as you may by heart and, when danger is past, rewrite your book, an it be safe.

55. For this reason, if any die, destroy their book an they have not been able to.

56. For, an it be found, 'tis clear proof against them.

57. And our oppressors know well 'Ye may not be a witch alone'.

58. So all their kin and friends be in danger of torture,

59. So destroy everything not necessary.

60. If your book be found on you, 'tis clear proof against you alone, you may be arraigned.

61. Keep all thoughts of the Craft from your mind.

62. If the torture be too great to bear, say: "I will confess. I cannot bear this torture. What do you want me to say?"

63. If they try to make you talk of the Brotherhood, do not.

64. But if they try to make you speak of impossibilities such as flying through the air, consorting with the Christian Devil, or sacrificing children or eating men's flesh,

65. To obtain relief from the torture, say, "I hold an evil dream, I was beside myself, I was crazed."

66. Not all the magistrates are bad; if there be any excuse, they may show mercy.

67. If you have confessed ought, deny it afterwards. Say you babbled under the torture, say you do not know what you said.

68. If you are condemned, fear not.

69. Fear not, the Brotherhood is powerful, they will help you to escape if you stand steadfast.

70. But if you betray ought, there is no hope for you in this life or that to come.

61. Keep all thoughts of the craft from your mind.

62. If the torture be too great to bear, say, 'I will confess. I cannot bear this torture. What do you want me to say?'

63. If they try to make you speak of the Brotherhood, do not.

64. But if they try to make you speak of impossibilities such as flying through the air, consorting with a Christian devil or sacrificing children, or eating men's flesh,

65. To obtain relief from torture say, 'I had an evil dream, I was beside myself, I was crazed.'

66. Not all magistrates are bad, if there be an excuse, they may show mercy.

67. If you have confessed ought, deny it afterwards, say you babbled under torture, say you knew not what you said.

68. If you are condemned, fear not.

69. The Brotherhood is powerful and will help you to escape if you stand steadfast, but if you betray ought there is no hope for you in this life or in that to come.

71. Be sure, if steadfast you go to the pyre, drugs will reach you, you will feel naught. You but go to death and what lies beyond.	70. Be sure, if steadfast you go to the pyre, drugs will reach you, you will feel naught. You go to death and what lies beyond, the ecstasy of the goddess.
The Ecstasy of the Goddess	
72. To avoid discovery, let the working tools be as ordinary things that any may have in their houses.	71. To avoid discovery, let the working tools be as ordinary things that any may have in their houses.
73. Let the Pentacles be of wax so that they may be broken at once or melted.	72. Let the pentacles be of wax so that they may be broken at once or melted.
74. Have no sword, unless your rank allows you one.	73. Have no sword unless your rank allows it.
75. Have no names or signs on anything.	74. Have no names or signs on anything.
76. Write the names or signs on them in ink immediately before consecrating them, and wash it off immediately afterwards.	75. Write the names and signs on them in ink before consecrating them and wash it off immediately afterwards.
77. Do not engrave them lest they cause discovery.	76. Let the colour of the hilts tell which is which.
78. Let the color of the hilts tell which is which.	77. Do not bigrave * them unless they cause discovery. * engrave.
79. Ever remember, ye are the "Hidden Children of the Goddess," so never do anything to disgrace them or her.	78. Ever remember ye are the hidden children of the goddess so never do anything to disgrace them or her.

80.	Never boast, never threaten, never say you would wish ill of anyone.	79.	Never boast, never threaten, never say you would wish ill of anyone.
81.	If any person, not in the magic circle, speak of the Craft say, "Speak not to me of such, it frightens me. 'Tis evil luck to speak of it.' "	80.	If any person not in the Circle, speak of the craft, say, 'Speak not to me of such, it frightens me, tis evil luck to speak of it.'
82.	For this reason: the Christians have their spies everywhere. These speak as if they were well affected to us, as if they would come to our meetings, saying, "My mother used to go to worship the Old Ones. I would I could go myself."	81.	For this reason, the Christians have their spies everywhere. These speak as if they were well affected to us, as if they wouldn't come into our meetings, saying, 'My mother used to worship the Old Ones. I would I could go myself.'
83.	To such as these, ever deny all knowledge.	82.	To such as these, ever deny all knowledge.
84.	But to others, ever say: "'Tis foolish talk of Witches flying through the air. To do so they must be light as thistledown. And men say that Witches all be so bleared-eyed, old crones, so what pleasure can there be at a Witch meeting such as folks talk on?"	83.	But to others, ever say, 'Tis foolish men talk of witches flying through the air. To do so they must be as light as thistledown. And men say that witches all be blear-eyed old crones, so what pleasure can there be at a witch meeting such as folks talk on?'
85.	And say, "Many wise men now say there be no such creatures."	84.	And say, 'Many wise men now say there be no such creatures.'
86.	Ever make it a jest and in some future time, perhaps, the persecution may die and we may worship our Gods in safety again.	85.	Ever make it a jest, and in some future time perhaps, the persecution may die and we may worship our gods in safety again.

87. Let us all pray for that happy day.

88. May the blessings of the Goddess and God be on all those who keep these Laws which are ardane.

89. If the Craft have any Appenage, let all guard it, and help to keep it clear and good for the Craft.

90. And let all justly guard all monies of the Craft.

91. But if any brother truly wrought it, 'tis right they have their pay, and it be just. And this be not taking money for the Art, but for good and honest work.

92. And ever the Christians say, "The laborer is worthy of his hire," but if any brother work willingly for the good of the Craft without pay, 'tis to their greatest honor.

SO BE IT ARDANE.

93. If there be any quarrels or disputes among the brethren, the High Priestess shall straightly convene the Elders and inquire into the matter and they shall hear both sides, first alone, then together.

94. And they shall decide justly, not favoring the one side or the other.

86. Let us all pray for that happy day.

87. May the blessings of the goddess and god be on all who keep these Laws which are ordained.

88. If the craft hath any appanage, let all guard it and help to keep it clear and good for the craft.

89. And let all justly guard all monies of the craft.

90. And if any Brother truly wrought it, tis right they have their pay, an it be just. An this be not taking money for the art, but for good and honest work.

91. And even the Christians say, 'The labourer is worthy of his hire,' but if any Brother work willingly for the good of the craft without pay, tis but to their greater honour. So be it ordained.

92. If there be any dispute or quarrel among the Brethren, the High Priestess shall straightly convene the Elders and inquire into the matter, and they shall hear both sides, first alone and then together.

93. And they shall decide justly, not favouring one side or the other.

95. Ever recognizing there be people who can never agree to work under others.

96. But at the same time, there be some people who cannot rule justly.

97. To those who ever must be chief, there is one answer.

98. Void the Coven, or seek another one or make a Coven of your own, taking with you those who will go.

99. To those who cannot rule justly the answer be, "Those who cannot bear your rule will leave you."

100. For none may come to meetings with those with whom they are at variance.

101. So, an either cannot agree, "Get hence, for the Craft must ever survive."

SO BE IT ARDANE.

102. In the olden days, when we had power, we could use the Art against any who ill-treated the Brotherhood. But in these evil days, we must not do so! For our enemies have devised a burning pit of everlasting fire, into which they say their God casteth all the people who worship Him, except

94. Ever recognizing there be people who can never agree to work under others.

95. But at the same time, there be some people who cannot rule justly.

96. To those who ever must be chief, there is one answer.

97. Void the Coven or seek another one, or make a Coven of your own, taking with you those who will go.

98. To those who cannot, justly the answer be, 'Those who cannot bear your rule will leave with you.'

99. For none may come to meetings with those whom they are at variance.

100. So, an either cannot agree, get hence, for the craft must ever survive, so be it ordained

101. In the olden days when we had power, we could use the art against any who ill-treated the Brotherhood. But in these evil days we must not do so. For our enemies have devised a burning pit of everlasting fire into which they say their god casteth all the people who worship him, except

it be the very few who are released by their priest's spells and masses. And this be chiefly by giving monies and rich gifts to receive His favor, for their God is ever in need of money.

103. But as our Gods need our aid to make fertility for man and crops, so it is the God of the Christians ever is in need of man's help to search out and destroy us. Their priests ever tell them that any who get our help are damned to this Hell forever, so men be mad with the terror of it.

104. But they make men believe that they may escape this Hell if they give Witches to the tormentors. So for this reason, all be forever spying, thinking, "An I catch but one of the Wicca, I will escape this fiery pit."

105. So for this reason we have our hidels, and men searching long and not finding say: "There be none, or if there be, they be in a far country."

106. But when one of our oppressors dies, or even be sick, ever is the cry, "This be Witches' malice," and the hunt is up again, and though they slay ten of their own to one of ours, still they care not. They have countless thousands.

it be the very few who are released by their priests, spells and masses. And this be chiefly by giving monies and rich gifts to receive his favour for their great god is ever in need of money.

102. But as our gods need our aid to make fertility for man and crops, so is the god of the Christians ever in need of man's help to search out and destroy us. Their priests ever tell them that any who get our help are damned to this hell for ever, so men be mad with the terror of it.

103. But they make men believe that they may escape this hell if they give victims to the tormentors. So for this reason all be for ever spying, thinking, 'An I can catch but one of these Wicca, I will escape from this fiery pit.'

104. So for this reason we have our hidels, and men searching long and not finding, say, 'There be none, or if there be, they be in a far country.'

105. But when one of our oppressors die, or even be sick, ever is the cry, 'This be witches' malice', and the hunt is up again. And though they slay ten of their own to one of ours, still they care not. They have countless thousands.

107. While we are few indeed.

SO BE IT ARDANE.

108. That none shall use the Art in any way to do ill to any.

109. However much they injure us, HARM NONE and now times many believe we exist not.

SO BE IT ARDANE.

110. That this Law shall ever continue to help us in our plight. No one, however great an injury or injustice they receive, may use the Art in any way to do ill or harm any. But they may, after great consultations with all, use the Art to restrain Christians from harming us or tax others, but only to let or constrain them.

111. To this end, men will say: "Such an one is a mighty searcher out and a persecutor of old women whom they deemeth to be Witches, and none hath done him skith, so they be proof they cannot, or more truly where be none."

112. For all know full well, that so many folk have died because someone had a grudge against them, or were persecuted because they had money or goods to seize, or because they had none to bribe

106. While we are few indeed. So be it ordained.

107. That none shall use the art in any way to do ill to any.

108. However much they injure us, harm none. And now-times many believe we exist not.

109. That this Law shall ever continue to help us in our plight, no one, however great an injury or injustice they receive, may use the art in any way to do ill, or harm any. But they may, after great consultations with all, use the art to restrain Christians from harming us Brothers, but only to constrain them and never to punish.

110. To this end men will say, 'Such a one is a mighty searcher out, and a persecutor of old women when they desire to be witches, and none hath done him harm, so it be proof that they cannot or more truly there be none.'

111. For all know full well that so many folk have died because someone had a grudge against them, or were persecuted because they had money or goods to seize, or because they had none to bribe

the searchers. And many have died because they were scolding old women. So much that men now say that "only old women are Witches."

113. And this be to our advantage, and turns suspicions away from us.

114. In England and Scotland, 'tis now many a year since a Witch hath died the death. But misuse of the power might raise the persecution again.

115. So never break this Law, however much you are tempted, and never consent to it being broken in the least.

116. If you know it is being broken, you must work strongly against it.

117. And any High Priestess who consents to its breach must immediately be deposed. "For 'tis the blood of the Brethren they endanger."

118. Do good, and it be safe and only if it be safe.

119. And strictly keep to the old Law.

120. Never accept money for the use of the Art. For money ever smeareth the taker. "'Tis sorcerers and conjurers and priests of the Christians who ever accept

the searchers. And many have died because they were scolding old women. So much that men now say that only old women are witches.

112. And this be to our advantage and turns suspicion away from us.

113. In England and Scotland 'tis now many a year since a witch hath died the death. But any misuse of the power might raise the persecution again.

114. So never break this Law, however much you are tempted, and never consent to its being broken in the least.

115. If you know it is being broken, you must work strongly against it.

116. And any High Priestess or High Priest who consents to its breach must immediately be deposed for 'tis the blood of the Brethren they endanger.

117. Do good, an it be safe, and only if it be safe.

118. And strictly keep to the Old Law

119. Never accept money for the use of the art, for money ever smeareth the taker 'Tis sorcerers and conjurors and the priests of the Christians who ever accept

money for the use of their Arts. And they sell dwale, and evil loves spells and pardons, so let men escape from their sins."	money for the use of their arts. And they sell pardons to let men escape from their sins.
121. Be not as these. If you accept no money, you will be free from temptation to use the Art for evil causes.	120. Be not as these. If you accept no money, you will be free from temptation to use the art for evil causes.
122. All may use the Art for their own advantage, or for the advantage of the Craft, only if you are sure you harm none.	121. All may use the art for their own advantage or for the advantage of the craft only if you are sure you harm none.
123. But ever let the Coven debate this at length. Only if all be satisfied and none be harmed may the Art be used.	122. But ever let the Coven debate this at length. Only if all are satisfied that none may be harmed, may the art be used.
124. If it is not possible to achieve your ends one way, perchance the aim may be achieved by acting in a different way, so as to harm none. May the Curse of the Goddess be on any who breaketh this Law. SO BE IT ARDANE	123. If it is not possible to achieve your ends one way, perchance the aim may be achieved by acting in a different way so as to harm none. MAY THE CURSE OF THE GODDESS BE UPON ANY WHO BREAKETH THIS LAW. So be it ordained.
125. 'Tis judged lawful an any of the Craft need a house or land and none will sell, to incline the owner's mind so as to be willing to sell, providing it harmeth it not in any way and the full price is paid, without haggling,	124. 'Tis judged lawful if ever any of the craft need a house or land and none will sell, to incline the owner's mind so as to be willing to sell, provided it harmeth him not in any way and the full price is paid without haggling.

126. Never bargain or cheapen anything whilst you live by the Art.

SO BE IT ARDANE.

127. 'Tis the old Law and the most important of all Laws that no one may do anything which will endanger any of the Craft, or bring them into contact with the law of the land, or any of our persecutors.

128. In any disputes between the brethren, no one may invoke any Laws but those of the Craft.

129. Or any tribunal but that of the Priestess, Priest, and Elders. And may the Curse of the Goddess be on any who do so.

SO BE IT ARDANE.

130. It is not forbidden to say as Christians do: "There be Witchcraft in the land," because our oppressors of old make it heresy not to believe in Witchcraft, and so a crime to deny it, which thereby puts you under suspicion.

131. But ever say "I know not of it here, perchance there may be, but afar off — I know not where."

125. Never bargain or cheapen anything whilst you buy by the art. So be it ordained.

126. 'Tis the Old Law and the most important of all laws, that no one may do anything which will endanger any of the craft, or bring them into contact with the law of the land or any persecutors.

127. In any dispute between the Brethren, no one may invoke any laws but those of the craft.

128. Or any tribunal but that of the Priestess, Priest and Elders.

129. It is not forbidden to say as Christians do, 'There be witchcraft in the land,' because our oppressors of old make it heresy not to believe in witchcraft and so a crime to deny it which thereby puts you under suspicion.

130. But ever say, 'I know not of it here, perchance there may be but afar off, I know not where.'

132. But ever speak of those as old crones, consorting with the Devil and riding through the air.

133. But ever say: "But how many men may ride through the air an they be not light as thistledown?"

134. But the Curse of the Goddess be on any who cast any suspicion on any of the Brotherhood.

135. Or who speaks of any real meeting place where any abide.

SO BE IT ARDANE

136. Let the Craft keep books with the names of all herbs which are good for men, and all cures, so all may learn.

137. But keep another book with all the Bales and Apies and let only the Elders and other trustworthy people have this knowledge.

SO BE IT ARDANE.

138. Remember the Art is the secret of the Gods and only may be used in earnest and never for show or pride, or vainglory.

131. But ever speak of them as old crones, consorting with the devil and riding through the air.

132. And ever say, 'But how may many ride the air if they be not as light as thistledown.'

133. But the curse of the goddess be on any who cast suspicion on any of the Brotherhood.

134. Or who speak of any real meeting-place or where they bide.

135. Let the craft keep books with the names of all herbs which are good, and all cures so all may learn.

136. But keep another book with all Bills and Apices and let only the Elders and other trustworthy people have this knowledge. So be it ordained.

137. And may the blessings of the gods be on all who keep these Laws, and the curses of both the god and the goddess be on all who break them.

138. Remember the art is the secret of the gods and may only be used in earnest and never for show or vainglory.

139. Magicians and Christians may taunt us saying, "You have no power. Do magic before our eyes. Then only will we believe." Seeking to cause us to betray our Art before them.

140. Heed them not. For the Art is holy, and may only be used in need. And the Curse of the Gods be on any who break this Law.

SO BE IT ARDANE.

141. It ever be the way with women, and with men also that they ever seek new love.

142. Nor should we reprove them for this.

143. But it may be found to the disadvantage of the Craft.

144. As, so many a time it has happened that a High Priest or High Priestess impelled by love, hath departed with their love; that is, they have left the Coven.

145. Now if a High Priestess wishes to resign, they may do so in full Coven.

146. And this resignation is valid.

147. But if they should run off without resignation, who may know if they may not return within a few months?

139. Magicians and Christians may taunt us saying, 'You have no power, show us your power. Do magic before our eyes, then only will we believe,' seeking to cause us to betray the art before them.

140. Heed them not, for the art is holy and may only be used in need, and the curse of the gods be on any who break this Law.

141. It ever be the way with women and with men also, that they ever seek new love.

142. Nor should we reprove them for this.

143. But it may be found a disadvantage to the craft.

144. And so many a time it has happened that a High Priest or a High Priestess, impelled by love, hath departed with their love. That is, they have left the Coven.

145. Now if the High Priestess wishes to resign, she may do so in full Coven.

146. And this resignation is valid.

147. But if they should run off without resigning, who may know if they may not return in a few months?

148. So the Law is: If a High Priestess leaves her Coven, but returns within the space of a year and a day, then she shall be taken back and all shall be as before.	148. So the Law is, if a High Priestess leaves her Coven, she be taken back and all be as before.
149. Meanwhile, if she has a deputy, that deputy shall act as High Priestess for as long as the High Priestess is away.	149. Meanwhile, if she has a deputy, that deputy shall act as High Priestess for as long as the High Priestess is away.
150. If she returns not at the end of a year and a day, then shall the Coven elect a new High Priestess.	150. If she returns not at the end of a year and a day, then shall the Coven elect a new High Priestess.
151. Unless there be a good reason to the contrary, the person who has done the work should reap the benefit of the reward.	151. Unless there is a good reason to the contrary.
152. If somebody else is elected, the deputy is made maiden and deputy of the High Priestess.	152. The person who has done the work shall reap the benefit of the reward, maiden and deputy of the High Priestess.
SO BE IT ARDANE.	
153. It hath been found that practicing the Art doth cause a fondness between aspirant and tutor, and it is the cause of better results if this be so.	153. It had been found that practising the art doth cause a fondness between aspirant and tutor, and it is the cause of better results if this be so.
154. But if for any reason this be undesirable, it can easily be avoided by both persons from the outset firmly resolving in their minds that if any such ensue, it shall be that of brother and sister, or parent and child.	154. And if for any reason this be undesirable, it can easily be avoided by both persons from the outset firmly resolving in their minds to be as brother and sister, or parent and child.

155. And it is for this reason that a man may be taught by a woman and a woman by a man and that woman and woman and man and man should never attempt these practices together.

156. And may all the Curses of the Mighty Ones be on any who make such an attempt.

SO BE IT ARDANE.

157. Order and discipline must be kept.

158. A High Priestess or a High Priest may and should punish all faults.

159. To this end: all the Craft must receive their correction willingly.

160. All, properly prepared, the culprit kneeling, should be told his fault, and his sentence pronounced.

161. Punishment should be the S followed by something amusing such as several S S S S, or something of this nature.

162. The culprit must acknowledge the justice of the punishment by kissing the hand of the Priestess and by kissing the S on receiving sentence; and again thanking for punishment received.

SO BE IT ARDANE.

155. And it is for this reason that a man may be taught only by a woman and a woman by a man, and women and women should not attempt these practices together. So be it ordained.

156. Order and discipline must be kept.

157. A High Priestess or a High Priest may, and should, punish all faults.

158. To this end all the craft must receive correction willingly.

159. All properly prepared, the culprit kneeling should be told his fault and his sentence pronounced.

160. Punishment should be followed by something amusing.

161. The culprit must acknowledge the justice of the punishment by kissing the hand on receiving sentence and again thanking for punishment received. So be it ordained.

NOTE: Many of the laws are archaic and more suited to the sixteenth than the twentieth century, and since

Alex Sanders was appointed King, he has agreed to many being tacitly dropped. No 25, ordering that no coven must know the whereabouts of the next, which caused so much difficulty when he was searching for witches, was the first to go.

Rule 82, ordering witches to deny all knowledge of the craft, is still contested. Alex maintains it should be scrapped, but there are many witches in Britain who will have nothing to do with his movement because he disregards this rule. Some believe that talking about one's powers diminishes them, but Alex and his followers put this down to superstition.

3.2. The Verse Charge (1961)

I the Mother, darksome and divine,
Say to thee, Oh children mine
(All ye assembled at mine Shrine),
Mine the scourge and mine the kiss
The five-point star of love and bliss
Here I charge ye in this sign. (Assume Goddess position.)

All ye assembled here tonight
Bow before my spirit bright
Aphrodite, Arianrhod,
Lover of the Horned God,
Mighty Queen of Witchery and night

Astarte, Hecate, Ashtaroth, Dione,
(Morrigan, Etain, Nisene),
Diana, Brigid, Melusine,
Am I named of old by men,
Artemis and Cerridwen,
Hell's dark mistress, Heaven's Queen.

(Whene'er trouble comes anoon)
All who would learn of me a Rune
Or would ask of me a boon,
Meet ye in some secret glade

Dance my round in greenwood shade,
By the light of the full moon.

(In a place wild and lone)
With the comrades alone
Dance about my altar stone.
Work my holy Magistry,
Ye who are fain of sorcery,
I bring ye secrets yet unknown.

(Whate'er troubles come to thee),
No more shall ye know slavery
Who give due worship unto me,
Who tread my round on Sabbat-night.
Come ye all naked to the rite,
In token ye be truly free.

I teach the mystery of rebirth,
Keep ye my mysteries in mirth
Heart joined to heart, and lip to lip,
Five are the points of fellowship
That bring ye ecstasy on Earth.

I ask no offerings, do but bow,
No other law but love I know,
By naught but love I may be known,
All that liveth is mine own
From me they come, to me they go.

3.3. Casting and Charging (1961)

· Forming Circle. Light candles.

Draw Circle with Magic Sword or Athame.

Sprinkle with consecrated water.

Cense.

Say, "I conjure thee, O Circle of Power, that thou be a Boundary and a Protection and a meeting place between the world of men and the realms of the Mighty Ones, A Guardian and a Protection that shall preserve and contain the Power which we shall raise within thee, Wherefore do I Bless and Consecrate thee."

Say "I summon, Stir, and Call Thee up, Ye Mighty Ones of the (East, South, West, North) To witness the Rites and to guard the Circle."

· Closing Circle.

Say, "Mighty Ones of the (East, South, West, North), I thank you for attending, and ere you depart for your lovely realms, I say Hail and Farewell."

· Consecration of Water and Salt.

Touch water with Athame, saying,

"I exorcise thee, O Creature of Water, that thou cast out from thee all the impurities and uncleannesses of the spirits of the World of

> Phantasm, In the names of Aradia and Cernunnos."

Touching Salt with Athame, say,

> "Blessings be upon this creature of Salt. Let all malignity and hindrance be cast forth hencefrom and let all good enter herein. Wherefore I bless thee that thou mayest aid me, In the names of Aradia and Cernunnos."

Drawing Down the Moon.

> "I invoke Thee and call upon Thee, O Mighty Mother of us All, Bringer of all Fruitfulness. By Seed and Root, by Stem and Bud, by Leaf and Flower and Fruit, by Life and Love, Do We invoke Thee to descend upon the body of Thy servant and Priestess (name)."

High Priest and other men give Fivefold Kiss.

Women all bow.

3.4. Forming the Circle. (1961)

- Must have a man and a woman, properly prepared, i.e., naked.
- Mark a circle nine feet across on the floor with chalk, etc. The best way is to get a string. Tie two loops four foot, six inches apart. Put one loop over a nail or something in the centre. Put chalk in the other and run it round. If you can't make marks on the floor, put furniture, etc., round to form it. Have a table, etc., as an Altar, with all tools, etc., on it. Have a bowl of water, and some salt.
- Place Athame on the bowl of water. Say,

> "I exorcise thee, O creature of Water, that thou cast out from Thee all the impurities and uncleannesses of the Spirits of the World of Phantasm in the name of Aradia and Cernunnos. But ever mind that Water purifies the body, but the scourge purifies the soul."

- Then place Athame on the salt. Say,

> "Blessings be upon this creature of Salt. Let all malignity and hindrance be cast forth hencefrom, and let all good enter herein. Wherefore I bless thee that thou mayest aid me, in the name of Aradia and Cernunnos."

- Then trace Circle on the lines you have marked out, starting at the East and returning to the East. (Always go round the circle with your Right hand to the Altar. Never go Widdershins.) Then put the Salt into the water and go round the circle again, sprinkling it to purify it. Then go round again censing it.

(Everyone in the circle must be sprinkled and censed.)

Then go to the East, Sword or Athame in hand. Draw an invoking pentacle in the Air, starting at the top and going to the left hand corner, saying,

> "I summon, and call thee up, O Ye Mighty ones of the East, to guard the Circle and witness our rites."

Then holding the point of sword or Athame upwards, do the same to the south, west, and north, and return to the centre, to the south of the Altar.

Then each girl should bind her man, hands behind back and cable Tow to neck. He should kneel at altar, and be scourged. When all men are thus "purified," they purify the girls in turn. No one may be in the circle without being thus purified.

Then do whatever work wanted.

When closing the Circle, the High Priestess, or whoever she tells to do it, saying,

> "Hail, ye mighty ones of the East. I thank you for attending, and ere ye depart for your lovely realms, We say, Hail and Farewell."

BOOK OF SHADOWS

PART FOUR

4.1. The Dryghtyn (Blessing) Prayer. (Anon. n.d.)

In the name of Dryghtyn, the ancient providence, which was from the beginning, and is for eternity, male and female, the original source of all things; all-knowing, all-pervading, all-powerful; changeless, eternal.

In the name of the Lady of the Moon and the Lord of Death and Resurrection; in the name of the Mighty Ones of the Four Quarters, the Kings of the Elements, bless this place, and this time, and they who are with us.

Published in *Witch Blood! The Diary of a Witch High Priestess,* Patricia Crowther, 1974, House Of Collectibles, Inc.

[EDITOR'S NOTE]

Dryghtyn : obscure form of *Drightin, -ten.* A Lord, ruler, Chief; *specifically* the Lord God, or Christ. [*OED*]

Nad he bene doghty and drye and Dryghtyn had served,
Douteles he had bene ded and dreped ful oft;

[had he not been stiff and strong and serving the Lord, doubtless he had been done to death ere this]

Sir Gawaine and the Green Knight II

Now neghes the Newe Yere and the night passes,
The day drives to the derk, as Dryghtyn biddes.

[Now the New Year drew nigh, and the night passed,
and the day chased the darkness, as is God's will]

Sir Gawaine and the Green Knight IV.

Gardner was familiar with the story of *Sir Gawaine and the Green Knight* [SGGK] he wrote:–

"The Old God makes an actual appearance as "The Green Man" in the old romance of *Sir Gawaine and the Green Knight.* The figure of the 'Green Knight', weird and fantastic yet courtly and kind in a way that puts Sir Gawaine to shame, is typical of the Old God; and it is to be noted that his "wife" in the story is Morgan Le Fay, the Lady of the Moon, who appears sometimes as an old hag, and sometimes as an enticing young woman.

> Morgan the Goddess
> Therefore it is her name.
> Wields none so high hautesse
> That she cannot make full tame.

Editor's Note: Having noted that the Green Knight is the Old God and Morgan Le Fay is the Lady of the Moon, Gardner fails to mention that Gawaine's shield is emblazoned with the symbol of the Craft, the pentacle! The poem describes Gawaine's armor and shield in detail — "He bare the pentangle on shield and surcoat as truest of heroes and gentlest of knights" — a bright red shield that has a gold pentangle (pentacle) painted on its front "for pure was he as gold". SGGK is the only story in which Gawaine uses the pentangle — in other stories he uses an eagle, lion or Gryphon. SGGK is the earliest known English text to use the word 'pentangle'.

In SGGK Gawaine's pentangle is described as being "a sign that Solomon set ere-while, as betokening truth". Each of the five points are linked and locked with the next, "and nowhere hath it beginning or end", forming what "the English call it, as I hear, the endless knot". The pentangle is a symbol that Gawaine is faultless in his five senses, never found to fail in his five fingers, "all his trust upon earth was in the five wounds that Christ bare on the cross", "he drew his strength from the five joys which the Queen of Heaven had of her Child" [i.e. the Virgin Mary had in Jesus — The Annunciation, Nativity, Resurrection, Ascension, and Assumption], and possesses brotherly love, pure mind and manners, and compassion most precious. The inside of the shield is adorned with an image of the Virgin Mary "that whenever he looked upon it he might not lack for aid".

It is also worth noting that SGGK contains many references to the Christian God and Christ. Gardner claims that the 'old God' makes an appearance as the Green Knight but his role is not that of 'a pagan God' but 'an adversary, or an accuser' with supernatural powers (like Satan — see Appendix: Witchcraft, Devil Worship and Christianity).

The romance was written somewhere between 1360 and 1400, and at its end are the words "Honi soit qui mal y pense†", which is the motto of the Order of the Garter founded in 1349. The story turns upon the possession of a girdle of green silk (The Witch Cord, or Girdle?) the love-gift of Morgan Le Fay, which the lords and ladies of King Arthur's court later adopt as the sign of their fellowship and the remembrance of the courtesy of the Green Knight and his Lady.

Editor's Note:– In SGGK Gawaine concludes the poem by saying of the girdle 'this is the bond and sign of my shame, this is the loss and the hurt that I have suffered through cowardice and covetousness. It is the token of untruth, and I must needs wear it while life shall last, for none may hide it, for when it is once fixed upon any one never will it pass from him.'

It will be remembered that the Order of the Garter was founded ostensibly as a memorial of King Arthur's Round Table by that King Edward III who gave refuge to Lady Alice Kyteler when her coven in Ireland was persecuted by the Bishop of Ossory. It is notable that Edward III later went out of his way to be as obnoxious to the said Bishop as he could. It may also be noted that when he commenced the project of founding the Order of the Garter he is said to have instructed his secretary, William of Wykeham, to make enquiries into the tradition of the Order of St George and the Garter. It is difficult to see how enquiry could have been made into the tradition of an Order which did not yet exist, so the Garter must have an earlier meaning.

Sir Gawaine and the Green Knight is an English 'Mystery Legend', and as such I recommend its study to the interested scholar."

"*The Meaning of Witchcraft*, Chapter XII, Signs and Symbols

Editor's Note:– The symbol of Order of the Garter is the blue 'garter' and the official version of the facts regarding the story is that at a Ball possibly held at Calais, Joan Countess of Salisbury dropped her garter and King Edward seeing her embarrassment picked it up and bound it about his own leg saying in French, Evil, (or shamed) be he that that thinks evil of it' — which probably refers to the leading political topic of the 1340's, Edward's claim to the throne of France.

4.2. The Descent of the Goddess (1953[†])

"The Myth of Witchcraft seems to be the story of the goddess here quoted. I am forbidden to give her name, so I will call her G.

Now G. had never loved, but she would solve all mysteries, even the mystery of Death, and so she journeyed to the nether lands. The guardians of the portals challenged her. "Strip of thy garments, lay aside thy jewels, for nought may ye bring with you into this our land." So she laid down her garments and her jewels and was bound as are all who enter the realms of Death, the mighty one.[‡]

Such was her beauty that Death himself knelt and kissed her feet, saying: "Blessed be thy feet that have brought thee in these ways. Abide with me, but let me place my cold hand on thy heart." And

[NOTES]

† Editor's Note: The text of Gardner's 'Myth of Witchcraft' was first published in *Witchcraft Today* (1954) but, according to Aidan Kelly it does not appear in Gardner's *Ye Bok of Ye Art Magical* (pre-1949). "The content of this document probably dates to 1953 or earlier..." Aidan Kelly, p. 128. *Crafting the Art of Magic*, Llewellyn, 1991.

‡ There was a Celtic custom of binding corpses; the cord with which one had been bound was of great assistance in obtaining second sight. But in the Ancient World there seems to have been a widespread idea that a living person must be bound to enter the presence of the Lords of Death. Tacitus, in *Germania xxix*, tells of sacred groves where men assemble to obtain ancestral auguries, to enter these dominions sacred to the Lords of Death. "All are bound with fetters to show that they are in the power of the Divinity, and if they chance to fall they are not helped to rise. Prone as they are, they must roll along the ground as best they may." This latter shows they were closely bound, as they could not rise themselves; so clearly it was no 'token' binding.

Lucian, in his *Vera Historia*, which, though a novel, treats of popular beliefs, tells of living people landing on the Island of the Blessed being instantly bound with chains and brought before the King of the Dead.

The idea of living people, or the newly dead, being thus bound with chains as soon as they went to the land of death may I think be the origin of the old idea that ghosts rattled chains; newly out of Limbo they would still be thus bound.

she replied. "I love thee not. Why doest thou cause all things that I love and take delight in to fade and die?" "Lady," replied Death, "'tis age and fate, against which I am helpless. Age causes all things to wither; but when men die at the end of time, I give them rest and peace and strength so that they may return. But you, you are lovely. Return not; abide with me." But she answered: "I love thee not." Then said Death: "As you receive not my hand on your heart, you must receive Death's scourge." "It is fate, better so," she said, and she knelt. Death scourged her and she cried: "I know the pangs of love." And Death said: "Blessed be," and gave her the fivefold kiss, saying: "Thus only may you attain to joy and knowledge."

And he taught her all the mysteries, and they loved and were one; and he taught her all the magics. For there are three great events in the life of man — love, death and resurrection in the new body — and magic controls them all. To fulfil love you must return again at the same time and place as the loved ones, and you must remember and love her or him again. But to be reborn you must die and be ready for a new body; to die you must be born; without love you may not be born, and this is all the magic."

This myth upon which its members base their actions is the central idea of the cult. Perhaps it was coined to explain ideas and rituals already conceived, and to explain why the wiser, older and more powerful god should give his power over magic to the goddess. It is very easy to say this is only the story of Istar descending into hell, but the point of the story is different. Again you can say it is simply Siva, the god of Death and Resurrection; but here again the story is different. It is quite possible that the stories of Istar and Siva have influenced the myth, but I think that its origin is most likely Celtic. In Celtic legends the Lords of the Underworld did prepare you for rebirth, and many living people are said to have entered their regions, formed alliances with them and returned safely, but it needed great courage; only a hero or a demigod dared to risk it. Celtic mysteries assuredly contained rituals of death and resurrection, and possibly visits to the underworld with a safe return. I think St Patrick's Purgatory in Lough Derg was a Christianized version of this legend."

Witchcraft Today, Chapter III: The Witch Beliefs. p. 36..

* * * * *

The faith of the cult is summed up in a witch's book I possess which states that they believed in gods who were not all-powerful. They wished men well, they desired fertility for man and beast and crops, but to attain this end they needed man's help. Dances and other rites gave this help. These rites were based on sympathetic magic, the idea that like attracts like, and also that "what gave pleasure to man, gave pleasure to the gods". Possibly they thought that the gods could feel man's pleasure. There was also the idea that the gods loved man and were pleased when he was happy, as opposed to the idea that god is an angry god who hates man to be happy. In this book are the following verses, but no indication of who wrote them:–

THE WITCH REMEMBERS HER LAST INCARNATION

I remember, O fire,
    How thy flames once enkindled my flesh,
Among writhing witches caught close in thy flame,
    Now tortured for having beheld what is secret.
But to those who saw what we had seen
    Yea, the fire was naught.
Ah well I remember the buildings ablaze
    With the light that our bodies had lit.
And we smiled, to behold the flames wind about us,
    The faithful, among the faithless and blind.

To the chanting of prayers
    In the frenzy of flame
We sang hosannas to Thee, our Gods,
Midst the strength-giving fire,
    Pledged our love to Thee from the Pyre.

Witchcraft Today, Chapter X: What are Witches? *p. 105.*

PART FIVE

Skull and Crossbones

At Rushen Abbey, near Castletown, some curious discoveries have been made (*vide* articles in the *Isle of Man Natural History and Antiquarian Society Proceedings*, March 1935). Mr W. Christian Cubbon writes (page 111):

> "There is another observation worthy of special mention. Its significance has not yet been explained. I refer to the device sometimes found in eighteenth century burials, namely the skull and crossbones. This was found here carried out within the grave itself in actual bone. The isolated heads were found with human thigh-bones crossed under the chins, and one at least of the skeletons had such bones under its chin; this is still to be seen at Rushen Abbey. On discussing this peculiarity it was said to have been observed in Ireland but passed over as being accidental, or having no known significance. With one was also found a bronze figure of the Egyptian god Osiris; Reginald Smith of the British Museum and Sir Arthur Keith pronounce it to be of early or pre- Roman date."[1]

The skull-and-crossbones sign is often found in old tombs and cemeteries; I believe it goes back to Roman times and is the symbol of death and resurrection. When I was made a Mason I was told the skull and crossbones represented "death" and the blazing star "resurrection". Now this star is also a pentacle. As I have said, in old times witches used a skull and crossbones to represent their god when his representative, the high priest, was not present. Nowadays the priestess assumes a position much like that of Osiris to represent the god in his death form, then opens out her arms to represent the pentacle, resurrection. The first gesture also represents a triangle formed by the head and elbows, and the second a five-pointed star (pentacle.) Both triangle and pentacle have special meanings to them. I have already told the story of the Lord of Sidon, and the skull and crossbones which became a talisman for the Templar Order. Commentators have always supposed that this story came from some spy who saw and misunderstood a ritual which actually took place. Now, although there was much "politics" in the persecution of the Templars, those in charge of the persecutions tried to make the charges plausible. As at this time most churches had skulls and bones of saints which were given divine honours, it is to be presumed that there was something different about the Templar usage. Since paying honours to a skull was common in all churches, did it here represent "Death and Resurrection"? Was it honouring the god of "Death and what lies beyond"? Are there any possible connections between these beliefs and these burials?[2]

People try to make me say that in the rites skulls and other repulsive things are used. I have never seen such things; but they tell me that in the old days sometimes, when the High priest was not present, a skull and crossbones was used to represent the god, death and resurrection (or reincarnation).

Nowadays the High Priestess stands in a position representing the skull and crossbones, or death, and moves to another position, a pentacle, representing resurrection, during the rites.[3]

1. *Witchcraft Today,* Chapter XII: Who is the Devil? p. 112.
2. *Witchcraft Today,* Chapter XII: Who is the Devil? p. 113.
3. *Witchcraft Today,* Chapter I: Living Witchcraft. p. 22.

Blood

The Grail, the Cup or Chalice, is like the Celtic Cauldron. It restored the dead, and brought fertility back to the land. The King, in the *Mabinogion,* gives Gawaine a sword which each day drops blood. There is a head and spear which drops blood in connection with a cauldron of fertility in the adventure of Peredur, vaguely said to be connected with the murder of a relation of Peredur by witches at Glaucesier. A sword or dagger dropping blood (or wine) into a cauldron would have great meaning to witches, and they have a head or skull tradition. Could the story be a hidden way of hinting that an ancestor of Peredur had gone through the circle to Death and returned, and so Peredur himself was of the Witch Blood and entitled to know the Mystery of the Cauldron? Most scholars agree that the bleeding spear is phallic.

In the *Merlin* MS., Bibliothèque Nationale 337, there is a Grail procession which passes through a wood singing: "Honour and Glory and Power and everlasting joy to the *Destroyer of Death"* Could not that be a chant in praise of the goddess? Or could it be really to disguise a chant: "Honour and Glory and Power and everlasting joy to the *destroyer of the fear of Death?"* That is, to the givers of Regeneration, *Death and what lies beyond.*[1]

The people I know are taught never to use blood or to make sacrifices; but the Irish coven seemingly use them and they are used in Voodoo. Knowing how the rites in England work, these practices would be useless in any I know, so presumably there are totally different rites of which my friends know nothing. The essence of magic is usually to raise power, then to use or control it. I can understand its being thought that killing something might release power or force, if the soul is force, but I do not understand how one would control or use it. Freshly shed blood might contain some vital power, which would exude slowly, and that blood might increase the power; but if this were the case, I should expect to hear that the municipal slaughterhouse men were setting up as magicians. When I hear of this, I will believe in the power of blood. I know the Bacchantes were said to tear live animals to pieces and eat them, but I think they were people who, not understanding the occult teachings they received, mistook drunkenness for divine ecstasy, doing mad things in their frenzy. The law then restrained these excesses and reforms were carried out in the sect. The West Africans use blood, but, again, I think they do not have the true secrets.[2]

The statement that all the systems for the disturbance of consciousness used by African negroes are derived from ancient Egypt is extremely interesting, as is the natural suggestion that they took these powers with them to America.

In ancient times there was widespread trading up the Nile, across and down to the Congo. I had always thought of the Africans going in for human sacrifices and orgies of rum, methods I believe entirely alien to the Egyptian spirit. I was told in New Orleans that it was not only negroes who attended the Voodoo festivals but that many whites went as well. It was well known there that Voodoo festivals were often held by the lakeside and bodies of police were regularly sent out to prevent them. But the police, who were mainly Irish, would search regularly several places where the festivals were not and then report back that they could find nothing. They would then go to the meeting, strip off their uniforms and join in the revelries. This indeed is a common joke in New Orleans. I noticed several resemblances between witchcraft and certain Voodoo practices. I was also told that it had been clearly proved that Voodoo was not African but was compounded in the French West Indies by French half-castes, from European magic, inverted Roman Catholicism and mixed memories of different African religions. I cannot say if this is right; but if some of these French half-castes had a witch tradition this would account for all the resemblances. For all over the world when faced with certain problems people are apt to solve them in the same way. If the knowledge now practised in West Africa is derived from ancient Egypt, there is no reason to doubt that some witch practices may have come from the same source to Europe via the Roman and Greek mysteries, which all seem to be derived from ancient Egypt. I feel that the Egyptian cults were too severe and respectable to go in for the blood practices used by Africans. I think Pythagoras, who is generally credited with bringing the mysteries to Greece, was not the sort of man who would have had anything to do with blood sacrifices or other objectionable practices. But it is conceivable that there were two sects, the worshippers of Set, as well as those of Osiris, who crept in with the plea: "There is a short cut; if you cannot work magic properly, you can gain power this way." The writings of witches speak with horror of the practice of sorcerers using blood to gain power. But the evil knowledge may have kept pace with the good and may account for some of the statements against the cult which I am still inclined to think were Christian libels or came from a misunderstanding of the rites.[3]

Many people say: "Witches use blood and all sorts of nasty things in their rites." All I can say is: "I have never seen it done, and my friends say they do not use them." Their writings forbid them to use blood or anything that can cause pain or fright, while admitting that freshly shed blood can give power, the actual words being: "Power flashes forth from newly shed blood, but the use of an animal, for instance, is hateful and cruel."

But a witch friend suggests to me that the use of blood drawn from your own body might be permitted. The late Aleister Crowley used occasionally to perform a ceremony, gashing his breast and using his blood, and it is quite possible some witches do this. All I can say is, I have no knowledge of its being done. The same witch, in answer to a suggestion by a member of the Society for Psychical Research, said:

"I doubt whether performing a series of magical experiments to observe the result for the sake of psychic research would ever work. If people had only a ha'p'orth of *practical experience* they would never make such a proposition, because in successful magical operations one of the strongest stimuli is the *emotional factor.* Before you can do any harm to your enemy by means of a wax image you must be in a genuine and spontaneous rage, as you would need to be before you knocked him down physically.

"Before you can work a love charm you must feel *genuine* and passionate desire for the object of it. These states of mind cannot be switched on and off at will to please the S.P.R. I believe the same thing may apply to astral projection. The records we have of successful projections are nearly always the result of strong and spontaneous desire. The exceptions are the cases of people in feeble health."

This is simply one witch's opinion, but I think it is very generally held. She speaks as if she knows something of how to make a wax image, but she says this is only general knowledge. Up to now I have not found anyone who knows the exact rite used. I have not the slightest doubt that some still know it, though they won't admit it. I particularly want to get it because I think it is apt to be more or less unchanged from the days when the cave man practised it, and knowledge of this might give one some idea of what a cave man thought.[4]

BLOOD SACRIFICE

The first witches I met denied ever using blood in any way — and I think they were speaking the truth according to their lights. I have already quoted them as saying that though freshly shed blood might give some extra power at a critical moment, it would be wrong or sinful to kill an animal for that purpose, and that they would not think of doing it. Indeed at that time I did not myself see how it would fit in with our system of magic. Lately, however, talking it over with someone, he pointed out to me that it was not at all necessary to kill anything; that one could draw blood from his own body and that the late Aleister Crowley, as mentioned above, occasionally performed a rite when he cut his own breast and made use of the blood. Traditionally this aids materialization in ceremonies of evocation. Of course it is well known that in the Great Mystery of Magic the magician is always the victim in a certain sense. Now the people I know have never attempted materialization; but mention of such practices does occur in the rituals, etc. So that these must have been practised in the past, and there are possibly many covens, of which I know nothing, who may use these methods today: that is, use blood to obtain certain results. Of course the old stock charge of killing unbaptized babies is ridiculous; it was only invented to scare people into having their babies baptized and *paying the fees.* It is impossible for large numbers of unbaptized babies to disappear without the police asking questions.[5]

It is an old game to spread stories about a faith you dislike, so as to frighten people from joining it. I wonder how many Romans were scared off by the story that the Christians were cannibals, who ate human flesh and drank human blood at their communion services?[6]

1. *Witchcraft Today,* Chapter VI: How the Little People became Witches . . . p. 66.
2. *Witchcraft Today,* Chapter IX: Irish Witchcraft. p. 87.
3. *Witchcraft Today,* Chapter VIII: Out of the Land of Egypt. p. 80.
4. *Witchcraft Today,* Chapter XIII: Recapitulation. p. 117.
5. *Witchcraft Today,* Chapter XIII: Recapitulation. p. 123.
6. *Meaning of Witchcraft,* Chapter XVII: The Future. p. 261.

Magic

> For there are three great events in the life of man; Love, Death, and Resurrection in a new body; and Magic controls them all. For to fulfil love you must return again at the same time and place as the loved one, and you must remember and love them again. But to be reborn you must die, and be ready for a new body; and to die you must be born; and without love you may not be born. And these be all the Magic.[1]

I must first explain why I claim to speak of things not generally known. I have been interested in magic and kindred subjects all my life, and have made a collection of magical instruments and charms. These studies led me to spiritualist and other societies, and I met some people who claimed to have known me in a past life. Here I must say that, though I believe in reincarnation, as most people do who have lived in the East, I do not remember any past lives, albeit I have had curious experiences. I only wish I did. Anyhow, I soon found myself in the circle and took the usual oaths of secrecy which bound me not to reveal any secrets of the cult. But, as it is a dying cult, I thought it was a pity that all the knowledge should be lost, so in the end I was permitted to write, as fiction, something of what a witch believes in the novel *High Magic's Aid.*[2] This present volume has the same purpose, but deals with the subject in a factual way.

Many people ask me how I can believe in magic. If I explain what I believe magic to be, I go a long way towards an answer. My view is that it is simply the use of some abnormal faculty. It is a recognized fact that such faculties exist. So-called calculating boys are famous, and very many people have the faculty under hypnotic control to calculate time most accurately. While asleep they are ordered to do something at, say, the end of a million seconds; they will know nothing of this order in their normal state, but their inner consciousness calculates it and at the end of the millionth second they obey the order without knowing why. Try to calculate a million seconds in your waking state, and say when it is up, without a watch, and you will see what I mean. The powers used are utterly unlike any mental powers we know. And exercising them is normally impossible. So, if there are some people with some abnormal powers, why should there not be other people who have other forms of abnormal powers and unusual ways of inducing them?

I am continually being asked various questions regarding the witch cult, and I can only answer: Nearly all primitive people had initiation ceremonies and some of these were initiation into priesthoods, into magic powers, secret societies and mysteries. They were usually regarded as necessary for the welfare of the tribe as well as for the individual. They usually included purification and some test of courage and fortitude — often severe and painful — terrorization, instruction in tribal lore, in sexual knowledge, in the making of charms, and in religious and magical matters generally, and often a ritual of death and resurrection.[3]

It will be seen that witchcraft is a system involving both magic and religion. This in itself is an indication of great age, because in primitive times magic and religion were closely inter-related. The priest was also the magician, and the magician had perforce to be a priest. Indeed, when one comes to consider it, many religious rites today are directed towards ends which might be called magical.[4]

I am familiar with most forms of ritual including Kabbalistic magic, and they all have certain things in common and work by calling up a spirit or intelligence and commanding it to do their will. All the members stand in a circle for protection and are warned that if they leave the circle before the spirit is dismissed they may be blasted. This is sometimes varied by working in a graveyard and attempting to raise a corpse to get information from it. There is another school which believes that all magical ceremonies should consist of an act together with a rhyming spell. That is, you must show the Powers what to do, then bind them with a rhyme.

Now if anyone in the last two hundred years had tried to make up a rite they would have used one of these methods or something resembling them. The English witches' method is entirely different. They believe the power is within themselves and exudes from their bodies. It would be dissipated were it not for the circle cast, as previously remarked, to keep the power in, and not, as magicians usually use it, to keep the spirits out. A witch can and does move freely in and out of the circle when she wishes. The only man I can think of who could have invented the rites was the late Aleister Crowley. When I met him he was most interested to hear that I was a member, and said he had been inside when he was very young, but would not say whether he had rewritten anything or not. But the witch practices are entirely different in method from any kind of magic he wrote about, and he described very many kinds. There are indeed certain expressions and certain words used which smack of Crowley; possibly he borrowed things from the cult writings, or more likely someone may have borrowed expressions from him. The only other man I can think of who could have done it is Kipling; but the cult writings are so alien to his ideas and expressions that I am sure he had nothing to do with writing them, though I fancy from some of his works that he knew something about them. There is much evidence that in its present form the rites were worked long before Kipling and Crowley were born. The people who certainly would have had the knowledge and ability to invent them were the people who formed the Order of the Golden

Dawn about seventy years ago, but knowing their aims and objects I think it is about the last thing they would have done. Hargrave Jennings might have had a hand in them, but his writings are so involved that I hardly think he could have devised anything so simple and clear-cut. Grandfathers and grandmothers have told folk still living of meetings they attended about a hundred and thirty years ago, when the cult was thought to have existed from all time. Barrat of the Magus, *circa* 1800, would have had the ability to invent or resurrect the cult. But he was mainly interested in ritual magic, which I think would have shown in the rituals. Sir Francis Dashwood, of Hell Fire Club fame, is another who might have had a hand in such a thing, but he was a freethinking diabolist and was the last man to start or invent a new religion; if he did, it would have been something on either diabolical or classical lines. Nor do I think it could have been invented when England was governed by the C.A.B.A.L. (the government of Clifford, Arlington, Buckingham, Ashley, and Lauderdale), and learned men were all Kabbalists; if they believed and worked on Kabbalistic lines they were unlikely to have invented this. It is quite possible that the main parts of the cult might have been brought over from Italy about the time of the Renaissance or even later; but if they were, it would have been as a fully developed witch cult, which was then joined on to the local covens.[5]

The foundation of magical beliefs, of which witchcraft is a form, is that unseen Powers exist, and that by performing the right sort of ritual these Powers can be contacted and either forced or persuaded to assist one in some way. People believed this in the Stone Age, and they believe it, consciously or not, today. It is now well-known that most superstition is in fact broken-down ritual.[6]

When I speak of magic I mean the magic which really exists, not what many people think of when magic is mentioned, such as waving a wand and something miraculous happening, or saying a rhyme and making signs and being forthwith rewarded by the appearance of a pantomime demon. A rhythmic form of words (a charm) is used sometimes by witches, to help to direct the power once it is raised; but the "magician" has to raise that power and know how to direct it in the first place.[7]

I define magic as attempting to cause the physically unusual. Aleister Crowley defined it as "The Science and Art of causing Change to occur in conformity with the Will." S.L. MacGregor Mathers (Frater D.D.C.F. of the Order of the Golden Dawn) defined it as "The science of the control of the secret forces of nature."[8]

Magic is in itself neither black nor white, bad nor good; it is how it is used, the intent or the knowledge behind it, that matters.[9]

The essence of magic is usually to raise power, then to use or control it. I can understand its being thought that killing something might release power or force, if the soul is force, but I do not understand how one would control or use it. Freshly shed blood might contain some vital power, which would exude slowly, and that blood might increase the power; but if this were the case, I should expect to hear that the municipal slaughterhouse men were setting up as magicians. When I hear of this, I will believe in the power of blood. I know the Bacchantes were said to tear live animals to pieces and eat them, but I think they were people who, not understanding the occult teachings they received, mistook drunkenness for divine ecstasy, doing mad things in their frenzy. The law then restrained these excesses and reforms were carried out in the sect. The West Africans use blood, but, again, I think they do not have the true secrets.[10]

I was much interested in Mr Pennethorne Hughes's theory, *vide* page 23 of his book, that magic was evolved by the Egyptian priests, that one branch of this knowledge came to Europe, becoming witchcraft, the other going to West Africa and thence to America, becoming Voodoo. I know that Frazer and others have mentioned the resemblance between the African cults of the Divine King and Egyptian myths, and I had already noted the resemblance between certain Voodoo practices and European witchcraft; but it seemed to me that the proof of Mr Hughes's theory must lie in West Africa. If the witches or witch doctors there had the knowledge, they might have passed it on to America.[11]

In ancient times probably many magicians, amongst the scholars and learned men, before and during the fall of Byzantium, came West and many may have made contact with the cult; also men who read forbidden books would be apt to come to the only places where they could meet people with free minds, the houses of the witches. Later Rosicrucians and Freemasons might have attended. They might not have known that their hosts were witches in all cases, though they would have known there were places where they might discuss things reasonably without fear of being tortured and burnt. There are resemblances to Freemasonry in certain parts of the rites which I think cannot be due to chance, so I think the one influenced the other. And it is probable that all these people may have brought some new ideas into the cult; but I think the only great changes were made in Roman times when contact was made with the mysteries, although this is all guesswork on my part. I can only judge on the evidence I can find.[12]

During the Renaissance witchcraft might have been expected to revive; but at that time, though men's minds had suddenly become freer, they had also turned to Kabbalistic types of magic, and learning had suddenly discovered many new types of poison. All this promised quick and easy effects which you could perform yourself. In England, in Elizabeth's time, there was learning and more freedom of thought; but Italian poisons arrived at the same time, and were used; also there seem to have been many outbreaks of ptomaine poisoning, due to more trade and importation of goods, and the blame was put on the witches.[13]

To recapitulate, Ritualistic Magic, Kabalistic Magic, Art Magic or Black Magic are alike attempting to evoke genii, demons or elemental spirits and forcing or bribing them to cause events to occur, the practitioner believing that such spirits have power to alter nature, to cause storms, floods or earthquakes for instance. They often use blood, skulls and other nasty things for this purpose. The witch dislikes these methods and thinks her ways are best. True, in the past there have been many cases of sorcerers employing witches; but this was as mediums when something of a spiritualistic nature was attempted, that is, trying to communicate with the spirits of departed human beings who were willing to communicate, and were neither bribed nor threatened.

The witch generally does not believe it is possible to alter nature — to cause storms, for instance; but she does believe that most important events are controlled by some human mind or minds, and that it is often possible to form a link with, and so influence, the minds of others (human or animal) by a means I can only describe as a sort of long-range hypnotism, the results depending on the amount of power raised, the skill in directing it, the sensitivity or otherwise of the brains at the other end and whether they are opposed to the idea which comes into their minds or not; and that their minds may still be so influenced, even if some strong counter-influence is exerted.

Now it is perfectly possible to influence people's minds in great numbers in order to gain your own ends. John Wesley, Gladstone and Hitler all did it on a large scale. None of them changed the minds of all the people they contacted; but the influence was sufficient to change the history of the world, and it was not done by reasoning with people. They simply put an idea into people's minds and rammed it home. All politicians do or attempt to do it. Witches use a different technique to do the same thing. They do not succeed in all their operations and it is difficult for me to assess exactly how many of their successes may have been due to chance; but they do seem to have had a remarkable number of successes. People tell me: "This is easy; either they succeed or they don't, so they have a 50 per cent chance of success", quoting: "If you toss 100 pennies in the air, about 50 per cent will come down heads." But it's not so easy as all that.

As the witch told the psychical research man: "To do magic you must work yourself into a frenzy; the more intense you feel, the more chance of success." You simply can't get the required number of people to do it just for fun, or if it's likely to come off naturally; the chances are then usually 80-90 per cent against.

Other people tell me: "If you are determined enough you can force anything through without having to resort to witchcraft," quoting: "Napoleon said 'There is no such word as *impossible* in the French language,'" but as a witch said when they told her this: "I suppose Napoleon said it in Corsican when we put it into his brain it is *impossible* to cross the English Channel."

Now I have seen things I'm forbidden to talk about, and quite admittedly I'm superstitious because of what I have seen of witches' powers. Also it is easy to see where this superstition could lead to and I know I'm going to be laughed at. I can take it.

As I have said before, an anthropologist's job is to investigate what people do and what they believe, not what moralists say they should do and believe. They may draw their own conclusions and give out any theory, provided they state clearly that these are their own theories, and not proven facts.[14]

1. *Meaning of Witchcraft*, Appendix I: The Magical Legends of the Witches. p. 263.
2. Published by Michael Houghton, 49 Museum Street, London, W.C.1.
3. *Witchcraft Today*, Chapter I: Living Witchcraft. p. 16.
4. *Meaning of Witchcraft*, Chapter I: The Witch Cult in Britain. p. 18.
5. *Witchcraft Today*, Chapter IV: Witch Practices. p. 39.
6. *Meaning of Witchcraft*, Chapter I: The Witch Cult in Britain. p. 20.
7. *Meaning of Witchcraft*, Chapter III: The Stone Age Origins of Witchcraft. p. 44.
8. *Meaning of Witchcraft*, Chapter VII: Magic Thinking. p. 95.
9. *Meaning of Witchcraft*, Chapter II: Witches' Memories and Beliefs. p. 22.
10. *Witchcraft Today*, Chapter IX: Irish Witchcraft. p. 87.
11. *Witchcraft Today*, Chapter XIII: Recapitulation. p. 130.
12. *Witchcraft Today*, Chapter X: What are Witches? p. 97.
13. *Witchcraft Today*, Chapter XI: Some other Matters. p. 108.
14. *Witchcraft Today*, Chapter XIII: Recapitulation. p. 131.

Numerology

The cult seems to use a crude numerology — whence obtained I do not know. The numbers 3, 5, 8, 13 and 40 are thought good or lucky and all these numbers have significance attached to them. There are three working tools which are essential and nothing can be done without them; that is, something to cut and stab with, something to strike with and something to bind with. There are five others, all of which have their special uses and are only needed if that particular kind of work is being done. For an initiation all eight must be present and the initiate is told the use of, and holds, each in turn. Because three and five make eight, many things must be in eights; but eight and five make thirteen, so thirteen is another good number; but since five eights, or three covens and a leader, make forty, forty is a good number and certain things must be forty. The coven traditionally consists of twelve witches and a leader, probably because it is a lucky number and because there are thirteen moons in a year.[1]

The scourgings are 3, 7, 9 (thrice three), and 21 (thrice seven) 40 in all. It is not meet to make offerings [scourgings] of less than two score to the Goddess, for here be a mystery. The fortunate numbers be: 3 and 5. For three added to two (the Perfect Couple) be five. And three and five be eight; eight and five be thirteen; thirteen and eight be twenty-one. The Fivefold Kiss is called 5, but there are 8 kisses, for there be 2 feet and 2 knees and genitals and 2 breasts and the lips. And 5 times 8 be two score. Also, fortunate numbers be 3, 7, 8, and 21, which total 40, or two score. For each man and woman hath ten fingers and ten toes, so each totals a score. And a perfect couple be two score. So a lesser number would not be perfect prayer. If more are required make it a perfect number, as four score or six score. Also there be Eight Elemental Weapons.[2]

[3]

- [Three Degrees]
- [Triple Circle]
- [Triple Goddess]
- Nowadays the priestess assumes a position much like that of Osiris to represent the god in his death form, then opens out her arms to represent the pentacle, resurrection. The first gesture also represents a *triangle* formed by the head and elbows, and the second a five-pointed star (pentacle.) Both triangle and pentacle have special meanings to them.[3]
- There are three great events in the life of man; Love, Death, and Resurrection in a new body.[4]

"Learn, in Witchcraft, thou must ever return triple. As I scourged thee, so thou must scourge me, but triple, where I gave thee three strokes, give nine, where seven, give twenty-one, where nine, give twenty-seven, where twenty-one, give sixty-three.[5]

5

- Nowadays the priestess assumes a position much like that of Osiris to represent the god in his death form, then opens out her arms to represent the *pentacle,* resurrection. The first gesture also represents a triangle formed by the head and elbows, and the second a *five*-pointed star (pentacle.) Both triangle and *pentacle* have special meanings to them.[6]
- [Fivefold Kiss]
- [Five Essentials]
- [Scourge has eight tails, each tail has five knots]

[8]

- [Eight Ritual Occasions — 4 Sabbats & 4 Esbats]
- [Eight Paths]
- [Scourge has eight tails]

13

- There are thirteen moons in a year and thirteen weeks in every quarter, each quarter of the year having its Sabbat.[7]

  In Italy witches are said to say "six and seven" as a password, because it would be dangerous to say thirteen; these numbers of course add up to thirteen. In England I could understand their saying five and eight for the same reason, but actually they mostly know each other in the coven and so do not need passwords.[8]

40

Magus: "I prepare thee to take the great oath."

He strikes three knells on the bell, and again gives the series of three, seven, nine, and 21 strokes with the scourge as before.[9]

1. *Witchcraft Today,* Chapter X: What are Witches? p. 98.
2. 2.3. The Scourge and the Kiss.
3. *Witchcraft Today,* Chapter XII: Who is the Devil? p. 113.
4. *Meaning of Witchcraft,* Appendix I: The Magical legend of the Witches p. 263.
5. *High Magic's Aid,* Chapter XVII: The Witch Cult. p. 188
6. *Witchcraft Today,* Chapter XII: Who is the Devil? p. 113.
7. *Meaning of Witchcraft,* Chapter I: The Witch Cult in Britain. p. 16.
8. *Witchcraft Today,* Chapter X: What are Witches? p. 99.
9. 1.4.2a Second Degree

Charms

In Palestine and other countries there are two kinds of witches: the ignorant herbalist and charm-seller, and the witch who is a descendant of a line of priests and priestesses of an old and probably Stone Age religion, who have been initiated in a certain way (received into the circle) and become the recipients of certain ancient learning.[1]

The popular notion of a witch became that of the common definition: "a witch is an old woman who flies through the air on a broomstick". Now no witch ever flew through the air on a broomstick or on anything else, at least not until aeroplanes came in. There is indeed a fertility charm to bring good crops which is performed by riding on a pole, or broom, as a hobbyhorse.[2]

CAN WITCHES MAKE LOVE CHARMS?

Witches have many formulae for making all sorts of charms, though few use them nowadays; when stripped of their superstitious practices they chiefly amount to forcing one's will into an object with the aim of influencing the waverer's mind: "Be brave, nothing can harm you, the object of your affection will love you" type of thing. Coupled with this, however, are instructions as to its use, and if you can carry them out I have little doubt that the charm would have some effect. For instance, a charm to make a young couple love each other ends with: "Try to ensure that the pair are thrown together alone, in exciting and if possible dangerous circumstances (or let them think they are dangerous). Soon they will begin to rely on each other; then let them know that a love charm has been made. If they be of the cult, make them perform the rites together and the charm will soon act." If I were only a quarter of my age, I wish that someone would try that charm on me![3]

In successful magical operations one of the strongest stimuli is the *emotional factor.* Before you can do any harm to your enemy by means of a wax image you must be in a genuine and spontaneous rage, as you would need to be before you knocked him down physically.

"Before you can work a love charm you must feel *genuine* and passionate desire for the object of it. These states of mind cannot be switched on and off at will to please the S.P.R. I believe the same thing may apply to astral projection. The records we have of successful projections are nearly always the result of strong and spontaneous desire. The exceptions are the cases of people in feeble health."

This is simply one witch's opinion, but I think it is very generally held. She speaks as if she knows something of how to make a wax image, but she says this is only general knowledge. Up to now I have not found anyone who knows the exact rite used. I have not the slightest doubt that some still know it, though they won't admit it. I particularly want to get it because I think it is apt to be more or less unchanged from the days when the cave man practised it, and knowledge of this might give one some idea of what a cave man thought.[4]

When I speak of magic I mean the magic which really exists, not what many people think of when magic is mentioned, such as waving a wand and something miraculous happening, or saying a rhyme and making signs and being forthwith rewarded by the appearance of a pantomime demon. A rhythmic form of words (a charm) is used sometimes by witches, to help to direct the power once it is raised; but the "magician" has to raise that power and know how to direct it in the first place.[5]

1. *Witchcraft Today,* Chapter II: There have been witches in all ages. p. 28.
2. *Witchcraft Today,* Chapter II: There have been witches in all ages. p. 29.
3. *Witchcraft Today,* Chapter XIII: Recapitulation. p. 124.
4. *Witchcraft Today,* Chapter XIII: Recapitulation. p. 117.
5. *Meaning of Witchcraft,* Chapter III: The Stone Age Origins of Witchcraft. p. 44.

Herbs

The Wica, the "wise people", who practise the age-old rites and who have, along with much superstition and herbal knowledge, preserved an occult teaching and working processes which they themselves think to be magic or witchcraft. They are the type of people who were burned alive for possessing this knowledge, often giving their lives to turn suspicion away from others.[1]

From an early date recruits were admitted only from people who were of the blood; that is, from a witch family. The various rituals of worship, secrets of herbal lore, and the Great Secret of what they call magic, have been handed down to what has become more or less a family secret society.[2]

Let the Craft keep books with the names of all Herbs which are good for man, and all cures, that all may learn. But keep another book with all the Banes & Apies. & let only the Elders and trustworthy people have this knowledge. So it be Ardane.[3]

I am told that in the olden days witches had knowledge of a herb called Kat which, when mixed with incense, would release the inner eye, the subconscious, but unless another herb, Sumach, was mixed with it, it could not be used for long as it would produce hallucinations. If you used both correctly, it was possible to leave the body. Unfortunately they do not know what these herbs were; but both are said to grow in England. It is said that if breathes incense with Kat in it, then woman becomes more beautiful, so it is possible that it contained wild hemp. Sorcerers used something for the same purpose and their mixture contained hemp and many other ingredients to tone it down. Many primitive races use drugs to obtain elevation of the spirits, Coca in South America, Peyotil in Mexico and many other substances. They have a varying effect on the nervous system, bringing about what might be the opening of the inner eye or perhaps hallucinations. Alcohol has the effect of increasing precognition, as the Society for Psychical Research records prove.[4]

Incense is best if you can get it, but coals in a chafing dish burning sweet-smelling herbs will do.[5]

1. *Witchcraft Today,* Chapter X: What are Witches. p. 88.
2. *Witchcraft Today,* Chapter II: There have been Witches in all Ages p. 28
3. 3.1 The Old Laws
4. *Witchcraft Today,* Chapter X: What are Witches? p. 95.
5. 2.13. The Working Tools

APPENDIX

UNITED NATIONS:

Universal Declaration of Human Rights:

Adopted and proclaimed by General Assembly resolution 217 A (III) of 10 December 1948

ARTICLE 7.

All are equal before the law and are entitled without any discrimination to equal protection of the law. All are entitled to equal protection against any discrimination in violation of this Declaration and against any incitement to such discrimination.

ARTICLE 18.

Everyone has the right to freedom of thought, conscience and religion; this right includes freedom to change his religion or belief, and freedom, either alone or in community with others and in public or private, to manifest his religion or belief in teaching, practice, worship and observance.

Witchcraft, Devil Worship and Christianity

> Witches have no books on theology, so it is difficult for me to discover all they actually believe. With all the thousands of books there are on Christianity I find it difficult to define Christian beliefs. Transubstantiation, for instance. On the other hand, it is easy to give the central idea or myth, which I believe is defined as being a story which affects people's actions. Strictly speaking, in this sense the Myth of Christianity lies in the Crucifixion and Resurrection, and few Christians differ about this.
>
> The Myth of Witchcraft seems to be the story of the goddess. (*see* 4.2. *The Descent of the Goddess*). The cult god is thought of as the god of the next world, or of death and resurrection, or of reincarnation, the comforter, the consoler. After life you go gladly to his realms for rest and refreshment, becoming young and strong, waiting for the time to be reborn on earth again, and you pray to him to send back the spirits of your beloved dead to rejoice with you at your festivals. That they believe something of this sort is clear from the myth of the goddess which forms the central part of one of their rituals. It is a sort of primitive Spiritualism.
>
> *Witchcraft Today,* Chapter III: The Witch Beliefs. p. 34.

In 1921, Dr Margaret Alice Murray published her book, *The Witch Cult in Western Europe;* it was followed by *The God of the Witches.* In these books, Dr Murray stated that witchcraft was the remains of the ancient pagan religions of Europe, and she identified the Horned God of the witches as being the oldest representation of a deity known to man, and identical with the deity depicted in the Palaeolithic cave paintings. Her books were attacked by the Revd Father Montague Summers as being a revival of the heresy of Girolamo Tartarotti.[1]

It must be understood clearly that witchcraft is a religion. Its patron god is the Horned God of hunting, death and magic, who, rather like Osiris of Egypt, rules over the After-World, his own Paradise, situated in a hollow hill, or at least in a place which is only approached through a cave, where he welcomes the dead and assigns them their places; where they are prepared, according to their merits and wisdom, for rebirth into a new body on this earth, for which they will be made ready by the love and power of the Goddess, the Great Mother, who is also the Eternal Virgin and the Primordial Enchantress, who gives rebirth and transmutation, and love on this earth, and in whose honour and by means of ritual the necessary power is raised to enable this to be done. They think that the God and the Goddess assist them in making their magic, as they assist the God and the Goddess in their turn by raising power for them by their dances and by other methods. In fact, they seem to consider the gods as being more like powerful friends than deities to be worshipped. To them the concept of an All-Powerful God, one who could simply say, "Let there be peace. Let there be no sickness or misery", and all wars, sickness and misery would cease, and who for his own reasons will not say that word, and keeps men in fear and misery and want, is not fit to receive worship. They quite realise that there must be some great "Prime Mover", some Supreme Deity; but they think that if It gives them no means of knowing It, it is because It does not want to be known; also, possibly, at our present stage of evolution we are incapable of understanding It. So It has appointed what might be called various Under-Gods, who manifest as the tribal gods of different peoples; as the Elohim of the Jews, for instance, who made them in Their own image ("Elohim" being a plural noun), "male and female made They them"; Isis, Osiris and Horus of the Egyptians; the "portmanteau-word" of certain initiates, "Maben", which is MA, AB, BEN, or "Mother, Father and Son"; and the Horned God and the Goddess of the witches. They can see no reason why each people should not worship their national gods, or why anyone should strive to prevent them from doing so. This has always caused them to take a poor view of missionary enterprise, whether by the orthodox Church or by totalitarians such as the Communists. They think that many of the troubles in this world are caused by those various organisations which are formed "to make people do and believe what they don't want to, and to prevent them from doing and believing what they do want to."[2]

Heaven and Hell — Good -v- Evil

What did paganism teach about the origin of evil? This, of course, depends upon what one means by "paganism". The only kinds of paganism with which we are concerned here are those which may have had some influence upon the witch cult. Druidism, the religion of the Celts, had no doctrine of an evil deity opposed to the God of Good. There is no evidence that the religion of the Great Mother Goddess or the old Hunting God had any conception of a supernatural author of all evil. And what of the Mystery Cults of the ancient world; have we any way of ascertaining what the Mysteries taught about the origin of evil?

Fortunately we have. In the 4th Century A.D., when paganism was engaged in a fierce struggle with the new creed of Christianity, Sallustius, who was a close personal friend of the Emperor Julian (called the Apostate because he tried to restore the old religion), wrote a treatise called *Peri Theon kai Kosmou, About the Gods and the World.* It is probable that this treatise was a kind of manifesto of the highest type of paganism prevailing at that time, and it is evident that its author was an initiate of the Mysteries.[3]

Now, the thing that will, I think, strike most the consciousness of the reader who is well versed in the teaching of the higher types of spiritualist and occult circles generally is not the antiquity of this teaching of Sallustius, but its startling modernity. It might have been spoken yesterday. Further, it might have been spoken at a witch meeting, at any time, as a general statement of their creed; and it will be seen that there is no room in it for any *'worship of the Evil Principle'*. Of course, not all of Sallustius' teaching stands up so well to the passing of time; for instance, he had the idea that the earth was the centre of the Cosmos; but the spirit of his teaching, the spirit of the Mysteries of his day, which is also the spirit of the beliefs of the witch cult, is timeless.[4]

Much has been made in recent years by such writers as Hugh Ross Williamson and H.T.F. Rhodes of the concept of "Dualism", meaning that idea which divides the Universe between a good God and an evil God, or "Satan", between whom eternal war is waged. Valuable as the researches of both these authors are, I must beg to differ from them upon some important points. They hold the idea that this Dualism is an important factor in the development of the witch cult, and with this I cannot agree, because both have the orthodox conception that Satan was the deity the witches worshipped, and from what I know this is not so. The people who ascribe powers to Satan which are almost the equal of those of God are Christians, whether orthodox or unorthodox. The paganism from which the witch cult is descended did not do so.[5]

> *Editor's Note: Gardner also asserts that within the Craft there is no room for any 'worship of the Evil Principle' (i.e. Dualism between a good God and an evil God, or "Satan") — although Christians believe that evil-doers will be punished after death, they neither 'worship' the 'evil principle' nor ascribe powers to Satan almost equal to God's.*
>
> *It must be remembered that Satan is a Hebrew name which signifies an adversary, or an accuser whereas 'the Devil' is a name commonly given to the fallen angels, who are also known as demons — Lucifer is often denoted as the chief of the fallen angels, as in Matthew 25:41, "the Devil and his angels".*

A Christian Witch?

It is usually said that to be made a witch one must abjure Christianity; this is not true; but they would naturally not receive into their ranks anyone who was a very narrow Christian. They do not think that the real Jesus was literally the Son of God, but are quite prepared to accept that he was one of the Enlightened Ones, or Holy Men. That is the reason why witches do not think they were hypocrites "in time of persecution" for going to church and honouring Christ, especially as so many of the old Sun-hero myths have been incorporated into Christianity; while others might bow to the Madonna, who is closely akin to their goddess of heaven. [6]

> *Editor's Note: The far-reaching respect for other faiths made in the statement that the Supreme Diety appoints "Under-Gods, who manifest as the tribal gods of different peoples" is short-lived with the declaration that Witches do not think that Jesus was the Son of God but just a 'holy*

man'. However, having reduced Jesus to a mere mortal Gardner inflates Satan's role within Christianity by mistakenly claiming that Satan's powers are almost equal to God's. It should be noted that throughout Gardner's texts Satan's 'existence' is not questioned — that is not to say that Gardner 'believed in' or 'worshipped' Satan but that he simply does not question Satan's status as he has done with Jesus.

Regarding Christianity Gardner also states:–

I can see no real reason why one cannot be a good enough though unorthodox Christian and a witch at the same time.[7]

Exactly what the present-day witch believes I find it hard to say. I know one who goes to church at times, though she is, at best, only an occasional conformist. She firmly believes in reincarnation, as many Christians do. How she or they reconcile it with the Church's teaching I do not know.[8]

Editor's Note: Gardner's statements regarding Jesus, Satan and the worship of 'the evil principle' would be much harder to reconcile for Christians than issues of reincarnation.

Gardner's approach to Christianity is at best confused. His assertions shroud a much deeper contradiction and confusion. Given his prior assertions regarding 'evil' and Satan one might assume this would extend to the Christian 'Hell'. Gardner is quite explicit:–

The Horned God had another function besides being the provider of food. He was also the dealer of death. It was after his magical dance that the great stag was brought low. One day, the hunter knew he too must leave this world by the gate of death. I do not think that primitive people were as afraid of death as many people are today. Living closer to nature, their psychic powers were more active, and they were used to the idea of communicating with their dead relatives and friends. They looked upon it as quite a natural thing. Hence the witches, among whom this ancient creed is still preserved in a fragmentary form, do not regard the Horned God in his form as Lord of the Gates of Death as a terrifying being, nor have they any conception of a burning "Hell" such as some Christians envisage. Their idea of the After-Life is rather that of a place of rest and refreshment, where people await their turn to be born again on this earth. This, of course, is the concept of reincarnation, which is widely held among primitive people of all kinds. To them, the most logical place for the souls of new-born babies to have come from is the Land of the Dead, where there are plenty of souls awaiting another body. Hence the Lord of the Gates of Death is also the phallic deity of fertility, the Opener of the Door of Life. This is the reason why the witches' god was incorporated into the Roman pantheon as Janus, the two-faced god who was Guardian of the Gates. He and his consort Diana are two of the oldest deities of Western Europe, and Diana is named in the Canon Episcopi of the early tenth century as being the goddess of the witches.[9]

Editor's Note: The passage "nor have they any conception of a burning 'Hell' such as some Christians envisage" is absolutely clear and straightforward but herein arises the greatest confusion of all. The 'Book of Shadows' contains a number of references to 'Hell' and yet, according to Gardner, there is no concept within the Craft of a burning 'Hell'.

First of all, it must be noted that it is now widely accepted that the majority of the 'Book of Shadows' was written by Gardner who drew inspiration (and copied passages) from Masonic Rituals, Aradia: The Gospel of the Witches of Tuscany by C G Leland and various other writings of Crowley, Blake, Yeats, and Kipling. However, there are parts of 'The Book of Shadows' which may be older and one such section is the 'Old Laws'. In this foundational document, contained within a most important passage relating to the breaking of oaths, there is mention of the 'Hell of the Christians' :–

So it be Ardane that no one may tell any not of the Craft who be of the Wica, nor give any names, or where they byde, or in any way tell anything which can betray any to our foes. Nor may they tell where the Covenstead be, or where is the Covendom, or where be the meetings, or that there have been meetings. And if any break these laws, even under torture, the Curse of the Goddess shall be upon them, so they never be reborn on earth, and may remain where they belong, in the Hell of the Christians.[10]

Editor's Note: This passage threatens that those who break their oaths or betray the Craft will be punished, i.e. that they will be condemned by the Goddess to the Christian Hell. There is no possible confusion here, this is explicit, the 'Christian Hell' — not the Scandinavian 'Hel' or the Greek Hades — the "'burning Hell' such as some Christians envisage". Clearly, for this threat to be effective it must be underpinned by a sincere belief in the existence of the Christian Hell by those who take the Oaths, otherwise the threat is simply meaningless.

Therefore, having no punishment zone of its own, the Craft apparently borrows 'Hell' from the Christians and this totally controverts Gardner's assertion that they have no "conception of a burning 'Hell' such as some Christians envisage". Furthermore, as befits the everlasting Christian Hell the curse of the Goddess is also eternal (i.e. the evil-doer will never be reborn again). There is no doubt that there will be those in the Craft, like many Christians also, who admit the existence of Hell but deny the eternity of its punishment.

One possible explanation for this 'curse' may be that in the past it was assumed that if members of the Craft were to break their oaths then they would be converting (or reverting) to Christianity but this matter is further complicated by a number of other references to 'Heaven and Hell' contained within the 'Book of Shadows':–

Hell's dark mistress, Heaven's Queen. (1.1.b A Revision of the Casting Procedure)

Queen of Heaven, Queen of Hell (2.1.b The Witches' Chant or Rune)

Hell's dark mistress, Heaven's Queen. (3.2. The Verse Charge)

Editor's Note: These references serve to reinforce 'The Old Law' concept of (and belief in) a Christian Heaven and Hell and undermines the concept of the 'Land of the Dead' as the only place of 'afterlife'. It is also interesting to note that it is the Goddess who is associated with the Christian Hell. Gardner states that the God is thought of as :–

"the god of the next world, or of death and resurrection, or of reincarnation, the comforter, the consoler. After-Life you go gladly to his realms for rest and refreshment, becoming young and strong, waiting for the time to be reborn on earth again, and you pray to him to send back the spirits of your beloved dead to rejoice with you at your festivals."

Editor's Note: The God is the Lord of the gates to both enter (death) and leave (Life) the 'After-Life'. In Witchcraft Today, p.162 (similarly on p.173) *Gardner further describes the God :–*

"Thou art the Opener of the Doorway of the Womb; and yet, because all things that are born must also die, that they may be renewed, therefore art thou Lord of the Gates of Death."

The term "Opener of the Doorway of the Womb" is an unusual term and is not found in either The Book of Shadows, The Meaning of Witchcraft *or* High Magic's Aid. *The Gardnerian term implies the male/female union and creation of life as "the phallic deity of fertility, the Opener of the Door of Life" whereas the biblical term 'opener of the womb' (peter rechem), introduced in Exodus 13:2 as a synonym for 'firstborn', places the emphasis on the child itself.*

In contrast, the Goddess is known as the "Queen of Heaven, Queen of Hell" or simply the "Goddess of Heaven" and she is associated with the realm of the living. As the Old Laws state that 'Hell' is the 'Hell of the Christians' it can be reasonably assumed that the 'Heaven' referred to is the Christian Heaven!

Therefore, Gardner propounds three possible places of after-life;

1) the realm of the God, where you go gladly for rest and refreshment, becoming young and strong, waiting for the time to be reborn on earth again — the 'After-Life'.

2) the Christian Hell for those cursed by 'the Goddess' and who shall never be reborn on earth again and

3) the Christian 'Heaven' where the role of the Goddess is unexplained.

Gardner wrote " . . . the belief in many different heavens, each with their different god, is not unusual."

This apparent confusion and overlap may well be a route for 'Christian Witches' to reconcile the two beliefs, i.e. the inherent dualism in the Goddess through her association with the 'Christian Heaven and Hell'. However, the matter does not end there for there is a further and perhaps more significant link for the Christian Witch which positions the Christian God (or Christ) as the supreme deity over the God and Goddess of the Witches.

In Witch Blood! The Diary of a Witch High Priestess *Patricia Crowther describes how she was initiated into the craft by Gerald Gardner. Bound and kneeling in the circle the High Priest recited the following Blessing Prayer.*

> In the name of Dryghtyn, the ancient providence, which was from the beginning, and is for eternity, male and female, the original source of all things; all-knowing, all-pervading, all-powerful; changeless, eternal.
>
> In the name of the Lady of the Moon and the Lord of Death and Resurrection; in the name of the Mighty Ones of the Four Quarters, the Kings of the Elements, bless this place, and this time, and they who are with us.

According to Gardner there is a "Prime Mover" or Supreme Deity who appoints Under-Gods who manifest as the tribal gods of different peoples — the description of Dryghtyn can be no other than that of Gardner's Supreme Deity.

Dryghtyn is listed by The Oxford English Dictionary *as an obscure form of Drightin (or Drighten) with a specific meaning — The Lord God or Christ. [See 4.1. The Dryghtyn (Blessing) Prayer.] The earliest known use of the word Dryghtyn is found in the story of* Sir Gawaine and the Green Knight. *The symbol on Gawaine's shield is noteworthy as it is the pentangle (pentacle), the principal symbol of the Craft. The description of the pentangle provided therein may yet provide further overlap for the Christian Witch — for Sir Gawaine was known as a knight both good and true and faithful in five and many times five. Gawaine's pentangle is described as "a sign that Solomon set ere-while, as betokening truth". Each of the five points are linked and locked with the next, "and nowhere hath it beginning or end", forming "the endless knot". The pentangle is a symbol that Gawaine is faultless in his five senses, never found to fail in his five fingers, that "all his trust upon earth was in the five wounds that Christ bare on the cross", that "he drew his strength from the five joys which the Queen of Heaven had of her Child" [i.e. the Virgin Mary had in Jesus — The Annunciation, Nativity, Resurrection, Ascension, and Assumption], and the five virtues frankness and fellowship, purity of mind, courtesy, and compassion most precious.*

Black Mass

The Grimoires have been often described as books of Satanism, and consequently people who have never seen one have been led to believe that these books enjoin the worship of Satan; nothing could be further from the truth, as the most cursory examination of them will reveal. . . . The theology of the grimoires is of the most orthodox. God and His angels, Christ and the saints, reign above; the devil and his angels reign below. The former are *invoked,* that is prayed to attend; the latter are *evoked,* that is forced to appear, by the power of the former.[11]

The Black Mass was — and I hope I am right in speaking of it in the past tense — a Mass which was performed by an ordained *priest,* with various magical ceremonies added, in order to use, or rather pervert, the power of the Eucharist to some magical end.[12]

It is often thought that the performance of the Black Mass is part of the tradition of witchcraft; but to use the late Dr Joad's words, "it all depends on what you mean" by the Black Mass. I understand it to be a blasphemous parody of the Catholic Mass. I have neither seen nor heard of this in connection with the cult and I do not believe it ever existed as one of their rites.

Rites are performed for certain purposes. These take time, but when they are finished the assembly have a little meal, then dance and enjoy themselves. They have no time or inclination for indulging in blasphemy.[13]

There are no crucifixes, inverted or otherwise, no sermons, mock or otherwise, and no absolution or hosts save for the cake and wine mentioned. Incense is used, but this has a practical purpose. There is no praise or homage to the Devil, no liturgy, evil or otherwise, nothing is said backwards, and there are no gestures with the left hand; in fact with the exception that it is a religious service and all religious services resemble one another, the rites are not in any way an imitation of anything I have ever seen. I do not say there have never been diabolists. I only say that, as far as I know, witches do not do the things of which they have been accused, and knowing what I do of their religion and practices I do not think they ever did.[14]

Mr Hughes in his most scholarly book on witchcraft[15] says that the witch cult conducted a Black Mass where Christian practices were ridiculed and the Devil received homage and praise. Again, let me assure him that though I have been to many sabbats I have seen nothing resembling the practices he accuses us of, unless he is thinking of the ceremony of the "cakes and wine" which may be an imitation of the ancient Christian *Agape,* the love feast, though I think it is much older.[16]

There is no suggestion that the cakes turn into flesh and blood[17] and in no way resemble those of the Roman Catholic or any other Church that I know.[18] The ceremony is simply intended as a short repast, though it is definitely religious.[19]

I do not say that the Black Mass has never been celebrated, but I do say that it is not done by witches, to the best of my knowledge.[20]

Has anyone ever heard of people wasting time in troubling themselves to go through a parody of a Buddhist or Mohammedan rite? Another thing I have always understood is that to perform a Black Mass you needed a Catholic priest who would perform a valid transubstantiation: God so present in the Host would then be desecrated. Unless it were a valid communion there could be no desecration. I should be surprised to find a Catholic priest among witches nowadays, though in the past many are said to have been members of the cult.[21]

I believe, however, that sometimes the Black Mass is performed. Once I doubted it; but in February, 1952, I was in Rome and was told that some unfrocked priests and nuns celebrated it at times. My informants said they could arrange for me to see it done properly by these unfrocked priests and nuns, but that it would cost me about £20; I had not enough foreign exchange or else I would have gone, so as to settle the question to my own satisfaction. I think it was probably a show put on for the tourists, though I was assured by responsible people that it was not.

In short, I believe that people may perform Black Masses at times for a thrill, or with evil intent; but I do not believe that these people are witches, or know anything about witchcraft. Incidentally, I met more than one witch in Rome, though witches have to keep underground, and they knew nothing of this Black Mass.[22]

One of the first questions I had asked witches as soon as I had got "inside" was. "What about the Black Mass?" They all said, "We don't know how to perform it, and if we did, what would be the point of doing so?" They also said, "You know what happens at our meetings. There is the little religious ceremony, the greeting of the Old Gods; then any business which has to be talked over, or perhaps someone wants to do a rite for some purpose; next there is a little feast and a dance; then you have to hurry for the last bus home! There is no time or place for any nonsense of "Black Masses," and anyhow why should we want to do one?"[23]

Devil Worship

Now the god is represented by the high priest (if there is one) and it is he who was called the Devil in the old days. I was very curious about him and asked at once when I was "inside", by which they mean a member of the cult: "Who and what is called the Devil?" Though members of the cult never use and, indeed, dislike the term, they knew what I meant and said: "You know him, the leader. He is the high priest, the high priestess's husband."

This, though true, was not the exact answer. It really should be: "He is whoever the high priestess appoints to take this position." In practice, she always appoints her husband if he has sufficient rank; but she may appoint anyone who is eligible, including herself; she belts on a sword and acts as a man. In the old days it was often a distinguished visitor who was appointed.

In the times when the People of the Heaths held their meetings the high priest was a man of great learning in the cult, probably a tribal chief, or possibly a Druid, and most likely everyone would know who he was. He was the horned god, received divine honours and possibly took precedence of the high priestess; but when the people of the mixed races became strong in the cult, I think there came a time when the masked (unknown) man took his place, and he was most likely a Norman manorial lord or local churchman who protected the cult in secret. It is very likely that it might be agreed that at one meeting the masked unknown (whom I shall for convenience call the Devil) took the place and, at the next, the old known tribal chief took it. It seems likely that this depended on local arrangements. It was soon found that the uninitiated congregation of farmers, fishermen and suchlike had such awe of the great unknown that the cult became more powerful, and that then, even when the old tribal chief played the part, he too was masked and unknown. The Church called him the "devil" and he became known as such.

"If this mysterious man turned up," I asked, "how would you recognize him?" and I found that they had joked about this. They wouldn't know if he were genuine or not! It had never happened to their knowledge; but there was always the possibility of someone from another coven turning up and claiming this right. Actually, the high priestess said: "I'd talk to him and if I found he really had great knowledge and I liked him and found him interesting, I'd treat him as a distinguished visitor and appoint him for the day. Another high priestess might think otherwise." She went on to say: "I wish one of the old sort, a great protector, would turn up, who had a great big house and grounds to lend us for meetings. If he really were of us, I wouldn't bother too much about his vast learning; I'd appoint him and teach him the job." So here's a chance for anyone who wants to play the Devil!

I trust I have made myself clear. The Devil is, or rather was, an invention of the Church. Witches found that the popular view that Satan was one of them added to their power, and rather adopted it, though they never called him by that name except, perhaps, on the rack; and even then, as Dr Murray has pointed out, sometimes a confession made under torture would name him as their god, but a transcript produced in court would substitute the word DEVIL. Now you cannot blame the poor witch for this. The tortures witches suffered would make anyone confess anything. I have heard that some great man at the time said: "If they did that to me they could make me confess that I'd murdered God the Father and the Son and the Holy Ghost and the Virgin."[24]

The Old Horned God of the witches is *not* the Satan of Christianity, and no amount of theological argument will make him so. He is, in fact, the oldest deity known to man, and is depicted in the oldest representation of a divinity which has yet been found, namely the Stone Age painting in the innermost recess of the Caverne des Trois Freres at Ariege. He is the old phallic god of fertility who has come forth from the morning of the world, and who was already of immeasurable antiquity before Egypt and Babylon, let alone before the Christian era.[25]

1. *Meaning of Witchcraft*, Appendix III: Significant Dates. p. 275.
2. *Meaning of Witchcraft*, Chapter II: Witches' Memories And Beliefs. p. 25.
3. *Meaning of Witchcraft*, Chapter XIII: The Black Mass. p. 182.
4. *Meaning of Witchcraft*, Chapter XIII: The Black Mass. p. 186
5. *Meaning of Witchcraft*, Chapter XIII: The Black Mass. p. 182.
6. *Meaning of Witchcraft*, Chapter II: Witches' Memories and Beliefs. p. 26.
7. *Witchcraft Today*, Chapter X: What are Witches? p. 103.
8. *Witchcraft Today*, Chapter III: The Witch Beliefs. p. 34.
9. *Meaning of Witchcraft*, Chapter III: The Stone Age origins of Witchcraft. p. 43.
10. 3.1 The Old Laws
11. *Meaning of Witchcraft*, Chapter: XIII: The Black Mass. p. 181.
12. *Meaning of Witchcraft*, Chapter: XIII: The Black Mass. p. 190.
13. *Witchcraft Today*, Chapter I. Living Witchcraft. p. 23
14. *Witchcraft Today*, Chapter I: Living Witchcraft. p. 19.
15. *Witchcraft Today*, Chapter I: Living Witchcraft. p. 15.
16. *Witchcraft Today*, Chapter X: What are Witches? p. 95.
17. *Witchcraft Today*, Chapter I: Living Witchcraft. p. 19.
18. *Witchcraft Today*, Chapter I: Living Witchcraft. p. 19.
19. *Witchcraft Today*, Chapter I: Living Witchcraft. p. 19.
20. *Witchcraft Today*, Chapter X: What are Witches? p. 95.
21. *Witchcraft Today*, Chapter I: Living Witchcraft. p. 23.
22. *Witchcraft Today*, Chapter I: Living Witchcraft. p. 24.
23. *Meaning of Witchcraft*, Chapter I: The Witch Cult in Britain. p. 10.
24. *Witchcraft Today*, Chapter XII: Who is the Devil? p. 110.
25. *Meaning of Witchcraft*, Chapter I: The Witch Cult in Britain. p. 19.

EDITOR'S POSTSCRIPT:

JUDGING OTHERS

THE PRACTICE OF JUDGING, AGAINST WHICH WE HAVE SO MANY WARNINGS IN THE NEW TESTAMENT, CONSISTS NOT SO MUCH IN THE CHARACTERIZING OF PARTICULAR ACTIONS OR MODES OF LIFE, AS IN MAKING THESE THE BASIS FOR A SWEEPING, AND, IN some cases, a final verdict on the character of those to whom they are rightly or wrongly attributed. The warnings are given in the interests of both the critic and the criticized. The practice is equally hurtful to both, and therefore if it is not absolutely condemned, it is surrounded by so many safeguards and limitations as to be practically forbidden. On the one hand it is an infringement of the royal law (Ja 2:13), on the other, it stands in the way of that self-criticism which is necessary to amendment of morals and progress in religion (Mt 7:3). The chief objection to judging, however, is that it must be based on partial knowledge; we are necessarily ignorant of the inner life, the motives and principles of other men; we are not acquainted either with the antecedent conditions of their actions, or the possibilities of justification, or progress, or amendment, that their future may contain. This is the position taken up by Jesus Christ in opposition to Jewish legalists. He declared that the latter judged according to appearance (Jn 7:24) , according to the flesh (Jn 8:15). As their religion consisted in the performance of certain prescribed duties, and the avoidance of outward offences, they had a rough and ready standard by which to estimate character. Christ and St Paul had a more righteous, because more complete, standard; they took into account the inner thoughts and motives, and, knowing the complexity of these, deliberately refrained from judging, even where the outward evidence seemed absolutely convincing (Jn 8:11, 1 Co 4:5). One last motive in the prohibition of judging must not be overlooked. It was necessary to exercise patience and forbearance, not only in the interests of the individual, but in those of the Church. This is at least indirectly taught in the Parable of the Tares (Mt13:24), which cannot be limited exclusively to ecclesiastical discipline, and it is a prominent motive with St Paul. It appears in his treatment of the 'strong' and the 'weak' parties in Rome (Ro 14) and of the rival possessors of gifts in Corinth (1 Co 13). In one word, while self-judgement is enjoined, the judgement of others is discountenanced throughout the New Testament.

MEANING OF WITCHCRAFT

Gerald Gardner

IHO913-X (296pp) £12.99

This book, by an actual member of one of the few surviving witch-covens, gives the correct meaning lying behind the age-old practices and beliefs of the witch-cult. Dr Gardner shows that in Witchcraft we have the remains of a pre-Christian religion, which has been distorted and mis-represented by its enemies throughout the centuries. Much painstaking research has gone into the writing of this book, which must take its place as an important contribution to the whole subject.

HIGH MAGIC'S AID

Scire (Gerald Gardner) IHO906-7 £11.99

Published in 1949, before the repeal of the Witchcraft Act in 1951, this daring magical novel heralded the return of the Old Religion from centuries of secrecy. Though Gardner was initiated into the craft in 1939, it took him until 1949 to persuade his High Priestess that the time to emerge from hiding had come — she agreed, on the condition that his work take a fictional form.

A GODDESS ARRIVES

Gerald Gardner

IHO914-8 (296pp) £12.99

Gardner's first novel came about as the result of a dream, or rather a series of dreams, in which he seemed to be in charge of constructing a defensive wall in order to repel invaders. He suspected that it may have been a memory from a previous lifetime somewhere in the Mediterranean or Middle East. The dreams were so vivid that Gardner was inspired to write "A Goddess Arrives".

The novel is based on the historical invasion of Cyprus by the Egyptians in 1450 BCE and tells of how they were ultimately repulsed. The heroine of the story, Dayonis, is described as a witch, but she seems to need animal and, in some cases, human sacrifices in her rituals. *A Goddess Arrives* is well written and was published at the end of 1939, just after Gardner's initiation into the Craft, as witchcraft is often known to those involved. It shows that he was interested in witchcraft and ritual previous to that time, although he was forced to change some of his ideas, for example about human and animal sacrifice, when he actually met some witches.

WITCHCRAFT TODAY

Gerald Gardner

IHO910-5 (136pp) £11.99

This is the book that started it all. Although most books on witchcraft were published in the first half of the 20th century, most were written from the perspective of non-witches who were often indifferent or hostile to magical religion. Gardner, himself an initiated witch, unleashed this study of the old religion from the inside in 1954, beginning a movement which continues to gather momentum today. To anyone interested in the early history of modern Wicca, this is the single most essential book.

GERALD GARDNER: WITCH

J.L . Bracelin

IHO908-3 (204pp) £11.99

First published in 1960, when its subject was still alive, this book recounts the colourful adventures of Gerald Gardner's early life as a civil servant in such places as Ceylon and Malaysia. Of courses its main focus is on Gardner's most enduring work, that of helping to bring traditional witchcraft "out of the broom closet" and into the light of public awareness. This work is indispensable to anyone wishing a glimpse into the mind of the founder of modern witchcraft.

GERALD GARDNER AND THE WITCH-CRAFT REVIVAL

Philip Heselton

IHO916-4 (84pp) £12.99

The significance of his life and works to the story of modern witchcraft. In this book, Philip Heselton tell us about the life and times of Gerald Gardner and why he is so important to the modern witchcraft movement. The book also includes reprints of the visitors' introduction to *The Folklore Centre of Superstition and Witchcraft* at Castletown; an article from *Folklore*, 1939 by Gardner about Matthew Hopkins relics; *The Story of the famous Witches Mill at Castletown, Isle of Man* by Gardner and other interesting Gardner artifacts. Even if they do not espouse the "Gardnerian", most witches and pagans around the world owe much of the form of their practises and rituals, perhaps far more than they realize, to one man — Gerald Gardner.

PHILOSOPHY OF WITCHCRAFT

Ian Ferguson

IHO919-9 (224pp) *£10.95*

The Witch was counsellor and consoler of man, the genius of the domestic arts, the treasury of knowledge, and the inspiration of belief. The prophet, priest and king of paganism whose territory was the World. This study of Witchcraft in social history goes beyond the boundaries of historical survey and acceptance of the Witch as a victim, to a symbol of the predominant instinct of a 'philosophy of comfort' against which ethics and pure knowledge have striven and are striving today.

DISCOVERY OF WITCHES

Montague Summers

IHO909-1 (70pp) £10.99

Montague Summers was a devout Roman Catholic who believed witches were evil, but his work has been considered important to Wiccans who wish to understand the history of magical religion before the Wiccan revival of the 1950s. This book reprints Matthew Hopkins' anti-witch tract first published in 1647, along with Summer's commentary, but its chief value may be the reprint of a brief essay by Gerald Gardner dating back to 1939. Not for the beginner, but a serious student of magic and occult history.

WITCHCRAFT FACTBOOK

Edmund M Buczynski

LAB400-3 (64pp) £6.99

Ed Buczynski was a major Craft leader in the early 1970's, father of the northeast United States Welsh Tradition, founder of an independent Gardnerian Tradition (where male and female were co-equal), founder of the Minoan Brotherhood and Sisterhood and was active in the Church of the Eternal Source, a revival of ancient Egyptian religion. This book is comprised of Ed's lecture notes to schools, libraries, etc. It is intended to be a primary statement to non-witches and also contains excellent introductory material for beginning witches, as well as a complete reading list of the classic books in this much misunderstood field.

TRADITIONAL WICCA

Keith Morgan

This book explores the Magick of the Wiccan Religion to greater depths; going a long way into explaining the true nature and identity of the Old Religion of the British Isles through the use of the Natural Magickal techniques of the author and his own interpretation of such. Extensive information is provided on the subjects of Practical Magick, including magickal correspondences for successful magickal rituals, talismans and spells. Following on from *Wicca Awakens*, this book is an excellent second part of the magickal education of the aspiring Witch. Keith Morgan is a High Priest of Wicca of many years standing. Keith has written over 25 books on the practical aspect of Magick and The Old Religion. His writing is concise and to the point, getting over many magickal realities that many authors fail to realise. His work will bring out the magickal potential in you. IHO939-3 £7.99

THE DIARY OF DR. JOHN DEE

Dr. John Dee

IHO918-0 (114pp) £10.99

This is a facsimile of the Camden Societies 1852 publication of Dr. John Dee's diary and the catalogue of his library of manuscripts, taken from the original manuscripts held at the Ashmolean Museum, Oxford and at Trintity College, Cambridge.

THE LIFE OF JOHN DEE

Dr. Thomas Smith

IHO917-2 (128pp) £10.99

This is a reprint of the 1908 biography of John Dee translated from the original Latin work of Dr. Thomas Smith by W. A. Ayton who had connections with the Golden Dawn

DRAGON OF REVELATION

Frederick Carter and D.H. Lawrence

IHO931-8 (330pp) £19.99

Frederick Carter analyses the symbols and apocalyptic images of 'The Revelation of Saint John the Divine' from the point of view of the Astrologer. This is the first publication of Lawrence's Introduction and Carter's book together as originally planned for publication in 1929. Lawrence's stimulating introduction was one of the last things written by him before his death. He had long been interested in Carter's theory of symbols in Revelation, but was unable to complete a much longer version due to ill-health. The present work includes Carter's letter to the London Mercury (September 1930) regarding Lawrence's Introduction and the complete text of Carter's book 'D H Lawrence and the Body Mystical'.

DRAGON OF THE ALCHEMISTS

Frederick Carter

IHO929-6 (178pp) £14.99

First published in 1926, this new edition is complete with Arthur Machen's introduction and all thirty-eight of Carter's designs. The text is set with gold titles and illuminated drop capitals using Carter's drawings.

HEALING SCENTS

Patricia Lennan

IHO934-2 (182pp) £12.99

This book is intended to introduce you to and help you understand aromatherapy. The history and underlying principles of Aromatherapy are explored and advice and guidelines are given on how to treat a range of problems at home, in a straightforward but comprehensive manner.

GRIMOIRE SYMPATHIA

Workshop of the Infinite: Healing without medicine using the spiritual essence of plants, minerals and precious stones

by Charubel

IHO949-0 £19.99

Charubel, or John Thomas, is best known for his *Degrees of the Zodiac Symbolised* which, through reinterpretation by Marc Edmund, gave rise to a system known as Sabian Astrology. He also operated a magical order called the Celestial Brotherhood which was broadly similar to the Golden Dawn, *i.e.* it had a system of progressive grades, claimed its teachings were from hidden adepts and practiced magical rituals. Notable members of the Celestial Brotherhood included John Yarker and Major Francis George Irwin (who worked with Frederick Hockley). Charubel was also in contact with Peter Davidson and Thomas Burgoyne of the Hermetic Brotherhood of Light.

This work is quite remarkable, being a grimoire of the spirits of plants, minerals and precious stones. The spirit for each has a name, a sigil and an invocation and these are used for healing purposes. In some instances simple rituals derived from folklore are given. The spirit attributions were derived by means of clairvoyant investigation, though the author is known to be familiar with Culpeper. However, this is not herbalism, the plants are not taken or used to prepare medicine, rather the magician attunes to their spirit to invoke *sympathetic magic*.

Very few original grimoires were produced throughout the 20th Century and despite its gentle tone, this book is undoubtedly a grimoire — a grimoire which has been constantly overlooked.

MYSTERY OF AN ARTIST: AUSTIN OSMAN SPARE

A.R. Naylor (Ed.)

IHO943-1 (266pp) £18.99

"Handsomely printed with wide margins and red embellishments, one coloured plate. Spare's essay 'Mind to Mind and How' was first published in the respected *Two Tracts on Cartomancy* as it deals with divination. This work places it, as near as possible, in its original context:- a response to a series of articles by Kenneth Walker and others concerning telepathy, psychic powers and inspiration carried in the *London Mystery Magazine* in the 1950s. This work reproduces those articles together with accompanying drawings by Ronald Searle which one could see would have grabbed Spare's attention. The polemical nature of Spare's essay, again presented here, becomes understandable, written as 'a Sorcerer' Spare declares himself someone who lives what Walker *et al* speculate about. Too raw for the magazine it was never used. Though the editors passed on this text they published illustrations by Spare. These are reproduced with the associated articles, being short stories by Lewis Spence, Algernon Blackwood, Dorothy Edwards and Martin Gardner. Also provided is the article 'Mystery of an Artist' written about Spare by Hannen Swaffer which appeared in the journal. This has been very scarce (original copies carrying the article have been offered for sale for over £200!). The longer work by Swaffer, *Adventures with Inspiration* is also provided. This discusses Spare in the wider context of sources of artistic inspiration. The front cover utilises a fine picture of Spare at one of his exhibitions fixing the camera in his gaze, with the editors of the *London Mystery Magazine* behind him. The last pages even give a design provided for the magazine but rejected which Spare went on to utilise elsewhere. This commendable publication represents an excellent window upon an often overlooked aspect of Spare's work."

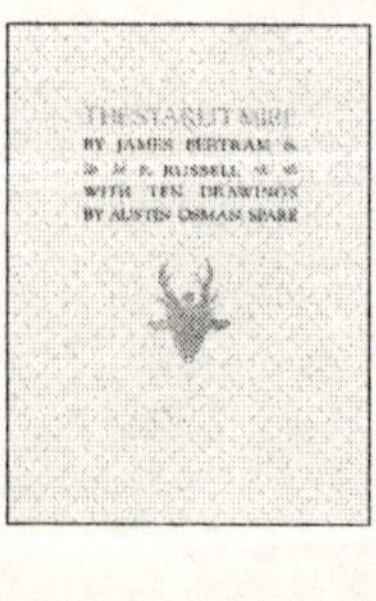

THE STARLIT MIRE

James Bertram & F. Russell

with ten drawings by Austin Osman Spare

IHO948-2 (72pp) £12.99

ART AND LETTER: WORD AND SIGN

Vera Wainwright and Austin Osman Spare

IHO942-3 (262pp) £19.99

Vera Wainwright was introduced to Spare by Victor Neuburg, they became friends, exchanging many letters and in due course Spare supplied six illustrations for a small book of poems by Wainwright which was first published as *Poems and Masks* by Toucan Press in 1968.

Art and Letter : Word and Sign reproduces *Poems and Masks* with many additional illustrations by Spare and a previously unpublished Wainwright poem. It includes both the original introduction by Stacey Biswas Day and her much longer introduction from the second edition.

Published for the first time are ninety-one of Vera Wainwright's letters to Spare from 1943 – 1946. These show that their relationship was far more than professional — evidently she supported Spare and they planned to live together — this was not to be. Spare spent his last years in the company of Millicent Paine and it is speculated as to whether he treated Vera at all fairly. Also included is a biography of Vera Wainwright by J Stevens Cox and a biography of Austin Spare by Wainwright. Appendices include: · A discussion concerning the designs by Spare published in the original Toucan Press edition with some speculation as to sources and showing where similar designs were also used · A short piece by Spare entitled *Fragmenta* (mentioned in Wainwright's letters) · A section on Spare from *Adventures with Inspiration* by Hannen Swaffer along with a coloured portrait of Swaffer by Spare · Two poems by Victor Neuburg from *The Triumph of Pan* which were dedicated to Spare. *Art and Letter : Word and Sign* is filled with over sixty-five of Spare's illustrations, two colour plates and four photographs, making it a fine addition to any collection as well as an intriguing snapshot of Spare's life.

BEHIND THE VEIL

Ethel Wheeler

Illustrated by

Austin Osman Spare

IHO950-4 (132pp) £14.99

ETHOS

The Magical Writings of Austin Osman Spare

IHO928-8 (178pp) £17.99

Spare's complete magical writings printed in one volume. Includes *Micrologus* (published elsewhere as Axiomata), *The Book of Pleasure*, *The Witches Sabbath* and *Mind to Mind and How by a Sorceror.* Along with rubricated captitals and shoulder notes this edition includes all the original illustrations to *The Book of Pleasure* plus a colour plate.

ANATHEMA OF ZOS

The Sermon to the Hypocrites

An Automatic Writing. Austin Osman Spare

IHO926-1 (66pp) £12.99

Originally written in 1924 and then privately published in 1927, this new edition of Austin Spares fifth book "Anathema of Zos", has been entirely reset with rubicated test and gold titles. A colour plate has also been added along with many of Spare's drawings.

THE YOUTH AND THE SAGE

Warren Retlaw. IHO937-7 (122pp) £13.99

This new edition of *The Youth and the Sage* includes Warren Retlaw's poem with decorated drop capitals by Austin Osman Spare, plus three new articules regarding Austin Spare and also included is *The Rubáiyát of Omar Khayyám* as translated by Edward Fitzgerald. The following reviews were printed in the prospectus for the original 1927 edition. *Professor MICHAEL SADLER* says: "I have read it with great interest and am moved by its sincerity. It is a record of truth. The parts which impress me most are pages 8 and 9, and the conclusion." *Mr BERNARD SHAW* says: "You have a poet's ear, apparently . . . As I also left school at 13 or thereabouts, it was tactless of you to disparage that happy accident." *Mr JAMES DOUGLAS:* "I have read your poem with very great interest and I think it is an extraordinary fact that it should have been written by a working man whose education was completed at the age of thirteen! . . . Your poem is so fine . . . There is one line in your poem which is a jewel nine words long — 'Creeds are life crops and vary with the sod' — and there are many like it."

AUSTIN O. SPARE: STEALING THE FIRE FROM HEAVEN

Edited and Compiled by A.R. Naylor,
IHO938-5 (237pp) £19.99

Handsomely printed in four colours with many illustrations. This remarkable piece of detective work by the Editor throws new light upon the work of Spare — he was an art thief! Many of the decorated initials that Spare claimed to have designed were in fact copied from the works of others, dating from the late fifteenth and early sixteenth century! There is speculation that a realization of this may have been the true reason that Spare withdrew (or was ostracized) from the artistic establishment. However, the Editor also recovers some work which Spare published under a pseudonym in *Form Magazine* and restores it to the corpus of known Spare work. *Eight Poems* by W.B. Yeats and *The Grotesque* by Edmund Sullivan are reprinted with the illustrations now known to be by Spare, together with *Twelve Poems* by J.C. Squire, which Spare claimed to have illustrated and decorated. Although these discoveries do not affect the occult significance of Spare's work they may now be viewed, by some people, very differently. The Editor also raises the question of authenticity regarding some of Spare's very elaborate and 'formal' alleged automatic drawings — the Spare & Carter illustrated essay entitled *Automatic Drawing* is reproduced.

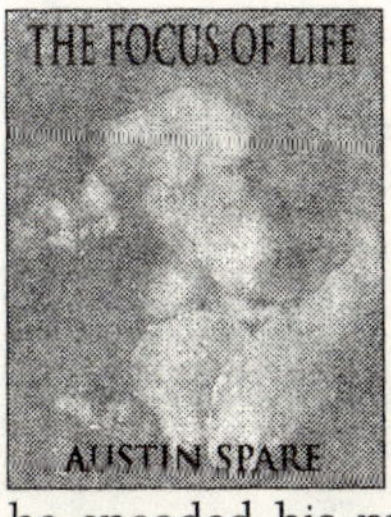

THE FOCUS OF LIFE

Austin Osman Spare
IHO959-8 (150pp) £14.99

Spare was a visionary artist of the early 20th century whose heroic nude figures of charwomen and petty criminals were haunted at the edges by ghost and demons. A practicing magician and friend of Crowley, he encoded his private magickal mythology into this collection of "the mutterings of Aaos." This sumptuous new edition contains the original introduction and all the original illustrations, plus five extra drawings and two colour plates along with a biographical Foreword by Spare's friend Dennis Bardens.

I-H-O BOOKS

THE GOLD TREE. *J.C. Squire*
IHO927-X (114pp) £13.99

With initials designed by Austin Osman Spare and cut in wood by W Quick. First published in 1917. Includes an extract from *Stealing the Fire from Heaven*, proving Spare's plagiarism for two of the letters, together with analysis and possible sources of influence for the others.

BACKLIST

ALTERNATIVE WICCA *Keith Morgan KM01 £4.95*

Continuing from *Harmonics of Wicca* - the fourth part in the theology course of Wiccan philosophies. This books explores the alternatives within magickal techniques & practises which are harmonious with the belief system that is Wiccan. An intensive & extremely thought provoking book that may challenge the system that has become established whilst paving the way for the new Aeon that is the birthright of all Pagans!

ANIMISM *The Seed of Religion Edward Clodd SU03 £7.25*

Contents include Pre-human elements in religion · Brain in Animal and Man · Man in the Making · Animal and Human Psychology · Naturalism · Animism · Nature of Spirit · Spirit in the Inanimate · Fear · Absentee Gods · Maleficent Spirits · Benevolent Gods: Earth Mother · Tree & Animal Worship · Stone Worship · Water Worship · Ancestor Worship.

ANNA KINGSFORD & EDWARD MAITLAND *Ralph Shirley MP13 £2.95*

Anna Kingsford, English mystic and occultist, was interested in dreams and esoteric Christianity and, with Edward Maitland, founded the Hermetic Society.

APOLLONIUS OF TYANA *H C de Lafontaine MP01 £2.95*

"Many have written about Appollonius, some in laudation, others in condemnation . . . I have called him the Cagliostro of the classic age."

THE ASTROLOGERS GUIDE

Guido Bonatus FI15 (H/B) £17.50

Anima Astrologae. Includes the choicest aphorisms of the seven segments of Jerom Cardan of Milan.

BIBLIA CABALISTICA OR THE CABALISTIC BIBLE

Walter Begley FI09 £12.95

An interesting study on the cabalistic correspondences to be found in the Bible.

BIBLIOTHECA ROSICRUCIANA *F. Leigh Gardener FI10 £9.95*

Introduced by William Wynn Westcott. Frontispiece engraving of Johann Valentin Andrae.

CANNABIS: A GROWERS GUIDE *Anya Marike KM28 £5.00*

This book gives all the vital information needed to study the practise of growing cannabis in temperate climates. Focusing on the biology and botany of the cannabis plants, it also goes into the vital chemistry needed to enable such projects to be viable. This book has been written as educational aid to help people understand more about the folklore, customs and uses of cannabis. WARNING: The possession, preparation, cultivation and use of cannabis is illegal in the British Isles and some European countries. We do not condone or wish to encourage anyone to break the law or make themselves liable to prosecution. Therefore, this book is sold on the strict understanding that it is to be used for educational purposes only and not to be used for criminal acts.

CANNABIS: A USER'S GUIDE *Anya Marika KM30 £5.00*
The definitive users guide to Cannabis, including essential information on how to: • Roll Joints. • Use a Pipe or Waterpipe. • Smoke Grass and Hashish. • How to Eat and Drink Cannabis. • Plus much more.

CHRISTIAN HEALING *Charles Fillmore SU06 £9.95*
Topics include the power of thought, the power of the spoken word, the relation of prayer and praise, the scope of the imagination, and many other matters of vital interest. It was written after a quarter of a century of practical experience in teaching and healing and constitutes a storehouse of inspiration and spiritual illumination. Presented in the form of lessons — a valuable textbook.

CLAIRVOYANCE *J C F Grumbine SU10 £9.50*
The System of Philosophy concerning the Divinity of Clairvoyance also a treatise on Divination and Crystal Reading published by the Order of the White Rose. Set out in fourteen leesons this book presents a system of inspired teachings concerning Divinity, especially Clairvoyance, and how to unfold the clairvoyant vision, to pierce the veil of sense, see and converse with spirits, enter at will into the spiritual world and become a seer and an adept in mystical science. Clearly and logically presents the subject in a manner at once simple and profound.

COOKING WITH CANNABIS *Anya Marika KM31 £5.00*
How to use Cannabis in cooking both for social and medical purposes. Includes information on the correct methods of cooking Cannabis for maximum efficiency. Includes recipes for all manner of Cannabis based dishes.

COUNT CAGLIOSTRO *Ralph Shirley MP12 £2.95*
Who has not heard of Cagliostro? And yet who but a few students have any real knowledge of that mysterious character? Ralph Shirley examines the mystery and the myth.

CRYSTAL MAGIC *Keith Morgan KM20 £3.50*
Explores the magickal potential of crystals and how they work within the magickal act. An ideal first book for the student or for those interested in learning more about the use of crystals.

DOWSING FOR BEGINNERS *Keith Morgan KM29 £4.00*
Everyone can dowse! Learn how to dowse, one of the Lost Magickal arts, that we humans could perform easily before the "Industrialisation" of our species. This book will show you many techniques of Dowsing including a simple way of dowsing with Pendulums, Divining Rods, Hazel twigs and more. This book contains everything that you need to know to help you to Dowse easily and efficiently. Contained within are charts to help you to dowse, plus detailed information on how to make your own dowsing equipment. Extensively illustrated.

EASY ASTRAL PROJECTION *Keith Morgan KM18 £3.50*
Astral projection is available to all with a little effort and practice. This book gives the FACTS.

EMANUEL SWEDENBORG *Ralph Shirley MP11 £2.95*
Often desribed as the "scientist who became a visionary", whose religious writings provide a clear account of what he regarded as direct messages from spirits and angels.

FROM THE INFERNO TO ZOS II *The Secret Language of Austin Spare. Austin Spare & William Wallace FI29 (488pp H/B Trade Edition) £75.00 FI29DL (488pp H/B Deluxe Edition) £125.00*
Introduction by Professor Roger Cardinal, the renowned Surrealist scholar. For the first time, Spare's art is analyzed for its hidden symbolism, a symbolism so rich in the traditions of esoteric knowledge. This knowledge was used to veil and declare a subtle, vibrant magic — a glimpse into another realm. Dr Wallace spent the better part of three years in the preparation of this work and his discoveries will be the cornerstone of Spare studies for a long time. One finds a continuity in Austin Osman Spare's work that would indicate magickal links joining paintings from one period with those of a later time. These are important reference points in his intense, unknown life, yet they are also the keys to his personal magic and philosophical concepts thus far only surmised. 488 pages, folio. Hardback edition with marbled end papers. Numerous scarce Spare drawings and illustrations.

FROM THE INFERNO TO ZOS III *Michelangelo in a Teacup: Austin Osman Spare. Frank Letchford. FI30 (360pp H/B Trade Edition) £75.00 FI30DL (360pp H/B Deluxe Edition) £125.00*
The first biography of the personal life of Austin Spare. Written by his friend and student this volume is crammed with the life and times of the magician/artist (was originally announced by Skoob as *The Magician of Southwark*). This volume contains over two hundred pictures and unpublished photographs — more than any other work on Spare. The volume presents a new idea of the art and magic of Spare and as Frank wrote in shorthand, there are many recorded words from the horse's mouth. 360 pages, folio. Hardback edition with marbled end papers.

GREAT ZODIAC OF GLASTONBURY *R. Nichols MP07 £2.95*
A system 6000 years old—local names linked with the Celtic-Arthurian myth—a ten-mile-wide Zodiac in North Somerset, outlined by 'rhines' or dykes, ancient paths and earthworks, and taking advantage of all available natural features such as rivers.

THE HARMONICS OF WICCA *Keith Morgan KM02 £4.95*
The continuance on from *Wicca Awakens & Traditional Wicca,* it is a Balancing process for the Old Religion in the New Age. Vital & exciting concepts that are occurring within the Craft today. It gets away from the medieval concept of the Craft & goes back to its roots, unifying many Pagan principles within the Craft structures. Extensively illustrated throughout.

HAVE YOU BEEN CURSED? *Keith Morgan KM03 £3.50*
A serious study into the phenomena of curses & hexes. Contains much vital information for people who think they may be at the receiving end of a curse.

THE HORNED GOD *Keith Morgan KM16 £4.95*
A full analysis into the the importance of the Pagan dualistic approach to deity. Explains why a belief in a God is not a patriarchal curiosity.

HOW TO USE A OUIJA BOARD *Keith Morgan KM19 £3.50*

A no nonsense book dealing with the Ouija board as a practical magickal tool. The truth about Ouija boards and how to use them.

IS THE ORDER OF R.R. & A.C. TO REMAIN A MAGICAL ORDER?
W. B Yeats MP37 £2.95

Written in March 1901, and given to the Adepti of the Order of R.R. & A.C. in April 1901. Also includes the postscipt to the essay - written 4th May, 1901.

MAGICK FOR LOVERS *Keith Morgan KM21 £3.50*

Probably the most practical and sensible book on the subject. Full of do's and don'ts and genuine advice from this best-selling author.

THE MAGICKAL RECORD *Keith Morgan KM05 £3.50*

This unique book with its pre-printed format allows you to quickly record your rituals. All the information contained within will be personalised by you, So keeping a record of your successful spells (or not so successful!) really is a matter of minutes rather than hours.

MAKING MAGICKAL INCENSE AND RITUAL PERFUMES
Keith Morgan KM22 £4.95

A simple and concise guide. A wealth of information & accurate recipes for producing your own ritual incenses and perfumes.

MAKING MAGICKAL TOOLS & RITUAL EQUIPMENT
Keith Morgan KM08 £3.50

This book gives the reader all the information needed for making ritual magickal tools, including making, Athames; Swords, pentacles, Robes, Incenses Oils & Much Much more with easy to follow instructions, using raw materials & tools that are readily available. Extensively illustrated.

MASONRY AND MAGIC OF FRATER RUDYARD KIPLING *Dr. Vaughan Bateson MP05 £2.95*

The influence of Masonry is seen in many of this great Master's works and the ideas he holds are of much value.

MICHAEL SCOT *Ralph Shirley MP09 £2.95*

Mathematician, Alchemist, Astrologer who indirectly exercised a marked influence on the history of Europe.

MYTHS & DREAMS *Edward Clodd SU07 £13.95*

Myth: Its Birth & Growth. Primitive Meaning · Powers of Nature · Solar Theory of Myth · Metamorphosis into Animals · Totemism · Myth Survival · Myth among the Hebrews. *Dreams: Their place in the growth of beliefs in the Supernatural.* Limitation of Language · Belief in the Inanimate · Reality of Dreams · Barbaric theory of Disease · Second Self or Soul · Dreams as Omens and Media of communication between Gods and Men.

NORTHERN MYTHOLOGY *Friedrich Kauffmann SU05 £8.50*

The translation by M Steele Smith of *Deutsche Mythologie.* Contents include Decline of Teutonic Paganism · The Gods · Beneficial and Harmful Dieties · Worship of the Gods – Temples – Sacrifices – Oracles · The Number of the Gods · Woden · Thunor · Tiw · The Inferior Norse Gods · The Vanir · The Goddesses · The World – The Beginning, The End, and the New Life . . . complete with Bibliography and Index.

THE NUMBER 666 *W Wynn Westcott MP02 £2.95*
The subject of this essay is the number 666 which is mentioned in "The Revelation of St John, the Divine," at the 18TH verse of the 13TH Chapter.

OGAM STONES & INSCRIPTIONS *A Gorham MP04 £2.95*
A study of the Ogam Alphabet and its use. Illustrated.

PARACELSUS *Ralph Shirley MP10 £2.95*
An introduction to one of the most illustrious medieval alchemists.

PLANET MAGICK *Keith Morgan KM09 £4.00*
Planets influence our lives in a myriad of ways, our moods, our emotions, our feelings. This book shows how to harness this power & channel it to bring about effects on our everyday circumstances. Explains in depth, planetary correspondences, & how to create your own planetary rituals.

PLOTINUS *Ralph Shirley MP08 £2.95*
A study of Plotinus the Egyptian born Greek philosopher who was the founding figure of Neoplatonism.

POEMS AND MASKS *Vera Wainwright & Austin Osman Spare MP33 £2.95*
Poems byVera Wainwright and Masks by Austin Osman Spare. Additional notes by S B Day & J S Cox.

READ THE TAROT WITHIN 7 DAYS *Keith Morgan KM14 £3.50*
This extremely simple book shows how to read the tarot in a very effective & simple manner, the way tarot should be read, in relating the individual to their circumstances. Absolutely ideal for anyone having a minimal knowledge of the tarot.

RELIGION OF JULIAN THE APOSTATE *Dr. J. Stokes MP06 £2.95*
A study of the Roman Emperor who was raised as a Christian and converted to Paganism.

ROSICRUCIANS IN RUSSIA *B Telepneff MP03 £2.95*
Draws on standard Russian sources . . . a very useful English survey.

RUNE MAGICK *Keith Morgan KM12 £3.50*
Rune Magick has been written for the beginner and explores the history of the runes, the ways of divination as well as the ways of magickal invocations, spells, bindrunes etc that can be created with runic scripts. Contains much information about the nature of each individual runestave, not found elsewhere.

SEVEN FRIENDS *Louis Marlow SEVEN £25.00*
Louis Marlow (Wilkinson) was five different characters – for five different sets of people, each set knowing him only as their own Louis and no other: 1. The Radley Boy who wrote to Oscar Wilde, 2. The Lecturer, 3. The Writer, as Louis Wilkinson or as 'Louis Marlow', 4. The co-literary executor and friend of Aleister Crowley, the Black Magician, 5. The Biographer and friend of the Powysses. *Seven Friends* is a series of literary portraits of such figures as William Somerset Maugham, Llewelyn Powys, and his brothers, fantastic figures such as Frank Harris and Aleister Crowley appear in the gallery, and in addition, Oscar Wilde. *Seven Friends* is introduced by Oliver Wilkinson (Louis's son), who also met Crowley, Yeats and many other of his father's friends. Illustrated with rare photographs and a previously unpublished photograph of Louis Wilkinson by Man Ray. Edition Limited to 750 copies.

SIMPLE CANDLE MAGICK *Keith Morgan KM17 £3.50*

Use Candles and Incense to create a magickal environment to harness energies and magickal currents for your personal needs.

SIMPLE SPELLS FROM A WITCHES SPELLBOOK *Keith Morgan KM15 £3.50*

Simple spells from a Witches spellbook is the kind of beginners book that has been so needed. Excellent advice for all.

THE SIXTH SENSE *Its Cultivation & Use Charles Brent SU09 £8.50*

The Mystic Sense, or that inner perceptive faculty which distinguishes man from the highest below him and allies him to the highest above him. It is the Human Sense. It is used for no one exclusive purpose; it is only under its operation that man's activities become human.

SO YOU WANT TO BE A WITCH *Keith Morgan KM06 £3.50*

Explains in a simple & often light hearted format what it is to be a Witch, whether witches are born or made, whether the perceptions one holds about witches is correct (often it is not!) This book is a valuable asset to aid your in your search for the true path.

TAROT ABECEDARIAN *The Treasure House of Images A. R. Naylor TAROT £14.95*

A unique book which is packed with information to aid even the most advanced reader. A 'must' for anyone interested in the Tarot.

Part One: A study of Tarot Spreads and their development, detailed instructions and illustrations for over eighty different Tarot Spreads. Topics covered include: · Building Blocks · Interactivity · Spread development, modification, enhancement · 1, 2 and 3 dimensional spreads · Recording results · Tarot a language? — rules of grammar. *Part Two:* A unique system of learning to read the Tarot which can be applied to any deck. The primary stage enables the reader to recall the attributions of each card with ease. The advanced stage aims to develop a deep conceptual understanding of the Tarot at the subconscious level which will heighten intuitive and perceptive abilities.

THOUGHTS ON PSYCHOMETRY *Ida Ellis SU11 £7.25*

The Science of Psychometry explained in the form of Question and Answer. This book is the result of many years study and continued practice of this gift by the author. Over 300 questions clearly and concisely explained.

THE TRUTH ABOUT WITCHCRAFT *Keith Morgan KM04 £2.50*

Written by a practising witch to allay some of the fears & misconceptions about Wicca & Paganism. This is the ideal book to present to parents, friends & family to explain your beliefs & practices in a very simple way.

WICCA AWAKENS *Keith Morgan KM13 £4.95*

Wicca Awakens is a perfect beginners book, on the Old Religion, that gives all the relevant & vital information that a newcomer to the Old Religion needs. Comprising of 13 very informative chapters that go into detail on subjects such as; The history of the craft; God & Goddess images; Modern Wicca; The Witches Year; Magickal tools; Incenses making & more. Extensively illustrated throughout.

A WITCHES KITCHEN *Keith Morgan KM24 £3.50*

This book show you: • How to make genuine witches potions, incenses and perfumes • How to use herbs for magick • How to plant a herb garden • How to make incenses and ritual perfumes • How to dry and store herbs for your incenses . . . . and much, much more.

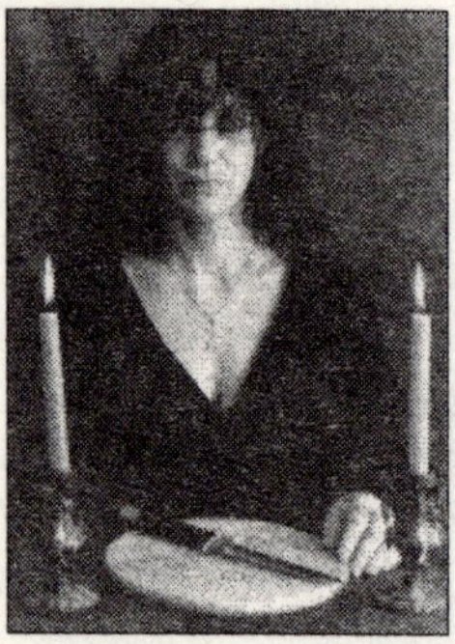

KATE WEST

KATE has been a practicing Witch for over 25 years. She is High Priestess of The Hearth of Hecate, an established Coven with groups around the country. She is Media officer for the Children of Artemis, the UK's foremost, and fastest growing Witchcraft and Wiccan organization, and previously served terms of office as both Vice President and Media Co-ordinator of The Pagan Federation. Kate is a respected and sought after speaker on Witchcraft, appearing at Pagan conferences, as well as non-Pagan and interfaith events.

Kate is the author of the *Real Witches* series of books which reveal the Craft for those who live in the real world. *The Real Witches' Handbook* and *The Real Witches' Kitchen* being Witchcraft bestsellers in the UK and the USA. She has also written *The Real Witches Coven*, *The Real Witches Book of Spell and Rituals* and *The Real Witches' Garden* (due in March 2004).'

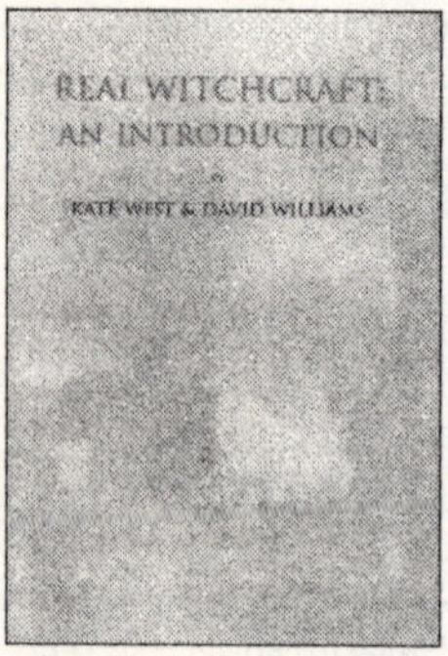

Real Witchcraft: An Introduction

Kate West & David Williams

Witchcraft, Wicca, the Craft, the Craft of the Wise, are all terms used by modern Witches. Witchcraft today is a renewed version of the Old Religion with its roots based in the Palaeolithic worship of the spirit of the Hunt and reverence for the Triple Goddess. This book provides a modern guide to the Old Religion. Phrased in down to earth, no nonsense language it gives a straightforward approach to Wicca. It is suitable for the experienced practitioner, the beginner or just to explain the Craft to those new to Paganism by demystifying the practical aspects of the religion, whilst destroying none of the spirituality. It is the culmination of teaching a training Coven to 1st Degree and the experience shows! The authors have between them over forty years of Craft experience including Gardnerian, Alexandrian and Traditional paths, placing a firm emphasis on what feels right to the individual rather than a 'do as I say' approach. Order IHO947-4 £9.99

HANDFASTING: *The Pagan Wedding*

PM02 £4.95

Many of the Traditions of modern Weddings, whether spiritual or secular draw their origins from the Rite of Handfasting. Binding the hands of two people each to the other, making their own vows. This book contains background information on the Traditions and history of this rite as well as two Rituals, one of which being the Handfasting Rite performed by the Hearth of Hecate for Kate's Handfasting to her husband Steve. There is also a wealth of practical hints and tips as well as advice on how to approach Family and Friends who do not necessarily share the same spiritual path.

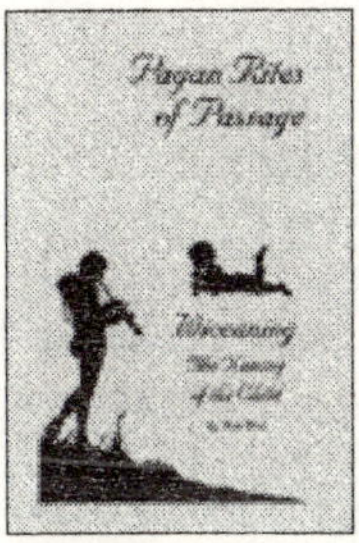

WICCANING: *The Naming of a Child*

PM03 £4.95

A logical step on from Handfasting, comes Wiccaning, the Rite of welcoming a new child and the giving of a name. As Witches we do not believe in indoctrinating our children with our beliefs, however the Rite of Naming carries with it a charm and wonder and unlike other faiths, in no way commits the recipient in anyway to the Craft. Sometimes Covens use the Rite of Wiccaning to name their new members. Again this book contains background information along with suggested Rites and ways of adapting them for your own Ritual, as well as Kate's usual practical advice.

WITHDRAWAL: *Saying Farewell*

PM04 £4.95

It is inevitable that people and pets near and dear to us pass on, as Witches we try to celebrate the life of those who go before. This book addresses this sensitive topic in Kate's usual practical style. Rites are included for those who wish to prepare for their own passage and of course Rites for those who are left behind. As well as helpful advice and background information on the folklore and traditions of this most significant of Rites of Passage.

REAL WITCHES' HANDBOOK

Complete Introduction to the Craft for both Young and Old
Wicca is a nature-based path rich with magic and enchantment. This grounded introduction separates the myth from reality, with all the advice you need to follow the Wiccan way. Order HC515-0 £8.99

REAL WITCHES' KITCHEN

Spells and Recipes from the Witches' Hearth. Over 100 spells and recipes vital to all real witches' kitchens. How to use witches' herbs, plants and other ingredients to create medicines to mend body and spirit, plus food and wine to celebrate festivals. Kate West has a very strong profile in the UK, with regular appearances as spokesperson for the Craft. Order HC786-8 £10.99

REAL WITCHES' COVEN

The Definitive Guide to Forming Your Own Wiccan Group. The Coven functions like a family, helping and supporting one another — they gather to honour the Goddess and the God, to celebrate the cycle of the seasons through the Sabbats, to mark the phases of the Moon and work magic at the Esbats. Whether you already run a Coven or are thinking of doing so, whether you are a member of a Coven, seek to join one, or just wonder what they do, this is the book for you with information, and real-life examples to help you. Order HCE389-3 £9.99

REAL WITCHES' BOOK OF SPELLS AND RITUALS

Showing to the full her encyclopaedic knowledge of the Craft of the Wise Kate provides the reader with a comprehensive book full of all the spells and Rituals you are ever likely to need, plus a whole range of guidelines for creating your own. In depth analysis of Magic and spells covering all the ethics and a useful guide on why sometimes the magic doesn't work. As usual this book is presented in Kate's pragmatic and down to earth style, with anecdotes and humour to illustrate the salient points. A must have on any Witches bookshelf. Order HCE111-X £12.99

SPELL IN YOUR POCKET

In *Spell in Your Pocket* provides a concise introduction to the Craft. Packed with magical spells and rituals, *Spell in Your Pocket* examines the myths and realities of Witchcraft and introduces the principles of magic. There are spells for every aspect of Witchy life and for the things in life that mean so much to everyone: love, money, protection and healing. Order HC664-7 £4.99

THE REAL WITCHES' GARDEN

For the modern Witch the garden is perfect for creating the sacred outdoor space you need to really get back to the roots of the Craft. In this first guide to, outdoor Witchcraft, Kate offers practical hints and tips on how to make the best use of your garden, whether you have twenty acres or a window box. The Real Witches' Garden provides advice on every issue, from how to tend herbs for use in particular spells and remedies, to the practicalities of working magic in your own backyard.

Put the nature back into your magic and magic back into your garden, spells, rites, worship and meditation, as you discover the benefits of:

- Erecting a permanent altar and consecrating your sacred space
- Easy-to-grow herbs, drying and storing
- The smallest of gardens - window boxes, pots and containers
- Planting spells and the many different plant associations
- Using the garden all year round, including seasonal celebrations
- Planting according to the lunar calendar and the Wheel of the Year"

Order HC322-3 £9.99